Financial Self-Defence

Financial Self-Defence

How to outsmart broken systems and financial predators

Darian Vos

Mindful Pages

Published in 2025

ISBN: 9789371346115 (PB)
ISBN: 9789371343350 (eBook)

Published by

Mindful Pages
Imprint of Alpha Editions LLC
312 W. 2nd St #1834
Casper, WY 82601, USA

This book was developed using advanced writing tools to support the drafting and ideation process. All content has been thoughtfully curated, refined, and reviewed to ensure quality and relevance.

Content

Introduction
The Invisible War on Your Wallet

You were never meant to come out ahead in the world of money. Not with the rules as they currently stand.

Now, before that sounds like some wild-eyed conspiracy, hear it out. This book isn't claiming that cloaked elites gather in smoke-filled rooms to fiddle with your interest rate. What it *is* saying, though, is arguably more unsettling: that the systems we're taught to respect—banks, government policies, financial advice, the lot—are structured first and foremost to protect their own interests. And, more often than not, those interests come at your cost. The real trap, then, isn't simply ignorance. It's participation. It's the quiet internalisation of norms, beliefs, and behaviours that make us willing players in a game we were never meant to win.

We've been conditioned to point the finger inward. Not saving enough? Your fault. Picked the wrong career? Should've known better. In debt? Must be irresponsible. Spend too much? Lack of discipline. The cruelest trick of the system is not just the extraction—it's the guilt it implants. It convinces you that your struggle is a personal failing. But perhaps it isn't. Or at least, not in the tidy, moralising way you've been led to believe.

Let's be clear: this is not a self-help book. You won't find bullet-pointed checklists here, no breezy "five hacks to retire by 40" nonsense. There's already a torrent of that sort of thing out there—some of it useful, much of it misdirected. *Financial Self-Defence* isn't offering hacks; it's presenting a manifesto. It's written for those who feel, even if only vaguely, that something's fundamentally askew. Those who've followed the rules, worked hard, stayed informed—and still find themselves on the edge, one crisis away from financial ruin. If you suspect the whole setup is rigged, you're not wrong. It is.

The heart of this book rests on a difficult but necessary assertion: you exist within a financial ecosystem that was not created with your flourishing in mind. It was constructed—deliberately, over time, and with great subtlety—to ensure wealth moves upwards, to reward docility, and to keep its inner workings hidden behind a facade of logic and positivity. Its strength lies not in brute force, but in camouflage. It mimics opportunity. It speaks in the language of empowerment. It cloaks itself in progress and "self-improvement", all the while tightening the net. This isn't a fight against villains. It's a reckoning with systems engineered to seem friendly.

Take a moment to consider: we are, collectively, more educated than any generation before us. And yet, most people today are less financially secure than their grandparents were. Wages have flatlined, debt has exploded, and the chasm between rich and poor yawns wider by the year. And curiously, at the same time, personal finance advice has never been more abundant. Blogs, influencers, courses, podcasts—you can drown in it. If knowledge were enough, we'd all be free by now. Clearly, something else is shaping the outcome.

That something is the infrastructure of the modern economy—one that thrives on manipulation, fabricated scarcity, and illusion. You're navigating a financial landscape designed to monetise your attention, amplify your fears, and reward constant activity over meaningful rest. The myth of the "rational economic actor"—that tidy figure of classical economics making clean, calculated choices—has long since been dismantled by behavioural science. Yet policies and products still lean on that outdated fiction. In truth, humans are not rational. We are reliably emotional—prone to shame, anxiety, aspiration—all of which are mined, measured, and monetised.

This book starts by naming the players. Not the ones in hiding, but the ones hiding in plain sight. The credit card companies selling debt as empowerment. The gig platforms pitching freedom while extracting control. The policymakers who, often without explicit malice, shape laws that reinforce a lifetime of struggle for the working class. But *Financial Self-Defence* doesn't stop at pointing fingers. Outrage without orientation just breeds helplessness.

What this book aims to provide is not false clarity—the kind dispensed by cheery financial gurus—but the real thing. And real clarity isn't always comforting. It can be disorienting, even painful. You'll begin to see the unconscious scripts you've internalised—about debt, success, ambition—and slowly start to erase them. You'll learn how corporations weaponise your insecurities, how inertia becomes revenue, how your data feeds a machine that sells you back your own fears. Most crucially, you'll learn how to begin stepping out. Not in the sense of disappearing into the woods, though some might dream of that—but in a deeper, more sustainable sense. Mentally. Emotionally. Structurally.

This kind of exit isn't about vanishing from society. It's about shifting your centre of gravity. It's about building your own scaffolding—psychological, economic, ethical—that the system can't easily bend or claim. It's about constructing a life with fewer points of capture. You regain control, not just over your finances, but over your time, your choices, your trajectory.

Why now? Because the stakes are only getting higher. Algorithms now judge your creditworthiness. You bleed money monthly through invisible subscriptions. Children are being taught—by the media, by advertising, by design—that convenience is worth any price, that flash equals value, and that playing inside the lines is the path to security. Meanwhile, those very lines are quietly being redrawn.

Arguably the most dangerous lie in today's financial landscape is that it's all on you. That success is purely a matter of willpower, discipline, and mindset. That your outcomes are entirely self-determined. This narrative serves power perfectly: it keeps scrutiny focused inward, while systemic forces go untouched. Of course, personal discipline is vital. Emotional self-awareness helps immensely. But without a clear-eyed understanding of the broader architecture, you're left running endlessly in place. Hustling harder while the treadmill speeds up beneath you.

To mount a defence, you need to understand the terrain. This book will walk you through the hidden anatomy of the financial world—its psychological tactics, its institutional games, its emotional traps. You'll look closely at why consumption feels so satisfying (and so empty), how debt becomes identity, and how the most insidious threats are the ones you no longer see. But this journey doesn't end in despair. It bends—firmly—towards agency. Not in the rah-rah, "just manifest it" sense, but in the grittier, more grounded sense of reclaimed authorship. The kind that sticks.

This isn't about playing the game better. It's about questioning the game itself. Throughout, this book will argue that wealth is not, ultimately, a number. It is your capacity to move through life without fear. And that freedom begins the moment you stop mistaking the illusion for truth, and withdraw your energy from the mechanisms that feed it.

The person this book was written for is not powerless, even if they've been disempowered. They are observant. Restless. Tired of surface-level fixes. They want to understand, truly and deeply, what's gone wrong—and what can still be made right. They're ready to stop internalising blame for circumstances they never stood a chance of controlling. And they're willing to do the hard work—not just for themselves, but for those they love, and those who come after.

If you are that person, know this: *Financial Self-Defence* won't tie up your confusion with a neat bow. What it offers is more elemental—clarity. It will challenge your assumptions, jolt you out of habitual thinking, and ask you to look unflinchingly at some hard truths. But it will also equip you. With insight. With strategy. With a lens that helps you see more sharply. It won't just leave you better informed. It will leave you more awake.

You don't have to become rich to be free. But you do have to become sovereign. And this, if you're willing, is your manual for beginning that journey.

Chapter 1
The Anatomy of Financial Deception

Most people don't knowingly step into a trap. And yet, each day, countless individuals do exactly that—not out of carelessness, but by design. The contemporary financial landscape doesn't need brute force. Its strength lies elsewhere: in subtle suggestion, calculated confusion, and the seamless absorption of its values. What's sold to you isn't so much a blatant lie, but a carefully crafted half-truth—packaged with authority, wrapped in complexity. This isn't trickery in the traditional sense. It's a structure. It's social. It's normalised. And it persists not because people are foolish, but because they've been trained not to notice.

This chapter lays bare the design of that training. It's not sufficient to wave a hand and say, "We're being manipulated." We must dissect it—see where it enters, understand why it works, and trace precisely which levers are pulled. The financial world around you—from that friendly budgeting app to the reassuring voice on a money podcast—isn't just a marketplace. It's a curated psychological environment. One designed to press against cognitive instincts that traditional economists, for decades, pretended weren't there. The collision between behavioural insight and economic dogma—that's the real story of modern financial deceit.

At the heart of the old economic worldview is a fiction that's proved remarkably persistent: the notion that people are rational actors. That we weigh options logically, digest information cleanly, and reliably pursue our best interests. This belief has shaped everything from public finance policy to how schools teach budgeting. It reassures us that the system is fair—and that if we're struggling, it must be a personal failing. After all, if the rules are sound, then falling behind must be down to laziness or poor choices. Rarely do we stop to consider whether the rules themselves are tilted, the instructions misleading, or the whole scoreboard fundamentally biased.

But behavioural science, over the past forty years, has torn that illusion to shreds. Human beings are not spreadsheets. We are guided—often blindly—by emotion, by impulse, by shortcuts of thought developed long before financial products existed. We fear loss more than we desire equivalent gain. We latch on to the first number we hear. We confuse the familiar with the wise. And perhaps most dangerous of all, we think we're immune to manipulation. The financial industry hasn't overlooked these vulnerabilities—it has commodified them.

Consider the architecture of financial choice. The layout of a banking app, the prompts on an insurance site, even the colours on a retirement planning portal—none of this is accidental. These platforms aren't neutral backdrops; they are scripts. Behavioural scripts, engineered with precision. The default settings, the timing of alerts, the labelling of options—all of it designed to steer your hand. Not towards your long-term welfare, but towards engagement, transaction, and data capture. Nudges are carefully chosen. Scarcity is simulated. "Recommended" choices often lead to products that serve the provider, not the user. It's less about what's good for you, more about what's good for their bottom line.

This brings us to one of the central tricks of the modern financial age: the illusion of scarcity. Now, scarcity is sometimes real—but often, it's a story. A script meant to keep you moving, keep you spending, keep you worried. Stillness, reflection, sufficiency—these are subtly recast as risky or naïve. Consider how many products and services are marketed with implied urgency. From subscription bundles to endless online courses, the message is the same: you are never quite doing enough. The insurance industry has perfected this. It doesn't just offer safety—it sells unease. Every policy is a whispered question: "What if?" What if you crash, get sick, live too long, or die too soon? The product is pitched as peace of mind. The pitch, however, is pure panic.

Fintech, too, plays its part. Investment apps frame volatility as a game. Notifications light up your screen, promising empowerment, delivering anxiety. The more you interact, the more they win. But wellbeing doesn't come from constant micro-decisions. In fact, it often requires less movement, not more. Yet we're prompted to monitor, to tweak, to act—as though vigilance itself could bring security. It doesn't. What it breeds is a restless state of alertness, mistaken for financial savvy. It's not literacy. It's tension, gamified.

And yet, all of that—the interfaces, the features, the marketing—is only part of the picture. The real machinery runs deeper. Beneath the apps and platforms lie stories. Inherited, absorbed, repeated. These are the grand narratives, the cultural assumptions that shape what we think money *means*. That debt is just part of growing up. That a job is the key to security. That buying things is proof of having made it. That owning a house equals success. These aren't truths. They're ideas, carefully seeded. Normalised not because they're universally correct, but because they serve a certain order. They shape not only your goals, but the framework within which you're allowed to imagine them.

Take debt. We're told it's a tool, a stepping stone, a marker of responsibility. Student loans are "an investment." Credit cards "build your history." Car finance is simply how things are done. But the language is gentle, the risks buried in fine print, the long-term cost easy to ignore. What debt often becomes is not a bridge, but a shackle. It quietly expands the years you'll need to work. It limits choice, constrains movement. And yet, it rarely feels shocking. Why? Because we've absorbed the script that says it's normal. Expected. Virtuous, even.

Employment offers another illusion. The "good job" is still held up as the bedrock of a responsible life. A steady salary, benefits, a path upwards. But in practice, those ladders have grown narrow and brittle. Roles are insecure. Wages lag. Support systems fade. And yet, straying from this model—pursuing self-employment, retiring early, questioning the premise—is often dismissed as foolish. Again, this isn't truth. It's containment. A cultural boundary masquerading as common sense.

Then there's consumption. We're sold more than objects—we're sold identity. A car is no longer just a vehicle, but a statement. A house isn't simply shelter, but validation. Even anti-consumption, in its trendy forms, can be packaged and sold. The result? A society where worth is measured not in peace or fulfilment, but in possessions and performance. Net worth becomes a stand-in for self-worth. And money ceases to be a tool—it becomes a test, a mirror, a pressure.

To challenge these scripts is not simply to think differently. It is to begin reclaiming your agency. Because so long as you operate within these inherited beliefs, your choices are not fully your own. Financial liberation doesn't begin with a spreadsheet. It begins with the ability to *pause*. To ask, before spending or borrowing or toiling: *Whose narrative am I acting out?*

This chapter aims to expose the machinery. Not in the abstract, but in the personal. You'll see how your mind is recruited into the system, how emotional responses are shaped, and how stories you didn't choose came to define what you think is possible. The traps, you'll discover, don't just sit out there in banks and policies. They live inside your habits, your self-talk, your fears. They whisper in your own tone of voice: *You should have more. You're behind. Everyone else is ahead.*

By the time you finish this chapter, you won't just see financial deception as a vague danger. You'll see its anatomy. You'll recognise that many so-called failures were not errors in judgment, but outcomes of design. That much of what you took as responsibility was, in truth, obedience to someone else's narrative.

This isn't a call to paranoia. It's a call to perception. Financial systems, by their nature, are not wicked—but neither are they impartial. They are shaped by incentives. And those incentives rarely align with your well-being. To navigate this terrain, you must learn to read it—fluently, critically, dispassionately. You must learn to question the frame before accepting the picture.

Only then can you stop playing a part and start making a choice. And that is where true autonomy begins—not in wealth, but in awareness.

Not in certainty, but in clarity. And not in playing to win, but in finally understanding the game.

1.1 The Age of the Financial Predator

The most dangerous predators do not pounce from shadows. They stand in the light, branded, licensed, and applauded. They speak the language of safety and wear the guise of service. They offer credit to the struggling, advice to the uncertain, and convenience to the overwhelmed. They do not need to lie outright. They simply ensure you never see the whole truth.

We no longer live in the age of the obvious scam. Nigerian princes and Ponzi schemes still exist, of course, but they are now relegated to the margins—amateur relics in a professionalised economy of extraction. The modern predator is institutional, systemic, and—crucially—legal. It operates through contracts, algorithms, advertising, and compliance departments. Its strength lies not in deception alone, but in its normalisation. You are not warned about these predators; you are told to trust them.

Banks, insurance providers, payday lenders, "buy now, pay later" apps, investment platforms, and even government policies now occupy the role once filled by street-level fraudsters. But the consequences of their actions are far more widespread, socially sanctioned, and economically entrenching. To understand how this came to be—and why it continues—we must first interrogate the conditions that allow exploitation to masquerade as assistance.

From Fraud to Framework: The Institutionalisation of Extraction

In the 19th and early 20th centuries, financial fraud was largely unregulated. Unscrupulous individuals could peddle bogus investments or predatory loans with impunity. The response—spurred by scandals like the 1929 stock market crash—was the birth of regulation: central banking, financial oversight, consumer protections. For a time, this worked. Trust in banks, pensions, and state-backed financial systems became a cornerstone of post-war economic life.

But regulation did not eliminate exploitation. It professionalised it. Over time, powerful institutions lobbied to shape the rules to their own advantage. Practices that would once have been deemed exploitative became codified into law. Consider the United States' repeal of the Glass-Steagall Act in 1999, which blurred the line between commercial and investment banking and paved the way for the 2008 global financial crisis. Or look to the UK, where the rise of zero-hour contracts and unaffordable housing policies have effectively privatised public precarity.

Predators evolved with the legal landscape. They stopped stealing. They started charging. Interest rates, penalty fees, hidden charges, and dynamic pricing are all mechanisms of modern wealth transfer—from the less informed to the more sophisticated, from the poor to the rich, from individuals to institutions. What separates today's financial predator from a criminal is not morality—it's a business licence.

The Language of Legitimacy: How Predators Rebrand as Protectors

The success of modern financial predation rests on more than structure; it rests on language. Words are weapons. *Interest* sounds neutral, even fair. *Premiums* imply exclusivity. *Late fees* suggest a personal failing. These terms obscure the nature of the transaction and shift moral responsibility onto the consumer.

Take "overdraft protection," a service banks offer that often results in exorbitant fees when an account dips below zero. Ostensibly a safeguard, it frequently traps users in a spiral of charges that far exceed the original deficit. Or consider payday loans, where annual percentage rates can exceed 1,000%, but are presented in terms of short-term cash flow assistance.

Even government policies contribute to the facade. Student loan schemes, for instance, are marketed as opportunities. They enable access to education—until repayment terms quietly metastasise into lifelong financial burden, with interest compounding faster than many graduates can earn. The UK's own student loan repayment structure, particularly after recent policy changes, effectively functions as a graduate tax—but without the same transparency, predictability, or equity.

Convenience as Camouflage: The Rise of the Platform Middleman

With the explosion of digital finance, a new breed of predator has emerged: the convenience broker. These are the apps, services, and platforms that insert themselves between you and your money, under the pretext of making your life easier. Some of them genuinely do. But others exploit your time pressure, cognitive load, and behavioural blind spots.

Take "Buy Now, Pay Later" services like Klarna or Afterpay. They sell the illusion of affordability. In reality, they encourage fragmented decision-making, delay financial reckoning, and lead to significant rates of delinquency—especially among younger consumers. The platform profits from every late fee and interest charge, while the user rationalises the decision as savvy budgeting.

Or consider micro-investment apps. They lower the barrier to entry, yes. But they also gamify financial risk, pushing users to trade more frequently than is prudent, often under the illusion that more activity equals more control. In truth, high-frequency trading by unsophisticated users tends to benefit the platforms through transaction fees and bid-ask spreads, not the investor.

These intermediaries are not neutral facilitators. Their business models depend on engagement, not outcomes. They profit when you borrow more, transact more, check more, fear more. And because they are sleek, mobile, and user-friendly, we forget to question their motives.

Regulatory Theatre: Why Oversight Isn't Protection

You might ask: if this is so exploitative, where are the regulators? The answer is complex, but deeply instructive. Oversight bodies often operate reactively, not proactively. They are slow to respond to innovation, limited by political capture, and frequently under-resourced compared to the institutions they are meant to supervise.

Moreover, financial predators are adept at staying just within the bounds of legality. Their lawyers design compliance into the product. They test thresholds, exploit grey areas, and use opacity as armour. Terms and conditions are deliberately complex, not to inform but to shield. By the time a regulatory response is mobilised, the damage is done—and the profits banked.

When regulators do act, they often settle for fines rather than structural reform. These fines are absorbed as the cost of doing business. For instance, Wells Fargo's fake account scandal led to billions in penalties. But the institution remains intact. No executive faced meaningful jail time. The brand was tarnished, but the model endures.

From Predation to Dependence: The Normalisation of Exploitation

Perhaps the most pernicious consequence of institutionalised financial predation is psychological: it shifts the burden of responsibility onto the individual, creating a population that blames itself for its entrapment. If you missed a payment, it's because you were disorganised. If you struggle with debt, it's because you didn't budget properly. If you can't buy a house, it's because you failed to hustle hard enough.

This narrative suits predators perfectly. It prevents scrutiny of the systems that exploit. It fosters shame, which inhibits collective action. And it maintains a market of compliant users who internalise failure and continue to engage with platforms and services that hurt them.

Worse still, dependence becomes habitual. Just as victims of abusive relationships may struggle to leave due to perceived security, users of exploitative financial systems may cling to them because the alternatives feel too risky, too complicated, or simply unavailable. A poorly designed pension is better than none. A predatory mortgage is still a way to own a home. A job with no future is still a paycheque. This is not choice; it is conditioned acquiescence.

Rethinking Trust in a Predatory Landscape

To navigate this environment, trust must be redefined. Traditional markers—regulation, branding, market share—are no longer reliable indicators of ethical intent or user benefit. Trust must now be earned through transparency, alignment of incentives, and demonstrable respect for user autonomy. Few institutions meet this standard. Many deliberately avoid it.

The implication for the reader is sobering but empowering: vigilance is not paranoia—it is prudence. Awareness is not cynicism—it is clarity. The only defence against predators dressed as providers is to remove the costume, piece by piece, until what remains is the truth of their intentions.

This does not mean rejecting all systems, abandoning modern finance, or descending into fatalism. It means recognising power dynamics and designing your financial life around autonomy, not dependence. It means reading contracts. Questioning defaults.

Valuing simplicity over convenience when convenience conceals cost. It means, above all, remembering that legality is not legitimacy, and trust must be earned, not assumed.

The age of the financial predator is not marked by violence, but by quiet erosion. Your task is not to become paranoid, but to become fluent. When you can see the predator's logic, you can stop playing their game.

1.2 The Myth of the Rational Actor

For decades, economic theory has rested on a seductive fiction: that humans are rational actors. That we assess options calmly, weigh risks logically, and optimise outcomes in our financial decision-making. This idea—known formally as the rational choice model—has been so influential that it underpins everything from national fiscal policy to the algorithms that determine your mortgage eligibility. But it is wrong. And dangerously so.

Humans are not rational calculators. We are emotionally charged, socially influenced, and frequently overwhelmed by complexity. The more we learn from psychology, neuroscience, and behavioural economics, the clearer this becomes. And yet, despite the mounting evidence, financial systems continue to be designed as if we were spreadsheet-minded machines. This mismatch—between how people actually behave and how systems assume we behave—is not merely academic. It is the root of widespread exploitation.

If a model misrepresents its subjects, it is not just inaccurate. It is weaponisable. The rational actor model does not just fail to protect people; it makes them easier to manipulate, because it ignores the very vulnerabilities that financial institutions now actively exploit.

The rational actor theory gained prominence in the 20th century through thinkers like John von Neumann, Oskar Morgenstern, and Milton Friedman. It presented a picture of economic life that was elegant, if simplistic: individuals act in their own best interest, make decisions by maximising utility, and respond predictably to incentives. Governments and markets, trusting this logic, built frameworks around it. Welfare policy, consumer protections, and even pension design were constructed on the assumption that people would save adequately for retirement, budget prudently, and invest according to risk tolerance.

Reality, however, is less tidy. People procrastinate, overspend, panic-sell, ignore small print, and make financially devastating decisions—repeatedly. The rational actor does not buy lottery tickets with near-zero odds. The rational actor does not go deep into debt for a depreciating car. The rational actor does not pay exorbitant fees for a convenience he could avoid with two minutes of planning. And yet, in the real world, these behaviours are not the exception. They are the rule.

Behavioural science has now catalogued a wide array of cognitive biases that consistently distort financial decision-making. *Loss aversion* causes people to avoid risks even when the odds are favourable. *Present bias* leads us to prioritise immediate gratification over long-term benefit—saving less, spending more, and delaying difficult but necessary choices. *Anchoring* causes us to rely on arbitrary reference points—like the first price we see or the salary we were offered—as if they held rational weight. *Confirmation bias* encourages us to seek information that affirms our existing beliefs, making us susceptible to persuasive marketing and financial echo chambers.

These are not isolated glitches in otherwise sound minds. They are baked into the human cognitive architecture. And they interact with emotional states—stress, fear, excitement—to create patterns of behaviour that are systematically irrational, but entirely predictable. Advertisers know this. App developers know this. So do payday lenders, casinos, and even certain credit card companies. They design with human error in mind, not in defiance of it.

Consider the design of modern fintech apps. Many are built to mimic the feedback loops of social media—instant notifications, micro-rewards, personalised nudges. Robinhood, a trading app once heralded for democratising finance, used digital confetti animations to celebrate trades. This wasn't frivolous; it was psychological. It encouraged users to trade more frequently, driven by dopamine rather than strategy. The average Robinhood user traded options—a complex and risky asset class—at a higher rate than clients at traditional brokerages. This wasn't empowerment. It was behavioural manipulation, camouflaged as convenience.

Or take the mortgage crisis of 2008. Subprime borrowers were given loans they didn't understand, under terms they couldn't sustain, for homes they couldn't afford. Rational actors would have avoided such arrangements. But the process was saturated with complexity, asymmetry of information, and targeted emotional appeal. Lenders pushed products with teaser rates and hidden resets. Borrowers were assured that housing prices always rise. The system assumed—and exploited—irrationality at every level.

And this is the point. When models of rationality are maintained despite evidence to the contrary, they cease to be neutral. They become ideological. They serve power by absolving institutions of responsibility. If individuals are rational, then financial missteps are personal failings. Debt is a lack of discipline. Poor investment decisions are a lack of intelligence. Financial ruin becomes a private tragedy, not a structural outcome. The system is always exonerated.

But let's be clear: these aren't isolated anecdotes. They are systematic effects, engineered by design. Financial products are not designed for rational actors. They are designed for real humans—fallible, busy, uncertain—and are often optimised not for user benefit, but for revenue extraction. High interest rates, default settings, complex terms, and late payment penalties are all built around behavioural expectations. If you were truly rational, many financial products would become unprofitable.

This misalignment also extends into public policy. Retirement savings plans in the UK and elsewhere often rely on the idea that people will voluntarily contribute enough over time, despite all evidence to the contrary. Auto-enrolment schemes have improved participation, precisely because they leverage inertia. But these programmes still assume that, once enrolled, individuals will make optimal choices about contribution levels, risk allocations, and withdrawal strategies. Few do.

Likewise, financial education campaigns often assume that providing information will change behaviour. It rarely does. Knowledge does not equal action. A person can know that carrying credit card debt is expensive and still carry it. They can understand compound interest and still fail to save. What's needed is not more information, but better environments—ones that account for human psychology rather than ignoring it.

There are, of course, economists and policymakers who now recognise this. The field of behavioural economics—pioneered by thinkers like Daniel Kahneman, Amos Tversky, Richard Thaler, and Cass Sunstein—has begun to reshape how we think about decision-making. Concepts like "nudging," choice architecture, and bounded rationality are slowly entering the mainstream. But progress is uneven, and often superficial. While governments have begun using behavioural insights to improve policy delivery, corporations have been quicker and more aggressive in using them to maximise profits.

This creates a profound ethical asymmetry. Institutions with massive data sets, behavioural scientists, and algorithmic power are interacting with individuals who may be stressed, distracted, or financially desperate. The playing field is not level. And when the system continues to treat people as if they were rational actors, it gives itself permission to blame them when they predictably behave otherwise.

What's the alternative? It begins with radical honesty—about what people are like, and what systems need to do to protect rather than prey on them. It requires moving beyond the mythology of the rational actor and designing financial products, services, and policies that support actual human behaviour. That means transparency, simplicity, safeguards, and aligned incentives. It means recognising that real empowerment is not about giving people more choices, but about helping them make better ones.

On an individual level, it also means cultivating awareness of your own behavioural patterns. Knowing the cognitive traps doesn't always mean you'll avoid them—but it does give you a fighting chance. Emotional regulation, decision boundaries, defaults that serve your interests rather than others'—these are the new competencies in a world that profits from your missteps.

The rational actor never existed. He was a fiction—a convenient one. But the human behind him is real: complex, emotional, sometimes irrational, but capable of learning. Financial self-defence begins with seeing yourself clearly—not as an economic agent in a vacuum, but as a person navigating a system designed for your imperfection. Not so that you can become invulnerable, but so that you can stop being predictable.

Once you understand that irrationality is not a flaw but a fact, you stop seeing yourself as broken—and start seeing the system more clearly for what it is.

1.3 Manufactured Scarcity and Fear Economies

Scarcity sells. That much is obvious. What is less obvious—and far more troubling—is how often scarcity is fabricated. Not by nature or necessity, but by design. In modern finance, fear is not just a by-product; it is a product. It is curated, scaled, and monetised across industries. Insurance providers, investment platforms, retailers, fintech apps, and even government agencies participate in the same psychological playbook: engineer a perception of risk, then offer yourself as the solution.

The market is no longer merely reacting to fear—it is creating it. And when fear becomes the organising principle of financial life, it distorts value, weakens autonomy, and renders decision-making reactive rather than strategic. Understanding this machinery is essential if one is to defend against it.

At its core, manufactured scarcity is a psychological manipulation that leverages our evolutionary wiring. Humans are not indifferent to loss. We are loss-averse. Behavioural research, particularly the work of Kahneman and Tversky, has shown that the pain of losing something is felt more intensely than the pleasure of gaining it. This makes us highly susceptible to threats—real or imagined. When scarcity is suggested, urgency follows. And when urgency kicks in, discernment shuts down.

Consider the insurance industry. Its entire model depends on presenting worst-case scenarios as looming possibilities. The marketing does not begin with probability—it begins with fear. Life insurance brochures don't open with actuarial data; they open with images of bereaved families and empty chairs. The message is clear: *what will your loved ones do when you're gone?* Travel insurance providers showcase tales of nightmarish hospital bills abroad. Health insurance advertisements feature smiling families juxtaposed with ominous statistics about disease prevalence. What you are being sold is not coverage—it is relief. And you pay handsomely for it.

This dynamic would be more defensible if pricing and products were transparent. But they rarely are. Policy details are obscured behind jargon and variable exclusions. Deductibles, co-pays, and limits are often buried. The fear is clear; the value is not. You are emotionally primed to act quickly but denied the tools to act wisely. This asymmetry of information is not incidental. It is commercial strategy.

Investment platforms operate under a similar logic but invert the emotion. Instead of fear of loss, they often stoke fear of missing out—FOMO, now so pervasive that it has become a driver of market behaviour. Retail investors are bombarded with images of others "getting in early" on the next big thing: crypto surges, meme stocks, IPOs. The message is urgent: *act now or be left behind.* Trading apps like eToro and Robinhood amplify this urgency by providing social feeds and rankings, nudging users to match the moves of others in real time. You're not just investing—you're playing not to lose, socially and financially.

What's crucial here is that the scarcity is synthetic. There is no actual shortage of investment opportunities. But by presenting time-sensitive windows, limited-supply offerings, or peer comparisons, platforms create the illusion of scarcity—and, therefore, the psychological imperative to act immediately. They turn the slow, deliberate task of building wealth into a fast-paced, high-stakes race.

The same tactic appears in consumer fintech. Budgeting apps, for instance, often deploy alert systems that flag you as "overspending" the moment you exceed arbitrary thresholds. Subscription managers colour-code your "danger zones" and flash red when your spending deviates from historical averages. While some degree of nudging can be helpful, the underlying effect is a constant drumbeat of insecurity. The suggestion is that you are always on the brink of failure, always just one forgotten payment away from collapse.

This dynamic extends well beyond fintech into consumer retail. Scarcity marketing—"Only 2 left in stock!" "Limited time offer!" "24 hours only!"—is now ubiquitous. Amazon, the world's most powerful retailer, uses real-time inventory prompts to signal urgency. Airlines and booking sites show how many people are "looking at this deal" or how few rooms are "still available." The result is not better decision-making but impulse purchasing. People buy not because of value alignment, but because they're afraid not to.

It is not that these tactics are new; it's that they've become universal, algorithmically optimised, and behaviourally engineered. Scarcity and fear are now embedded into the user experience itself. And they are being deployed against users who are increasingly time-poor, cognitively overwhelmed, and financially vulnerable.

This is especially problematic because it alters the perceived value of money and goods. When fear drives action, we stop evaluating based on utility and start evaluating based on avoidance—of pain, regret, exclusion. We pay premiums not for actual quality or fit, but to silence anxiety. In such a climate, value becomes subjective and fragile, distorted by emotional urgency. You are not choosing between products; you are choosing between fears.

The most insidious effect of the fear economy is cumulative: over time, it reshapes your worldview. When scarcity becomes normalised—when you're always on alert for loss, exclusion, or deficiency—you begin to operate from a defensive crouch. Financial decisions are made not from sovereignty, but from stress. You hoard out of fear of inflation. You overspend out of fear of social exclusion. You underinvest out of fear of loss. In each case, fear shrinks the range of viable action.

This dynamic also has broader sociopolitical consequences. When entire populations are kept in a state of manufactured precarity, they become easier to govern and harder to mobilise. People bogged down in financial stress are less likely to protest, organise, or vote against exploitative systems. The fear economy thus serves not only private enterprise, but also entrenched power structures. Scarcity is not just a business tactic; it is a tool of social control.

Some will argue that fear has a legitimate place in economic decision-making. And indeed, not all risk is illusory. Insurance, for instance, exists for a reason. But the issue is not fear per se; it is its amplification and monetisation. When risk is exaggerated, when probabilities are warped for commercial gain, and when transparency is deliberately reduced, we are no longer in the domain of prudence—we are in the machinery of manipulation.

It is also worth noting that this manipulation is not evenly distributed. The poorest are most vulnerable to it. They are less likely to have time, energy, or access to decode complex terms. They experience greater anxiety and urgency in financial matters, which makes them more susceptible to fear-based decision-making. Payday loans, high-interest credit, and predatory insurance products flourish in precisely these demographics—not because of moral failing, but because of systemic targeting.

So how does one resist this apparatus? The answer begins with awareness—not just of tactics, but of the emotional terrain they seek to exploit. Recognise the emotional cues that precede financial decisions: is the purchase grounded in need, or in fear? Is the urgency real, or artificially induced? Is the product's value clear, or obscured by narrative?

Secondly, embrace slowness where possible. Manufactured scarcity relies on speed. Pausing undermines its grip. Delayed decisions are often better decisions—not because they guarantee optimal outcomes, but because they allow room for reflection over reaction.

Thirdly, treat simplicity as a strategic asset. Financial tools and decisions should be intelligible without anxiety. If a product requires 40 pages of terms and conditions, it likely profits from your confusion. The goal is not to avoid risk entirely, but to engage with it on your own terms—not the ones written by an anxious copywriter or a conversion-optimised interface.

Fear will always exist. But when it becomes the default setting of your financial life, something has gone wrong—not in you, but in the system designed to profit from your discomfort. Manufactured scarcity and fear-based economics are not anomalies; they are the new norm. Seeing them clearly is the first—and most critical—step in reclaiming agency.

1.4 The Story You Were Sold

You were told a story. Not out loud, not in a single sitting, and not by any one person. It arrived in fragments—over dinner tables, in classrooms, through television ads and glossy university brochures. It was reinforced by bank campaigns, economic policy, and the proud tone of HR departments offering long-term contracts with modest annual reviews. And if you're like most people, you absorbed it without question, because it never asked for permission. It came wrapped in the tone of common sense, of "how the world works."

This is the story: Debt is normal. Jobs are security. Success is visible and expensive. That's the narrative architecture of modern financial culture. And like all well-told stories, it functions best when you forget it's fiction.

This subchapter is about making that story visible—deconstructing the invisible scripts that shape how you relate to money, work, and status. Because before you can change your financial outcomes, you must identify the assumptions you've inherited. Not the ones you *consciously* believe, but the ones that operate like background code: unquestioned, automated, and quietly limiting. These aren't personal quirks. They're *cultural malware*—belief systems seeded by interests that profit from your compliance.

Let's start with the most corrosive and widely accepted myth: *that debt is normal.* The average Briton enters adulthood already carrying student loans. For many, this is followed by credit card balances, auto loans, mortgages, and Buy Now, Pay Later agreements. Each debt is framed as a rite of passage. Borrowing is presented not as a risk, but as a tool—a way to access adulthood, invest in your future, or build creditworthiness. The problem is not that all debt is inherently evil. The problem is that it has been *systematically normalised*, often without fully informed consent.

When student loans were first introduced in the UK in the early 1990s, they were modest and optional. Today, the average graduate leaves university owing £45,000 or more, with interest rates well above inflation and repayment mechanisms designed more to generate revenue than to ensure equity. What was once a subsidy is now a profit stream. Yet society still markets higher education as an unquestionable necessity and positions the debt that funds it as inevitable.

This same pattern plays out across other domains. A mortgage is framed as a "good debt"—a smart investment in your future. Yet this framing often obscures the long-term financial, psychological, and geographic constraints that 25- to 35-year fixed payments impose. What's more, the metrics used to determine mortgage affordability (typically income multiples) are rooted in market assumptions, not individual well-being. You are told what you *can* afford by someone who profits from your stretching to the limit.

Credit card debt is the most revealing case. The majority of people carrying balances do not do so out of indulgence. They do it out of necessity—an emergency expense, a shortfall between paycheques, or a period of unemployment. And yet the cultural narrative around credit card debt remains saturated with moral judgement: overspending, irresponsibility, living beyond one's means. These judgements are not accidental. They serve a function: they deflect scrutiny from the systemic conditions that make debt a survival strategy for many.

Debt, then, is not simply a financial instrument—it is a social control mechanism. It locks people into jobs they no longer want. It discourages risk-taking, such as starting a business or relocating. It forces short-term thinking, narrows opportunity, and keeps people compliant. And all of this is justified through the idea that debt is "just part of life." That's not a financial principle. That's a story you were sold.

Next comes the myth of *job as safety*. From childhood, most people are conditioned to equate employment with stability. The message is simple: study hard, get a good job, climb the ladder, retire well. It is a vision of linear progress and institutional reliability. But this vision is outdated—and in many sectors, dangerously misleading.

Today's labour market is not structured for stability. It is structured for flexibility—*employer* flexibility. In the UK, the rise of gig work, zero-hour contracts, and freelance arrangements has steadily eroded the social contract once offered by employers. The pensions are smaller, the benefits thinner, and the ladder—if it exists at all—is shaky at best. And yet the cultural messaging remains frozen in time. We still ask children what they want to "be" when they grow up, as though professions are static identities rather than economic negotiations.

The modern economy doesn't reward loyalty. It rewards leverage. And yet people are taught to equate staying put with safety, even when the data suggests otherwise. Job redundancy, sudden re-skilling requirements, and toxic workplace cultures are real and rising risks. But the belief that "a steady job equals a secure life" persists—because it is functional for institutions. A workforce that views salary as sanctuary is less likely to challenge poor treatment, wage stagnation, or structural inequity.

This is not a critique of employment per se. Some people find meaningful, well-compensated work within organisations. But the point is *you were sold a narrative of safety that no longer matches the architecture of the system*. When reality and expectation diverge, suffering increases. That gap is not your failure. It's the result of an obsolete script being force-fed through modern mechanisms.

Finally, we come to the crown jewel of consumer capitalism: the idea that *success equals consumption.* From luxury cars to branded tech, from designer clothing to five-star holidays, the markers of financial "arrival" are external, curated, and conspicuous. We are taught not just to succeed, but to be seen succeeding. The effect is corrosive—not only on wallets but on identity.

Social media has accelerated this dramatically. Platforms like Instagram and TikTok function as curated theatres of consumption, where people perform prosperity in increasingly stylised formats. "Lifestyle content" is often indistinguishable from advertising. And the result is a subtle but powerful inflation of expectations. You begin to feel poor not because you lack necessities, but because your life lacks *display value.* This is not a flaw in the system; it is the business model.

The problem is that this performative consumption rarely brings sustained satisfaction. The hedonic treadmill ensures that each purchase, once made, becomes the new normal. The dopamine hit fades. The next upgrade becomes necessary. The cycle continues. Meanwhile, savings remain stagnant, debt increases, and genuine well-being is deferred indefinitely.

This cycle is reinforced by financial institutions that directly benefit from overconsumption. Credit card companies design reward schemes that encourage spending. Retailers offer point-of-sale credit as a frictionless option. Even banks use transactional data to upsell products based on past spending behaviour. The idea that "you deserve it" is not a message of empowerment. It is a lever of control.

To begin rewriting these scripts, one must first name them. Observe them not as truths, but as cultural constructs. Interrogate inherited phrases like "a house is always a good investment," "it's just what adults do," or "you can't put a price on peace of mind." Ask who benefits when you believe these things without question. Then experiment with alternatives.

What if debt were a last resort, not a default? What if a job were a tool—not a destination? What if success were defined privately, not performed publicly? These are not abstract questions. They are strategic reframings. And they are necessary because once you see that much of your financial thinking is inherited, not chosen, you reclaim agency. You stop living out someone else's script.

This is not about becoming contrarian for its own sake. It is about identifying which parts of the financial story serve you—and which serve others at your expense. Culture is not just something we passively inherit. It is something we can edit, one belief at a time. The story you were sold has power only for as long as you accept its terms. Once you expose it, you get to write a new one. One aligned with clarity, not compliance. With sufficiency, not status. And most importantly, with values that are truly your own.

Chapter 2
The Psychology of Money Traps

No one sets out in life aiming to be entangled in financial fog, yet that's exactly where so many find themselves. In an age brimming with budgeting apps, financial advice at every turn, and ever-expanding avenues for earning, it's a striking paradox. People still spend on things they don't truly value, earn less than they're capable of, and bounce between periods of meticulous control and financial disarray. The issue is rarely intellect, and rarely a failure of will. More often, it's the result of a deeper compromise: their internal compass—the system guiding those choices—has been quietly rewritten. Shaped not by intention, but by lingering emotions, cultural narratives, and automatic behaviours that serve agendas not their own.

This chapter isn't a guide to budgeting or timing the market. It drills further down—into the foundations beneath your financial behaviour. Into the beliefs, emotions, reactions, and neurological defaults that silently sculpt the way you spend, save, earn, and give. If the previous chapter exposed the external architecture of financial manipulation, this one maps how those forces nest within us—how they hijack self-perception, occupy attention, and install reflexes that feel uniquely personal but are, in fact, systematically conditioned.

At the heart of this lies a quiet but catastrophic confusion: the conflation of net worth with self-worth. It starts young. A child receives praise not only for curiosity or kindness, but for marks on a report card, stylish trainers, or being well put together. As adolescence sets in, achievement and identity begin their courtship. By adulthood, the union is complete. Your job title stands in for dignity. Your salary feels like a statement of intelligence. Your lifestyle becomes a billboard for who you believe yourself to be. This isn't coincidence. It's the culmination of decades of cultural scripting, reinforced by marketing departments, economic policy, and social institutions that benefit from the fusion.

And that fusion is ruthlessly exploited. Entire sectors—from the high street to professional networking sites—depend on your readiness to measure your value by what you earn, what you wear, and what you post. Because the emptiness of external validation is never fully resolved, the chase never ends. You work extra hours, spend beyond your values, or remain underpaid—not for lack of financial knowledge, but because money has become tangled with identity. You may overextend to feel momentarily whole, or undercharge to sidestep the anxiety of seeming greedy. Both behaviours stem not from calculation, but from a logic rooted in emotion—misaligned and misunderstood.

This emotional fog is thickened by the modern economy's emphasis on instant gratification. Neuroscience offers a blunt reality check: we don't make financial decisions purely from our rational minds. The limbic system, our emotional engine, plays a central role—especially in moments of spending. When you tap a card or hit 'buy now,' you're lighting up the same reward circuits activated by sugar, sex, and social approval. And today's financial technologies are built to keep those circuits firing. Everything—from banking apps to payment interfaces—is optimised for ease, speed, and unconscious action. The faster the transaction, the less time your rational faculties have to intervene.

Take subscriptions. They're not just convenient—they're psychologically cunning. They automate assent. They thrive on our brain's resistance to effort. You forget you're even paying because remembering would require effort, and effort creates friction. Or consider one-click purchases, tap-to-pay features, or investment apps wrapped in candy-coloured UX. They abstract the reality of money leaving your account. You don't feel like you're spending—

you feel like you're interacting. The pain of paying is dulled; the dopamine of acquiring remains intact.

These aren't glitches in the system. They *are* the system. The financial landscape is increasingly gamified—engineered not for your wellbeing, but for your interaction. You're not meant to win. You're meant to engage. To return. To click again. In this context, being merely informed isn't enough. Information doesn't cancel manipulation. What's needed now is something sterner: awareness. Not passive awareness, but active, embodied, practiced vigilance. In an economy of nudges and triggers, consciousness becomes a kind of financial armour.

But let's not be naïve. Awareness alone won't fix what's broken if the operating system running underneath—the emotional and cognitive architecture—is still corrupted. That's why the final section of this chapter shifts focus. It moves from diagnosis to repair. Drawing from neuroscience, behavioural psychology, and mindfulness, we'll explore ways to rewire the patterns that compromise your clarity. This isn't theory for theory's sake. It's lived, applicable practice: the art of pausing before a reaction. The skill of separating emotional reflex from values-aligned action. The habit of questioning inherited assumptions before they harden into choices.

None of this is about becoming hyper-controlled or perfectly rational. That's not the point. The aim is to move from autopilot to agency. To trade reactivity for reflection. Consider, for instance, how mindfulness—a term often tossed around casually—can materially change financial behaviour. Studies show that mindfulness increases *interoception*, the body's internal sensing ability, which in turn enhances emotional regulation. Translation? You're less likely to blow your budget after a bad day if you can detect the physiological signs of stress before they drive your decisions.

Likewise, cognitive reframing—a method of consciously reinterpreting events—can help shift the meaning of financial failure. Instead of viewing a setback as shameful, you can begin to understand it as information. That shift doesn't just feel better. It enables action. Instead of freezing, you can adapt.

Just as vital is the idea of values-based financial design. It's a different starting point entirely. Instead of asking, "How can I spend less?" or "How can I earn more?", it invites a more meaningful inquiry: "What is enough—for me?" What's the point of all this earning and budgeting, if you haven't stopped to ask what you're trying to build? Without a clear answer, it's far too easy to be pulled into cycles of anxious accumulation and empty control.

Speaking of control—beware its seduction. In an increasingly volatile world, financial control can become a proxy for safety. Budgeting tools, expense trackers, performance dashboards—they whisper promises of mastery. But beneath that sense of order often lies unease. The kind of hypervigilance that doesn't soothe, but inflames. And the need to monitor every penny isn't always a reflection of responsibility; sometimes it's just fear dressed up in metrics. True peace with money doesn't come from obsessing over every detail. It comes from alignment. From coherence. From the confidence that, even amidst uncertainty, your actions reflect your values—not your fears.

The deeper irony in all this is that most people aren't imprisoned by a lack of money. They're trapped by what money represents. By how they imagine others see them. By how they believe they should behave. Money becomes not just medium, but metaphor. Not just currency, but story. And unless you learn to see those layers for what they are, they'll keep running the show—silently, relentlessly, and often destructively.

This chapter isn't selling quick wins. It won't feed you platitudes or turn financial psychology into a checklist. Instead, it offers a lens. A way to examine, with honesty and rigour, why you do what you do with money—and how to break free from the scripts that no longer serve you. Because financial literacy is never just about numbers. It's about emotional fluency. Behavioural insight. Psychological courage.

You're not "bad with money." You were simply never taught how to recognise the architecture shaping your behaviour. And let's be blunt: the systems profiting from that ignorance are well-resourced, sophisticated, and largely invisible. They won't disappear. But they *can* be defused—once you learn to name them. Once you choose, again and again, to respond from awareness, not impulse.

The psychology of money is not an accessory to your financial life. It *is* your financial life—until you claim it. Until you rewrite the defaults. Until the decisions you make truly belong to you.

2.1 The Wounds We Spend From

Most financial decisions don't begin in spreadsheets. They begin in memory. Behind the act of tapping a card, declining a raise, hoarding cash, or spending compulsively lies something older and less visible: a psychological residue, often formed in childhood, shaped by emotional imprinting, parental modelling, and moments of unprocessed instability. This is what psychologists and financial therapists refer to as *financial trauma*—an under-acknowledged but pervasive force that can shape an individual's relationship with money for decades, often without their awareness.

To call it trauma is not to exaggerate. It is to name a reality backed by evidence. Trauma, in its broadest psychological sense, is not just about catastrophic events. It is about overwhelming experiences that exceed a person's ability to integrate or make meaning from them. When applied to money, trauma can take many forms: growing up in a household where resources were chronically scarce, where arguments about bills created a backdrop of anxiety, or where abundance was present but used manipulatively—as a tool of control, guilt, or conditional love. Each of these situations can leave lasting imprints, not only on one's beliefs about money but also on their sense of safety, identity, and agency.

Financial trauma is not evenly distributed. It is influenced by socioeconomic background, race, class, family dynamics, and cultural norms. But what unites all manifestations is the way it *internalises threat.* Money becomes not just a tool or necessity but a symbolic battleground. For some, it represents freedom; for others, shame. For some, it triggers urgency and fear; for others, inertia and avoidance. And these reactions are rarely conscious. They are patterns—repeated actions that make sense only when viewed through the lens of unresolved experience.

Consider the adult who compulsively under-earns despite qualifications and talent. On paper, it looks irrational. But dig deeper, and a pattern emerges: a parent who resented high earners, a childhood where ambition was shamed, or a belief that asking for more invites conflict or rejection. Conversely, take the executive who constantly overspends, not on luxuries but on gifts, dinners, or "taking care of others." Behind the generosity may lie a younger version of themselves who had to earn love through usefulness—or who feared that financial security made them emotionally expendable.

In both cases, the money behaviour is not about numbers. It is about unmet emotional needs, distorted beliefs, and the coping strategies that once protected someone but now quietly limit them.

Neuroscience supports this understanding. The brain's threat detection system—particularly the amygdala—does not distinguish between physical and financial threats. If scarcity or volatility defined early experiences, the brain wires itself to detect and react to any cues that resemble those moments. This hypervigilance manifests as over-saving, chronic financial anxiety, or decision paralysis, even when external conditions have changed. The body doesn't "know" that the crisis has passed. It continues responding as if survival is still at stake.

Cultural messaging further complicates recovery. In many societies, financial struggle is pathologised. Poverty is moralised, wealth is idolised, and financial mistakes are seen as personal failings rather than symptoms of structural forces or psychological adaptations. This creates what some researchers call *compound shame*: not only does the individual suffer from past wounds, but they also carry the shame of having them. The result is silence. Financial trauma becomes a private burden—unspoken, unexplored, and reinforced by the absence of honest discourse.

Silence, however, doesn't mean dormancy. Trauma that is unspoken is often acted out. It appears in self-sabotaging financial decisions, in compulsive saving or spending, in sudden surges of guilt when receiving money, or in an inability to plan beyond the next pay cycle. It shows up in relationships—where money becomes a proxy for control, trust, or intimacy. And because these patterns are rarely traced back to their origin, they are misinterpreted as personality traits rather than trauma responses.

There is growing recognition in both clinical psychology and financial therapy that *healing is not about fixing behaviour first*. It is about surfacing the beliefs, memories, and emotional charges that drive the behaviour. For instance, a person who feels chronically unsafe with money may need not another budgeting tool, but a structured process to explore when and how that sense of unsafety began. Was it the eviction they watched their parents endure? The time a parent lost a job and spiralled into depression? Or was it subtler—an absence of communication, where money was always a taboo, and thus became a source of quiet dread?

Crucially, not all financial trauma stems from poverty. Some of the most entrenched patterns arise in environments of apparent stability. Children who grow up in wealthier households but experience financial manipulation—being rewarded or punished through money, having love equated with gifts, or being used as pawns in divorce settlements—often carry equally distorted money stories. They may grow up either fearing money's power or seeking to replicate it at any cost. In both cases, their financial decisions are shaped by emotional inheritance, not conscious strategy.

Identifying financial trauma requires more than introspection. It requires a willingness to question inherited scripts. What did your family *teach* you about money—not explicitly, but through tone, behaviour, and atmosphere? Was money discussed openly or shrouded in secrecy? Was it framed as something earned with dignity or as a necessary evil? Were you praised for saving or criticised for wanting? These questions are not philosophical; they are diagnostic.

Answering them provides the foundation for *rewriting your financial operating system*, a theme explored in later sections. But for now, the key insight is this: financial behaviour is rarely about money alone. It is about what money represents, how it was modelled, and how past instability has shaped your default responses to uncertainty, value, and control.

Importantly, recognising trauma does not mean blaming the past. It means reclaiming authorship. It means seeing that the budgeting "failure" or the refusal to raise your rates may not be about laziness or fear—but about an outdated emotional contract with money, one written by circumstances you didn't choose. Once seen, it can be edited.

There is no financial calculator that can account for this. No interest rate formula can factor in the weight of inherited shame or the fear of repeating your parents' struggles. But these are the forces that most deeply influence financial life. Healing them does not happen overnight. It begins with awareness, progresses through self-compassion, and culminates in small, sustained acts of clarity—saying no to spending that masks discomfort, saying yes to opportunities that once felt too threatening, or simply acknowledging that your financial instincts were shaped for survival, not success.

You may never be able to completely erase the wounds you spend from. But you can stop letting them decide the terms of your future. And that is the quiet revolution this chapter invites: *to make financial decisions not from past pain, but from present alignment.* Not because the past didn't matter, but because you've finally seen it clearly enough to choose differently.

2.2 Money as Identity: Status, Shame, and Self-Worth

Few forces shape the architecture of modern identity more powerfully than money. Not because we all aspire to wealth, but because money—consciously or not—has become the dominant metric through which value is perceived, status is assigned, and self-worth is internalised. You are not simply judged by what you earn, own, or owe. You judge yourself. And that judgement is rarely rational, often corrosive, and deeply embedded.

This chapter explores the entanglement between money and identity—not as an abstract philosophical idea, but as a psychological and cultural reality with profound behavioural consequences. When your net worth becomes your self-worth, you enter a double-bind: financial decisions are no longer about utility or logic; they become acts of self-definition or self-protection. You spend to signal value, even if it erodes your security. You undercharge or self-sabotage, because asking for more triggers discomfort that feels existential. You begin to confuse financial outcomes with moral character—and that confusion is reinforced by nearly every social and institutional structure around you.

To understand how this happens, we must start early. Children do not learn about money only from banks or schoolbooks; they absorb it through the emotional climate of the household. Was money a source of tension or pride? Was it weaponised, withheld, idolised, or ignored? These early emotional exposures shape more than attitudes—they shape *identity scripts*. A child who sees a parent panic over bills may internalise a belief that financial safety is fragile and conditional. Another who hears a parent ridicule "rich people" may associate wealth with arrogance or corruption. A child praised only when saving or earning may come to equate self-worth with financial performance. These associations are not intellectually chosen. They are emotionally imprinted.

By adolescence, identity becomes entangled with economic display. Teenagers learn quickly that possessions signal social value: the right trainers, phone, or branded clothing can make or break social acceptance. This logic carries into adulthood, reinforced by advertising and social media—both of which thrive on comparison. Instagram doesn't just show people's lives; it shows their spending. LinkedIn doesn't just show employment history; it signals earning potential and hierarchy. In this environment, *money becomes not only a means but a mirror*—one that constantly reflects back a distorted image of what success and adequacy look like.

The psychological consequences are predictable and well-documented. Shame, in particular, plays a pivotal role. Unlike guilt, which focuses on behaviour ("I made a financial mistake"), shame attacks identity ("I am a financial failure"). People living with chronic financial shame often describe themselves as "bad with money," "irresponsible," or "not the kind of person who can be rich." These aren't observations; they're identity statements. And identity, once fixed, becomes a powerful behavioural anchor. You act in accordance with who you believe you are—even if that belief is outdated or inherited.

This entanglement has two primary behavioural outcomes: *overspending to compensate* and *under-earning to self-protect.*

Overspending is often misunderstood as a lack of discipline. But in many cases, it is a coping strategy. People spend to access a temporary sense of worth, visibility, or control. The purchase is not about the item itself—it is about what it symbolises: success, belonging, relief. The problem is that these emotional boosts are short-lived. The debt, however, is not. And so the cycle continues, often driven by what psychologists call *emotional substitution*: using money to regulate states that would be better addressed through connection, rest, or validation.

Under-earning, on the other hand, is frequently driven by a subconscious belief that one is undeserving. This belief may originate from family narratives, cultural programming, or formative experiences of rejection. It manifests in people who hesitate to negotiate, feel guilt around charging for their time, or subconsciously sabotage promotions. They may say things like "I don't want to seem greedy" or "I'm just grateful to have a job." On the surface, these statements sound modest. Underneath, they often reflect a limiting identity narrative: that financial success and integrity are incompatible.

Both patterns are self-reinforcing. The overspender incurs debt, which triggers shame, which fuels further spending. The under-earner receives less, which confirms their perceived value, which reduces their motivation to ask for more. In both cases, money is not the root cause—it is the vehicle through which deeper psychological patterns express themselves.

This is where cultural narratives must be examined. Western capitalist societies in particular promote a dual message: that money is both a private matter and a public measure. You are told not to discuss your income, but judged by your lifestyle. You are encouraged to hustle for wealth, but warned against "talking too much" about money. This contradiction creates confusion and further internalisation. If you succeed, you may feel the need to justify it: "I just got lucky." If you struggle, you may feel the need to hide it. Silence becomes the norm—and in silence, shame thrives.

Philosophers and sociologists have long warned of the consequences of equating value with productivity or possession. Hannah Arendt, in *The Human Condition*, argued that modern societies confuse *labour* with *worth*, reducing people to economic functions. More recently, thinkers like Alain de Botton have highlighted the epidemic of "status anxiety"—the psychological distress caused by constant economic comparison. Their insight is as relevant as ever: *when worth is indexed to wealth, everyone is vulnerable—because everyone is always being measured.*

So how does one begin to untangle this knot?

The first step is recognition. Observe how you speak about yourself when it comes to money. Are your descriptors factual or judgmental? Do you view financial difficulty as circumstantial or as evidence of inadequacy? Pay attention to the internalised language—"I'm terrible with money," "I'll never be rich," "People like me don't earn that much." These statements are not insights; they are inherited scripts, often absorbed from family, media, or formative experiences.

The second step is *reframing.* This does not mean positive thinking. It means *truthful re-contextualisation.* For example: if you've struggled with saving, perhaps it's not because you're lazy, but because saving was never modelled in your household. If you avoid asking for a raise, perhaps it's not about humility, but a fear rooted in past rejection. Reframing invites compassion—not as indulgence, but as accuracy. It allows you to examine behaviour without reducing it to identity.

Thirdly, begin *de-identifying* from financial outcomes. Your bank balance is a data point, not a personality trait. Your income reflects a market interaction, not your moral worth. This is not to minimise financial hardship or success—but to *depersonalise* it. Financial performance may reflect skill, effort, luck, or circumstance—but it is not the sum total of who you are. If this seems abstract, consider the inverse: would you judge a friend's character based on their salary or savings? Probably not. So why do you do it to yourself?

Finally, create *alternative markers of self-worth.* If money has become your primary scoreboard, what other metrics could you use? Integrity, generosity, creativity, contribution, resilience—these are forms of wealth that cannot be measured in currency. They don't pay rent, but they shape how you relate to yourself. And that relationship is the foundation of all sustainable financial behaviour.

Money will always play a role in how we navigate society. But when it starts defining who we are, the costs become invisible and profound. Not just in pounds or debt, but in self-concept, emotional resilience, and life choices. Detangling money from identity is not a one-time shift. It is a practice—a deliberate, daily refusal to let external metrics dictate internal value.

Until you see the difference between who you are and what you earn, your financial decisions will always be distorted by a need to prove, perform, or protect. Clarity begins when that need dissolves—and you stop asking money to answer questions about your worth that it was never meant to answer.

2.3 The Addiction to Convenience and Control

Convenience has become a default virtue of modern life. It is framed as progress, a reward for innovation, and a marker of efficiency. You can summon food, transport, entertainment, and financial products with a few taps on a screen—no queues, no friction, no human interaction. This seamlessness is often celebrated. But behind the user-friendly interfaces and rapid fulfilment lies something less benign: *a behavioural architecture designed to override reflection, trigger compulsion, and monetise impulsivity*. What looks like empowerment is often engineered dependence. What feels like control is, more often than not, carefully curated illusion.

This subchapter examines how the convenience economy—anchored in dopamine-driven design and marketed as consumer liberation—has become one of the most underestimated drivers of financial sabotage. It explores how instant gratification, digital frictionlessness, and the illusion of control are shaping our financial behaviour in ways that appear rational on the surface but are deeply irrational beneath it.

Let us start with the neurological core of this phenomenon. Dopamine is a neurotransmitter often misunderstood as the "pleasure chemical." In truth, dopamine does not produce pleasure per se—it fuels *anticipation*, *desire*, and *motivation*. It is released in anticipation of reward, and its release is amplified by unpredictability, novelty, and perceived control. These are precisely the dynamics optimised by digital finance and e-commerce platforms. When you receive an alert about a limited-time deal, when you see your stock portfolio update in real time, or when you "win" a cashback reward for spending, your brain produces a spike of dopamine—not because you are better off, but because you *feel* involved, responsive, active. The reward is psychological long before it is financial.

Companies understand this. They employ behavioural scientists not to encourage better decision-making, but to *increase engagement*. Apps are designed to keep you tapping, scrolling, checking. This is not neutral architecture—it is a form of conditioning. And when applied to financial behaviours, it creates patterns that mimic addiction. Not in the moralistic sense, but in the neurological one: compulsive, reward-seeking activity that continues despite negative consequences.

Consider the phenomenon of *frictionless spending*. One-click purchases, contactless payments, auto-renewing subscriptions—these features are sold as conveniences, and technically they are. But psychologically, they decouple the act of spending from the pain of parting with money. Behavioural economists refer to this as *decoupling*, and it significantly lowers the mental barrier to spending. Cash, once a tangible representation of value, created a moment of pause. Digital transactions do the opposite. The ease with which we spend becomes a liability when reflection is removed from the process.

This is especially evident in the subscription economy. What began as a model for newspapers and gyms has become ubiquitous—entertainment, meal kits, software, fitness, vitamins, even razors. Subscriptions operate on a powerful cognitive loophole: they automate choice. You don't decide every month whether the product or service is still valuable; you only decide whether it's worth the effort to cancel. Most people don't. Not because they are passive, but because *the system is built to exploit passivity*. Free trials convert to paid plans. Reminders are opaque or buried. Cancellation requires navigation through multi-step processes. This isn't inertia. It's design.

And the cost? Often invisible, until it accumulates. A few pounds here, ten more there, and suddenly a quarter of your monthly outgoings are quietly draining into services you no longer use or barely value. These aren't extravagances. They are micro-leaks—death by a thousand frictionless cuts. And because they feel small, they escape scrutiny. The result is a widening gap between intention and behaviour. You believe you are budgeting, planning, in control. But your bank statement tells another story.

Control is a particularly insidious part of this dynamic. Many digital finance tools market themselves as instruments of empowerment: real-time spending alerts, personal finance dashboards, investment tracking apps. Superficially, these tools offer transparency. But what they often deliver is *hypervigilance*: a constant stream of information that stimulates anxiety rather than agency. You don't feel more in control—you feel more responsible for outcomes you can't influence in real time. This leads to over-monitoring, reactive decisions, and an illusion of mastery that masks deeper vulnerabilities.

A prime example is the gamification of investing. Apps like Robinhood and Freetrade have made markets more accessible, which is a commendable goal. But access without context is dangerous. By turning investing into a game—with confetti, leaderboards, and instant feedback—these platforms activate the same neural pathways as slot machines. Users trade more frequently, take greater risks, and confuse activity with intelligence. The sense of control is intoxicating, but it is often unearned. Markets are not games. Volatility is not entertainment. And "being in control" of your portfolio minute by minute is not the same as having a long-term strategy.

This confusion between *interaction* and *influence* is key. Many tools give you the ability to act, but not the power to change outcomes. You can monitor, adjust, respond—but that doesn't mean you are steering the ship. The illusion of control arises when action is available, even if that action is ineffective. And the more you act, the more emotionally invested you become—not in your goals, but in the act of managing.

The larger cultural context matters too. We live in a time when convenience is sold as self-care, and control as competence. Saying "no" to friction is seen as rational; outsourcing difficulty is celebrated. But there is a cost to this emotional outsourcing. When every inconvenience is removed, we lose opportunities to exercise discernment. When everything is available instantly, we weaken our tolerance for delay, discomfort, or discipline. These are not moral judgements. They are psychological observations with financial implications. The less we practise patience and reflection, the more likely we are to chase short-term ease at the expense of long-term stability.

None of this is to suggest that digital tools are inherently harmful. Used mindfully, they can enhance clarity, reduce unnecessary labour, and support strategic decisions. The problem is not the technology—it is the way it is designed and deployed. Most platforms are not optimised for your wellbeing. They are optimised for revenue per user, engagement time, conversion rate. You are not the customer; you are the product.

So what does resistance look like in this context? It begins with *slowness*. Pause before signing up. Before clicking "buy now." Before downloading a new finance app. Create *manual moments* in your financial life—spaces where you must decide consciously, rather than be led by automation. This might mean reviewing subscriptions quarterly, using cash for discretionary spending, or disabling push notifications from investment platforms.

It also involves *redefining control.* True control is not constant management. It is the ability to set a direction, establish rules, and stick to them without needing to watch every metric. It is about building systems that work in the background—automated saving, value-based spending limits, time-gated purchasing decisions—rather than chasing the illusion of perfect oversight. Control is not about micromanaging your finances; it's about designing a financial life that doesn't need micromanagement.

Above all, it requires *psychological distance.* Notice what financial decisions feel like in your body. Is your heartbeat elevated? Are you rushing? Are you reacting to a notification, a fear, a need to prove something? These cues matter. They reveal when you are no longer choosing, but being led.

Convenience is not inherently bad. Nor is control. But when they become compulsions—when they replace reflection with reaction and agency with impulse—they become traps. Traps built by algorithms, designed for profitability, and dressed in the language of freedom.

The antidote is not rejection of the digital world. It is intentionality within it. When you stop confusing convenience with value, and control with wisdom, you begin to reclaim your ability to choose—not just faster, but better.

2.4 Rewiring Your Financial Operating System

If you've ever looked back on a financial decision and asked yourself, "What was I thinking?", you're not alone—and you weren't necessarily thinking at all, at least not in the way you assumed. Most money behaviour is not driven by logic, spreadsheets, or conscious goals. It is driven by an internal operating system—a set of emotional, neurological, and cognitive defaults that guide your financial responses in the background. Until this system is made visible and deliberately restructured, no amount of financial literacy or technical advice will result in lasting behavioural change.

Rewiring your financial operating system is not about adopting a better budgeting app or reading another book on passive income. It is about recognising that beneath every money decision is a complex interaction between your brain, your nervous system, and your belief structures—many of which were formed long before you ever earned a paycheque. Neuroscience and mindfulness offer tools not just to understand this complexity, but to begin reshaping it. The goal is not perfection, but *clarity-based agency*: the ability to make values-aligned money choices, even under pressure, ambiguity, or emotional intensity.

To begin, we must understand how the brain processes financial stimuli. From a neurological standpoint, money is not treated as a neutral object. It activates circuits in the brain associated with threat, reward, and social judgement. Neuroimaging studies have shown that areas like the amygdala, ventral striatum, and anterior insula light up when people engage with money-related tasks—areas also involved in detecting danger, craving, and disgust. In other words, *your brain treats money like an emotional event, not a mathematical one.* This helps explain why people act against their own interests: they're not "irrational," they're emotionally hijacked.

One of the core mechanisms at work here is *limbic hijack*—a term used to describe moments when the emotional brain overrides the rational prefrontal cortex. In financial terms, this might look like panic-selling during a market dip, impulse-buying during a stressful week, or avoiding account statements entirely due to anxiety. These are not character flaws. They are predictable consequences of an outdated neurological model being applied to a highly complex and often emotionally charged modern financial environment.

This is where reframing becomes essential. Reframing is a cognitive technique rooted in both neuroscience and psychotherapy. It involves consciously shifting the lens through which you interpret an event or belief. The power of reframing lies in its ability to change your *emotional* response—not just your intellectual understanding.

For example, consider the belief: "I'm bad with money." This is not simply a description; it is a conclusion, often rooted in early experiences of scarcity, shame, or failure. Reframing does not deny past experiences, but interrogates the meaning ascribed to them. A reframed version might be: "I've never been taught to manage money in a way that aligns with how I think and feel—it's a skill I can now develop." That shift may seem small, but neurologically, it is significant. It changes the emotional tone from shame to curiosity, which opens the door to learning and change.

Mindfulness practices add another layer to this work. Unlike intellectual reframing, mindfulness focuses on increasing *interoceptive awareness*—the ability to sense what is happening in your body and nervous system in real time. This is crucial in financial contexts, where decisions are often made in states of unconscious stress or reactivity. If you can recognise the rising tightness in your chest before clicking "buy," or the tension in your jaw when you open your budgeting app, you create a space for choice. That space is the intervention.

Studies on mindfulness and financial behaviour are still emerging, but preliminary research suggests that regular mindfulness practice improves delay of gratification, reduces impulsivity, and enhances financial self-efficacy. It also strengthens the connection between present actions and future consequences—an essential function of the prefrontal cortex, which mindfulness appears to support through increased grey matter density in relevant regions.

Practical application means integrating these insights into routines, not just reflections. For instance, if you find that spending is often driven by emotion, you might implement a "pause protocol"—a fixed rule that any non-essential purchase must be delayed by 24 hours. This is not about restriction; it is about creating time for your prefrontal cortex to catch up to your limbic system. Similarly, if certain financial tasks consistently trigger anxiety—checking your account balance, opening a bill—you can pair them with a grounding practice: three deep breaths, a short body scan, or even a self-reminder of your long-term goals. These are not hacks. They are neurological recalibrations.

Values-based decision-making is the final layer of the rewiring process. Most people think their money problems stem from not having enough, or not knowing enough. In reality, much dysfunction arises from a lack of *alignment*—from spending, saving, or earning in ways that contradict core values. This misalignment creates cognitive dissonance, which the brain resolves through avoidance, rationalisation, or emotional numbing. By clarifying values—autonomy, generosity, stability, contribution—you create a personal compass against which decisions can be measured.

This requires more than listing values. It demands operationalising them. What does "autonomy" mean financially? Perhaps it's a six-month emergency fund, or the ability to say no to work that compromises your ethics. What does "generosity" mean? It might involve a standing donation to causes you care about, or budgeting time for unpaid mentorship. The point is not the answer, but the intentional connection between money and meaning. When that connection is clear, decisions feel less burdensome. You stop asking, "Can I afford this?" and start asking, "Does this reflect what I stand for?"

None of this is instantaneous. Neural pathways take time to reshape. Emotional patterns take repetition to rewrite. But the brain is not static—it is plastic. Neuroplasticity, the brain's capacity to form new connections, is not limited to childhood. It persists throughout life, especially when learning is coupled with emotion, repetition, and reflection. Each time you make a values-based financial decision, you are literally strengthening the neural architecture of clarity and control. Each time you override a compulsion with conscious choice, you weaken the power of your old operating system.

It's important, too, to approach this work with *compassion rather than perfectionism*. Financial self-improvement is often laced with shame-driven urgency—"I need to get it together," "I should know better." But shame narrows focus and triggers defensive behaviour. Sustainable change requires a different posture: one of curiosity, self-respect, and patience. Not because money doesn't matter, but because *you do*—and the operating system you build will ultimately shape not just your bank account, but your relationship with autonomy, trust, and self-worth.

To rewire your financial operating system is to recognise that your money behaviour is not a fixed trait, but a dynamic reflection of your beliefs, your biology, and your environment. It is not a moral failing to act from old programming. But it is an act of power to interrupt it.

The shift is not from irrational to rational, but from unconscious to conscious. Once you understand what's driving your financial decisions beneath the surface, you can begin to choose—not just react. That's where freedom begins—not in more control, but in better alignment.

Chapter 3
Rigged from the Roots – Systems Built to Exploit

There's a particular betrayal that stings deeper than most—not the kind orchestrated by crooks in alleys, but by the very institutions that promise protection. To live cautiously in a clearly dangerous world is one thing. But to build your life on the assumption of safety, only to find out—usually at the moment of greatest need—that the supposed safeguards were a façade? That is something altogether different. This chapter deals with those structures: systems sold as safety nets that, in truth, function as engines of quiet extraction. Institutions that speak the language of care while carefully engineering dependence. Bureaucracies that wrap private profit in the rhetoric of public responsibility.

It's a comforting myth, isn't it—that financial exploitation is the province of rogues and scammers, operating at the fringes of legality? That if you're careful, informed, and responsible, you'll be spared? Unfortunately, that myth is as dangerous as it is widespread. The most potent forms of economic exploitation today don't sneak around the rules—they codify them. They're not illegal. They are policy. They dictate where your wages are deposited, how your retirement is structured, how insurance is priced, and what kind of digital trail you leave every time you scroll, click, or tap.

These aren't aberrations on the margins—they are the mainstream. So commonplace they've become invisible. And that, precisely, is their power. Large-scale exploitation rarely resembles a stick-up. More often, it looks like a line item on your payslip. A checkbox you never unticked. A subscription you meant to cancel. A payment gateway's "convenience fee." It's small enough to ignore, yet persistent enough to accumulate. Always trickling upward.

To grasp the depth of this manipulation, we must move beyond blaming individual choices and examine the scaffolding itself. Take public safety nets—the pension, the student loan, the NHS. Once considered pillars of a civilised society, many of these were meant to buffer citizens from the market's worst swings. That was the theory. In practice, these very institutions have been gradually reconfigured to serve commercial interests under the guise of public service. Support has been financialised. Protection has been privatised.

Look at pensions. On paper, a simple concept: defer part of your income, pool it, and retire with dignity. But that simplicity is long gone. The traditional defined-benefit schemes—once the norm—have largely given way to defined-contribution plans, which shift the risk entirely onto the individual. What used to be a shared responsibility has become a personal gamble. Fees are buried in jargon. Returns are volatile. And the reassuring narrative—that if you just save and invest wisely, you'll be fine—conveniently ignores the fact that the system was never calibrated for your security. Meanwhile, regardless of market performance, fund managers pocket their fees without fail. Risk is yours. Reward? Optional.

Student loans follow a familiar pattern. Framed as the ticket to upward mobility, they've morphed into a lifetime drag on financial freedom—particularly for those already marginalised. In the UK, graduates regularly begin their working lives saddled with debts in excess of £45,000. Repayment feels less like a loan and more like a second, invisible tax. Universities raise fees, government funding shrinks, and the student loan book becomes an asset class in the portfolios of private investors. You thought you were buying an education. In reality, you were underwriting a financial instrument.

Insurance is no less instructive. Once rooted in the principle of shared risk, it has evolved into a deeply individualised game of actuarial warfare. Premiums are calculated with eerie precision—not merely by age or postcode, but by your online behaviour, shopping habits, and even the websites you visit. You're told it's about personalisation. In truth, it's about extraction. Terms are shrouded in exclusions. Discounts are illusory. Claims processes are labyrinthine by design. The more data they collect, the better they get—not at protecting you, but at predicting and profiting from you.

Which brings us to the most insidious development of all: the commodification of your financial data. Every transaction, every delay, every app you authorise, feeds a data economy that tracks, profiles, and packages your behaviours. Credit scores no longer reflect just your borrowing history—they're increasingly shaped by your online footprint, your social circle, your patterns of consumption. Often, this data is harvested without your explicit understanding. Lenders, insurers, even potential employers use it to make decisions that affect your future. You think you're using financial products. But they're using you.

This isn't some dystopian fever dream. It's already here. When your browsing habits impact the terms of your loan, or your delivery postcode influences your insurance premium, data privacy ceases to be a philosophical issue—it becomes a financial one. And yet most people have already relinquished that privacy, unaware that the true cost of "free" apps and smooth transactions was always their behavioural data.

So, why do these systems persist, even thrive? The answer is disarmingly simple: because they are profitable. Distributed exploitation—legal, incremental, anonymised—is incredibly resilient. It rarely makes headlines. There's no dramatic exposé, no single villain. Just a web of interests—consultants, hedge funds, insurers, fintech startups—all with a stake in preserving the illusion of fairness. And on the other side? Ordinary consumers, fatigued and distracted, gradually trained to accept complexity not as strategy, but as reality.

The term "legalised theft" might sound alarmist. Yet consider the mechanics. When a pension scheme charges 1.5% in annual fees and delivers less than 1% in returns, the shortfall isn't an error—it's baked in. When payment platforms skim nearly 3% off donations or school fees, that's not convenience—it's capture. When a late fee is levied after a single missed payment—even after years of good behaviour—that's not risk management. It's opportunism.

All of it is hidden in the footnotes. The cumulative impact? Not just financial, but psychological. People begin to disengage. They feel inadequate for not understanding. They start to believe the system is too complex to question. This is not an accident. It's the intended result. Confusion discourages resistance. Complexity prevents scrutiny. And exhaustion guarantees passivity.

This chapter aims not to stoke despair, but to illuminate the machinery. To help you trace the fault lines in systems that masquerade as support. To unpack how your data is used against you. To spot the charges that aren't really optional. And, most crucially, to equip you with the mindset and strategies required to resist quietly sanctioned forms of exploitation.

This isn't a rallying cry to abandon civilisation or retreat into an off-grid fantasy. It's a call to see—properly, plainly. Because the danger isn't always external coercion. Often, it's the internalised trust in systems that no longer deserve it. In this light, financial literacy stops being about APRs or compound interest and starts being about power. About understanding *who* benefits from your choices, and *why* those choices are shaped to be convenient, rushed, and unexamined.

Once you see the root structure, you stop trimming weeds—and start redesigning the garden, on your own terms.

3.1 The Illusion of Meritocracy

Few concepts are more deeply embedded in modern economic narratives than the promise of meritocracy—the belief that hard work, intelligence, and perseverance are sufficient to climb the ladder of success. It is the founding story of contemporary capitalism, an ideological glue that binds diverse populations to systems they did not design but are conditioned to trust. It reassures the struggling that their effort will eventually be rewarded, and flatters the successful with the comforting belief that they earned it all. But beneath this elegant fiction lies a structural reality: *the ladder of upward mobility is not just uneven—it is greased in favour of those already at the top.*

Meritocracy, in practice, is less a system of opportunity than a story told about how opportunity supposedly works. The idea that economic outcomes reflect individual merit ignores how the architecture of privilege is fortified—not by overt discrimination alone, but by subtler mechanisms: inherited capital, tax optimisation strategies unavailable to the general public, elite social networks, and cultural codes that signal belonging in spaces of influence. This is not a matter of envy or victimhood. It is a matter of precision—of seeing clearly how systems operate to preserve advantage while advertising fairness.

Consider taxation, often presented as a neutral tool of redistribution. In reality, it is one of the most strategically gamed elements of the modern economy. High-net-worth individuals and corporations do not simply work harder or invest smarter—they *hire access to loopholes.* Through offshore trusts, shell companies, carried interest provisions, and jurisdictional arbitrage, they can reduce effective tax rates to levels unimaginable for a salaried worker. The UK's "non-domiciled" tax regime, for instance, allows foreign residents to legally shield global income from taxation—a privilege utterly unavailable to the average Briton. What's marketed as complexity is often little more than engineered opacity.

The same principle holds in education, a domain frequently cited as the great equaliser. Yet access to elite institutions—Oxford, Cambridge, or top-tier grammar schools—is disproportionately concentrated among children from wealthier families. Whether through private tuition, postcode advantages, or legacy admissions, the appearance of meritocratic selection is undercut by deep structural bias. Even when entry is "earned," the cultural capital required to thrive in these environments—knowing how to network, speak the language of power, or navigate implicit norms—is typically passed down through families, not classrooms.

The job market reflects similar dynamics. Hiring processes that claim to reward skills often mask preferences for cultural fit, pedigree, or aesthetic presentation. CVs bearing certain surnames, accents, or university affiliations are filtered differently by both human recruiters and algorithmic systems. Those raised within circles of influence understand unwritten codes: how to speak in a job interview, when to ask for equity, how to negotiate a contract. These behaviours are not innate—they are taught, modelled, and reinforced through proximity to power.

Gatekeeping is perhaps most insidious when cloaked in the language of inclusion. Professional associations, startup incubators, investment opportunities, and even philanthropic boards all maintain *formal openness but informal exclusivity*. They are accessible in theory, but in practice require networks, endorsements, and insider fluency. This is not conspiracy—it is continuity. Systems protect themselves by rewarding those who resemble existing beneficiaries. The result is a feedback loop: capital begets capital, and proximity to power begets more access to power.

A useful lens through which to examine this is Pierre Bourdieu's concept of *social capital*—the resources available to individuals through their networks of relationships. Unlike financial or human capital, social capital is less visible but often more decisive. It determines who gets the first call when a promotion opens up, who is offered mentorship, and who is invited into rooms where decisions are made. It is also the least formally taught and the hardest to access without pre-existing ties. When success depends not just on what you know, but *who* you know—and how you know how to behave around them—meritocracy becomes a performance, not a principle.

Even the myth of the "self-made" entrepreneur, lionised in business media, often collapses under scrutiny. Behind many unicorn founders are early capital injections from family, elite education, or well-placed advisors. Venture capital flows disproportionately to those who already speak the language of finance and whose social profiles align with funders' implicit biases. Meanwhile, equally capable entrepreneurs without those connections struggle for visibility. What appears as market validation is often social pattern recognition. Innovation is less funded than familiarity.

It is worth noting that the meritocratic ideal persists not because it is entirely false, but because it is selectively true. There are indeed individuals who rise through grit and ingenuity. But the existence of exceptions does not invalidate the rule. A few upward trajectories do not negate the structural downward pressure on the majority. In fact, the visibility of exceptional cases can serve to reinforce the myth: *if they did it, why can't you?* The implication is that failure reflects personal inadequacy rather than systemic constraint.

This framing has profound psychological consequences. Belief in a pure meritocracy generates internalised shame among those who struggle—*I must not be trying hard enough*—and moral entitlement among those who succeed—*I must be more deserving.* It discourages collective scrutiny of institutional design by individualising outcomes. And it fosters a cultural climate in which questioning the rules is mistaken for bitterness, rather than discernment.

A genuinely honest society would not demand we abandon the concept of merit altogether, but that we disaggregate it. Talent, effort, and discipline *do* matter—but they are not sufficient when the infrastructure is skewed. Recognising this is not defeatist; it is foundational to building fairer systems. It allows us to distinguish between a person's effort and their environment, and to identify where structural reform—not just motivational rhetoric—is needed.

The illusion of meritocracy is not just a moral problem. It is a practical one. It distorts incentives, misallocates talent, and wastes human potential. When resources are channelled toward those already resourced, and when innovation is evaluated through a lens of pedigree rather than value, societies stagnate. The result is not just inequality, but inefficiency.

So what does it mean to move beyond the illusion? It begins with literacy—the capacity to decode how advantage is manufactured and maintained. It means understanding how tax systems are written, how hiring pipelines are shaped, how financial privilege is converted into cultural legitimacy. It means recognising that fairness is not the default outcome of open markets—it is a condition that must be actively engineered.

And it means learning to navigate the system with both clarity and conscience. Not by pretending the ladder is fair, but by refusing to internalise its distortions. By building parallel structures when necessary. By mentoring across boundaries. By interrogating one's own advantage and using it with intention rather than denial.

The point is not to abolish aspiration, but to ground it in reality. A society that truly values merit must dismantle the architectures that obscure it. Only then can we begin to imagine mobility not as a fantasy marketed to the many, but as a principle accessible to all.

3.2 Broken Safety Nets

For much of the twentieth century, public safety nets were heralded as the great equaliser of capitalist society—mechanisms through which governments could counterbalance market volatility and extend a baseline of dignity to their citizens. Pensions, unemployment insurance, student loans, and healthcare subsidies were introduced not merely as economic supports, but as moral commitments. They represented a promise: that no matter the instability of the outside world, there would be systems in place to catch you if you fell. That promise, once the cornerstone of post-war social contracts, has decayed—not by collapse, but by design. What remains today is often not protection, but performance: systems that simulate security while outsourcing risk to the very people they claim to protect.

Nowhere is this transformation more evident than in the pension system. In theory, pensions are a form of intergenerational solidarity: workers contribute today to support retirees, and in turn, are supported when they themselves exit the labour force. But in many Western countries, particularly in the UK and United States, the defined-benefit pension—once the gold standard of retirement security—has been steadily dismantled in favour of defined-contribution schemes such as personal pensions or 401(k)s. The distinction is not semantic. Under the old model, employers bore the investment risk and guaranteed a fixed income in retirement. Under the new model, individuals shoulder the risk, manage their own investments, and hope the markets are kind.

This shift has turned what was once a collective promise into an individual gamble. Savers are encouraged to "take charge" of their financial futures, but the reality is that most people are not—and should not be expected to be—investment strategists. The complexity of pension products, the opacity of fees, and the psychological burden of long-term financial planning in an era of short-term economic insecurity create conditions ripe for suboptimal decisions. Worse still, the financial industry profits regardless of outcomes: fund managers and pension providers extract fees on contributions, even if the underlying investments underperform or collapse.

Moreover, the narrative around pensions is heavily moralised. We are told that failing to save is a personal failure, that living in retirement poverty is the result of poor planning. Yet this framing deliberately ignores structural constraints: stagnant wages, precarious employment, rising housing costs, and unpredictable inflation—all of which erode the capacity to contribute in the first place. When the average worker is navigating an economy in which full-time work no longer guarantees a liveable income, to speak of "retirement planning" as an individual responsibility is both cynical and absurd.

Education loans follow a similarly deceptive trajectory. Marketed as a "ticket to the middle class," student debt is now one of the most profitable financial products in the global economy. In the UK, tuition fees were introduced in 1998 and have since ballooned, saddling graduates with debt that, in many cases, they may never fully repay. The design of the loan system is deliberately obtuse: repayment thresholds, interest rate structures, and inflation-linked adjustments are wrapped in bureaucratic language that makes it difficult to calculate the actual cost of borrowing.

More troubling is the psychological toll. Graduates enter adult life with a debt burden often equivalent to a mortgage—before they have even secured stable employment or housing. This debt is not just financial; it shapes career choices, delays family formation, and creates a persistent undercurrent of anxiety. And because the repayment system is collected through the tax code, many borrowers do not experience their debt as a distinct loan but as an indefinite financial drag. The sense of ownership over one's future is quietly replaced by a feeling of structural indebtedness—legally sanctioned, culturally normalised, and economically regressive.

Insurance, too, has become a broken safety net masquerading as protection. The original function of insurance was mutualisation: pooling collective resources to cover individual misfortunes. But contemporary insurance markets have inverted this ethic. Risk is now not only priced, but *predicted*—using increasingly invasive data analytics that extract behavioural, demographic, and geographic information to set personalised premiums. On the surface, this appears efficient. But in practice, it creates a stratified system in which the poor, the sick, and the already marginalised are charged more for being poor, sick, and marginalised.

Take car insurance, for instance. In many urban areas, policyholders pay higher premiums simply for living in postcodes associated with higher claims—even if their personal driving record is spotless. Or consider life and health insurance policies that use wearable data, social media activity, and even grocery shopping habits to determine eligibility and cost. This is not protection. It is surveillance repackaged as service. And it ensures that the people most in need of security pay the highest price for it.

The same logic extends to unemployment benefits, which are increasingly conditional, means-tested, and administratively punitive. Far from being a cushion for economic shocks, welfare systems in many countries now function as a deterrent—designed to discourage claims, reduce caseloads, and create bureaucratic friction that wears down applicants. In the UK, the Universal Credit system is a case study in administrative cruelty: payments are delayed, sanctions are frequent, and recipients are treated as potential fraudsters rather than citizens in need. The result is not just material deprivation, but psychological harm—fuelled by a rhetoric that frames need as weakness and assistance as failure.

What all of these systems share is a fundamental shift in responsibility. Public safety nets have not disappeared; they have *mutated.* Where once they were premised on solidarity and shared risk, they are now structured around *individualisation*: you are responsible for your pension returns, your student debt, your premiums, your job search. If the system fails you, the problem is *you.* This reframing absolves institutions of responsibility while preserving their legitimacy. It transforms policy failures into personal ones, and disguises structural traps as market choices.

This ideological sleight of hand is not accidental. It is the product of decades of neoliberal policy, which has systematically undermined the public sphere while outsourcing key functions to the private sector. Public pensions become private funds. Public universities operate like corporations. Insurance providers lobby for deregulation while digitising exclusion. At every turn, the rhetoric of empowerment—"choice," "freedom," "personal responsibility"—masks a deeper withdrawal of collective commitment.

To critique these systems is not to deny the value of safety nets. On the contrary—it is to demand that they live up to their name. Real safety nets are designed to hold you without humiliation. They are transparent, accessible, and grounded in a belief that social protection is not a luxury for the fortunate, but a foundation for a just society. They recognise that economic shocks are not moral failings and that resilience is not built by forcing individuals to navigate broken systems alone.

So what does it mean to reclaim the idea of a safety net in the 21st century? It means rejecting narratives that frame debt as investment, insurance as empowerment, and retirement as a gamble. It means demanding clarity, accountability, and equity in the design of these systems. And it means recognising that financial security is not the outcome of good character or clever planning—it is the result of political choices, institutional design, and collective values.

The next time someone tells you the system is there to protect you, ask who profits when it fails. Until that question is answered honestly, what we call safety nets will remain traps in disguise.

3.3 Your Data Is Currency

Walk into any financial institution today, and you may notice something curious: they don't ask *who you are*, they ask *what you are worth*—not just in money, but in metadata. Your past transactions, shopping habits, browsing behaviour, click patterns, repayment history, insurance choices, postcode, and even the time of day you're most likely to respond to a notification are all part of a new valuation protocol. The question is no longer *if* your personal financial data is used—it is *how extensively*, and *to whose benefit.* In the digital economy, data has eclipsed oil as the most valuable commodity. But unlike oil, most people are unaware that their data is being drilled, refined, packaged, and sold—often in real time, and with their implicit consent.

This transformation didn't happen overnight. The shift from analogue ledgers to algorithmic modelling was incremental—starting with basic credit scores and ballooning into predictive profiling systems that now underpin nearly every major financial decision made *about* you. The language of creditworthiness has become a proxy for trust in modern capitalism. But trust, in this context, is not about your integrity; it's about your *trackability*—the extent to which your behaviours can be captured, quantified, and forecasted.

Let's begin with the cornerstone: credit scoring. Originally conceived as a straightforward tool for assessing lending risk, the credit score has metastasised into an all-purpose gatekeeper for economic participation. Want to rent a flat? Secure a mobile phone contract? Apply for insurance? The number assigned to you—based on proprietary formulas you are not permitted to inspect—can determine access, pricing, and terms. The algorithms that generate these scores ingest thousands of data points: missed payments, length of credit history, types of credit used, and, increasingly, behavioural proxies such as spending rhythms or online activity patterns. This is not a neutral system. It encodes assumptions, penalises deviation from normativity, and often reproduces existing inequalities under the guise of objectivity.

For instance, consider the impact of "thin files"—a term used for individuals with limited or no credit history. Young people, immigrants, gig workers, or those who opt out of mainstream financial products are disproportionately affected. Not because they are irresponsible, but because they haven't yet—or choose not to—participate in the traditional credit ecosystem. In response, fintech companies have begun exploring "alternative data": analysing everything from utility payments to social media activity to determine creditworthiness. In theory, this broadens access. In practice, it introduces new layers of surveillance and bias. What happens when a single late bill, an irregular income stream, or a poorly worded tweet becomes the basis for financial exclusion?

This commodification of data extends well beyond credit scores. Take insurance underwriting. Traditionally based on actuarial tables, risk is now algorithmically personalised. Auto insurers harvest data from telematics (black box devices or apps) to track how fast you drive, how hard you brake, what time you travel. Health insurers experiment with wearable integration—monitoring your sleep, steps, diet, and heart rate in exchange for "wellness discounts." On the surface, this seems fair: healthier behaviours = lower premiums. But such framing masks coercion. It nudges people into hyper-monitoring, blurs the line between voluntary sharing and mandatory compliance, and creates a two-tiered system where privacy is a luxury good.

The deeper problem is asymmetry. While you are profiled in minute detail, you rarely see the full picture of how your data is used, stored, interpreted, or shared. Terms and conditions obfuscate more than they reveal. Consent is often bundled and vague. And even when explicit permission is sought, it is frequently presented as a take-it-or-leave-it proposition: use the service *or* walk away. There is no real negotiation. And because data is collected passively—through cookies, device fingerprinting, app permissions, and default settings—opting out becomes an exhausting game of whack-a-mole. The system is designed not for transparency, but for frictionless extraction.

This data asymmetry creates profound ethical challenges. Financial firms now possess what Shoshana Zuboff calls "behavioural surplus"—predictive insights that not only track what you've done, but anticipate what you *will* do. This shifts power in subtle, dangerous ways. A lender doesn't just assess whether you're likely to repay; it can tailor the offer, set the terms, or deny the opportunity based on invisible behavioural flags. A payment app doesn't just process your transaction; it learns your triggers, your financial weak points, your late-night cravings—and it can nudge, upsell, or exploit accordingly.

Such dynamics erode financial agency. When every tap, scroll, and swipe feeds a machine learning model designed to optimise *their* profits, not *your* well-being, autonomy becomes a managed illusion. Consider the rise of buy-now-pay-later (BNPL) services. These tools integrate seamlessly into online checkouts, often using background data to instantly "pre-approve" microloans without traditional credit checks. While framed as convenience, BNPL exploits impulse psychology, targets the vulnerable, and reinforces cycles of short-term thinking. Many users don't even realise they are entering debt arrangements.

And what happens to the data once it is collected? It enters vast ecosystems of resale and recombination. Data brokers aggregate financial records, purchase histories, geolocation patterns, demographic attributes, and psychographic profiles to create dossiers that can be sold to marketers, lenders, insurers, or surveillance contractors. These dossiers are not regulated with the same stringency as the financial institutions that feed them. In the UK, the ICO (Information Commissioner's Office) has raised concerns, but enforcement is patchy. In the US, there's no federal law equivalent to the GDPR. The result: *you* are for sale, and often without even knowing it.

The implications extend beyond economics. When access to capital, housing, education, or even employment is filtered through proprietary models built on your data, the line between discrimination and "personalisation" becomes blurred. Algorithmic opacity ensures that appeals are futile: try asking a chatbot to explain why your loan was rejected. Try correcting a mistake buried in a dataset compiled by a third-party broker you've never heard of. The feedback loops are closed. The accountability is vanishing.

And yet, data-driven finance is expanding. Open banking initiatives, which allow third-party apps to access your account data with your permission, are framed as empowering tools for financial innovation. In reality, they risk further entrenching the commodification of your personal information. While there are upsides—price comparison, tailored advice, budgeting tools—they also introduce vulnerabilities: security breaches, misuse by unauthorised actors, or the subtle erosion of consent over time.

To navigate this reality, we must rethink the language of "free" and "convenience." Free apps are rarely free. They are funded by monetising your attention, your habits, your predictive profile. Convenience is not neutral—it is engineered to favour the data collectors, not the user. When finance is wrapped in frictionless design, the real cost is often obscured.

So what would genuine data ethics in finance look like? It would begin with radical transparency: not just "we use your data," but *how*, *why*, *who profits*, and *how you can opt out.* It would include meaningful consent—not buried in 48-page legalese, but as clear, revocable, and specific permissions. It would involve data minimisation—collecting only what is necessary, and deleting what is no longer needed. And it would include algorithmic explainability: the right to know *how* decisions are made about your money, *on what basis*, and *by whom.*

Until then, we are living in a financial landscape where your data *is* your currency—and everyone is spending it *except you.* The question is no longer whether this dynamic exists, but whether you understand the stakes clearly enough to push back. Autonomy in the age of algorithmic finance requires more than budgeting skills; it demands vigilance, literacy, and a willingness to challenge systems that feed off opacity.

If money is power, then data is the lever that moves it. And those who control the data increasingly control the terms of economic life itself. The time to reclaim that control is not someday—it is now.

3.4 Silent Fees, Hidden Costs, and Legalised Theft

The average consumer is far more financially exploited than they realise—not through spectacular scams or outright fraud, but by a slow drip of "legitimate" fees so deeply embedded in the financial system they appear normal, even necessary. These costs, often camouflaged by complexity or buried in the fine print, represent a form of legalised theft: a steady erosion of wealth by institutions that frame themselves as helpful intermediaries. From your pension plan to your everyday payment apps, the system is littered with mechanisms that quietly siphon value while evading scrutiny. The danger lies not in what is obvious, but in what is designed to go unnoticed.

Let's begin with banks—the most publicly trusted and least publicly understood agents of micro-extraction. Take overdraft fees. On paper, they serve a purpose: to discourage consumers from spending more than they have. In reality, they have become a major profit centre. UK banks collectively make hundreds of millions annually from unarranged overdraft fees, many of which are triggered by transactions as small as a cup of coffee. The charges are often disproportionate to the offence—a £1.50 transaction can lead to a £30 penalty. And crucially, these fees disproportionately affect those already financially vulnerable. Rather than functioning as a deterrent, they form a regressive tax on the poor—coded as 'service'.

Then there's the issue of foreign exchange markups. When you use your card abroad, or make online purchases in a foreign currency, you are typically charged not only a flat fee but also a hidden markup on the exchange rate. That markup—often 2–3%—is rarely disclosed transparently. The bank or payment provider simply applies a less favourable rate than the market value and pockets the spread. Multiply this across millions of transactions, and the result is a multi-billion-pound ecosystem of extraction built on opacity.

But perhaps the most insidious cost structures live within long-term financial products—pensions, investment funds, and insurance policies. These are arenas where trust is high and scrutiny low, making them ideal for hidden charges. Fund management fees, platform fees, transaction costs, performance fees, advisory fees—all compound, year after year, quietly diluting the returns of the average saver. A seemingly small annual fee of 1.5% on a pension pot may not sound alarming, but over 30 years it can reduce your final value by *more than 30%*. That's not incidental—that's structural.

Consider the example of "active" versus "passive" investment funds. Active funds, managed by financial professionals who claim to beat the market, typically charge higher fees. But extensive research shows that most of these funds *fail* to outperform cheaper, passive index funds over time. The added cost is rarely justified by added value, yet millions continue to invest in actively managed products because of outdated advice or persuasive marketing. Financial institutions know this—and they capitalise on inertia.

The pension industry is particularly egregious. Many pension schemes, especially legacy ones, are riddled with "scheme charges" and "administrative costs" that most users do not understand and rarely question. Worse still, many employers and financial advisors fail to clearly communicate the impact of these costs. The Financial Conduct Authority (FCA) has attempted to enforce fee caps and standardisation, but loopholes remain. Variable exit fees, for instance, can punish savers for transferring their pension pots to more efficient providers—effectively charging them for exercising autonomy.

Technology hasn't solved this; in many ways, it's made the problem more elegant. Fintech platforms often market themselves as disruptors—transparent, user-centric, democratising finance. And to some extent, they have introduced more accessible tools. But many of these platforms also monetise through covert means: spread-based pricing, "freemium" models that lock key features behind paywalls, and default settings that nudge users towards more profitable choices for the platform, not the user. A zero-commission trading app may still earn money by selling your order flow to market makers, a practice that creates subtle misalignments in execution pricing.

Subscription models are another prime example. Financial tools that offer budgeting, credit monitoring, or tax assistance often begin with free trials—only to auto-renew into costly monthly fees. These amounts are small enough to avoid detection, yet large enough to generate meaningful revenue when scaled. What matters is not whether a product is worth its cost, but whether the cost is being *transparently conveyed and continually consented to*. Many people pay for tools they don't use, for services they didn't know they activated, or for benefits that could have been obtained elsewhere for free.

Then there's the "dark design"—interfaces crafted not just for usability, but for manipulation. From pre-ticked boxes to confusing opt-out processes, the architecture of choice is often rigged. The goal is not clarity, but conversion: how to get users to sign up, stay in, or spend more without noticing. In many cases, the burden of diligence is shifted onto the consumer—forcing them to scrutinise small-print PDFs or hunt through obscure account settings to protect their own interests. The system is adversarial by design.

Insurance is no different. Premiums are often opaque, shaped not just by actuarial logic but by behavioural profiling and loyalty penalties. Existing customers are frequently charged more than new customers—a phenomenon known as "price walking"—simply because the algorithm assumes they're less likely to switch. The UK's Financial Conduct Authority banned this practice in 2022 for home and motor insurance, but similar patterns persist across other domains. Extended warranties, payment protection insurance, and add-on coverages are often upsold with minimal scrutiny, exploiting the consumer's lack of information or time.

These hidden costs are not anomalies. They are *business models*. Financial institutions, like all businesses, seek profit. But unlike most sectors, they operate under a veneer of necessity—embedding themselves in life's most unavoidable transactions: housing, retirement, health, education, debt. This dependency makes pushback more difficult. We trust these institutions with our futures, and they, in turn, capitalise on that trust by structuring fees that are hard to detect, hard to decode, and hard to escape.

The language itself is engineered to disarm. Terms like "maintenance fee," "processing charge," or "account service cost" sound procedural, even protective. Rarely are they described in terms that reflect their actual impact. A bank doesn't say, "We'll take £60 of your money annually for doing almost nothing"; it says, "This account includes a bundled monthly service fee." Semantic laundering helps transform aggressive monetisation into bureaucratic routine.

What is particularly insidious is that the cumulative effect of these silent fees is often more financially destructive than a one-off scam. A fraudulent call might steal £200. But an unchecked pension fee could cost someone £60,000 over a lifetime. The difference is that the former is criminal, while the latter is contractual. Both erode wealth. Only one is policed.

So what can be done? Awareness is the first defence. We must move from passivity to interrogation—from assuming good faith to demanding clarity. This means asking hard questions of your providers: What are all the fees, explicitly and implicitly? How are they calculated? How do they change over time? What would it cost me to leave? If they can't answer clearly, that's a red flag.

Next comes diversification. Relying on a single institution for all financial services increases your exposure to exploitative practices. Seek platforms and advisors who offer transparency not just as a tagline but as a structural principle. Use independent tools to audit fees, compare services, and simulate long-term cost impacts. Understand the incentives of anyone giving you financial advice: are they fiduciaries legally bound to act in your best interest, or salespeople with commission targets?

Finally, we need to elevate financial literacy to include *fee fluency*. It is not enough to know how to save or invest; we must also know how to decode statements, read fund prospectuses, and understand cost compounding. Schools don't teach this. Advisors often won't. So the burden falls to us—to study, to question, and to share what we learn.

Silent fees are not the price of financial progress. They are the tax on financial complacency. And in a system that profits from your inattention, vigilance is not just wise—it is radical. You have every right to demand clarity. You have every right to protect your value. And you have every reason to start now.

Chapter 4
The Cult of Consumption — Introduction

Walk through the bustling heart of any modern city, browse the curated illusions of a social media feed, or step inside a home seamlessly wired into the digital hive, and you'll witness a truth so omnipresent it now hides in plain sight: we no longer consume to live—we live to consume. The transaction is no longer just economic; it's existential. We don't merely buy objects—we assemble identities, posture values, and perform belonging through them. Consumption, once a tool, has become the stage and the script, and in many cases, the performance itself. This chapter pulls back the lacquered surface of that spectacle. It asks not only *what* we buy, but *why* we buy it, how often, and—most revealingly—who we imagine we're buying it for.

Let's be clear: this isn't a finger-wagging lament over modern materialism, nor a wistful ode to simpler, pre-digital times. It's something sharper, colder, more deliberate. A forensic analysis of how commercial systems have quietly infiltrated the psyche—how they've learned to trade in insecurity, engineer habit, and convert emotion into profit with surgical precision. Because much of what we take to be individual taste or personal financial behaviour is anything but. These preferences, these decisions—they've been sculpted. Not for your wellbeing, but for someone else's margin. The game isn't just rigged. It's rehearsed.

At the centre of this evolution is a digital economy that transforms lifestyle into spectacle. "Influencer culture," once an auxiliary to celebrity branding, is now its own industrial force. Instagram's clean grids, TikTok's unboxings, Pinterest's hygge-soaked mood boards—these are not innocent showcases of individual flair. They are commercial artefacts, finely tuned to manufacture appetite. And it's rarely the product itself that's being sold. It's a constructed ideal: the life you ought to be living. A neutral-hued living room whispers calm authority. A capsule wardrobe telegraphs discipline. A frothy matcha latte implies mindfulness and success. And underlying each image, there it is—that quiet accusation: *you're behind.*

This is not advertising in the traditional sense. This is a more refined species of manipulation. The influencer economy thrives on the porous boundary between aspiration and self-worth, feeding on the human tendency to equate visibility with value. The algorithm doesn't reward sincerity; it rewards spectacle. And what trickles down to the consumer is a nagging, half-formed belief that one can purchase their way into the lives they observe. What economics once labelled "demand" is now, in truth, cultivated unease—disguised as opportunity.

Then there's convenience—a seductive promise that has become a modern Trojan horse. In today's consumer landscape, friction is the enemy. One-click checkouts, auto-renewals, predictive product placements, and same-day shipping all conspire to eliminate the pause between desire and decision. That pause, by the way, was once called discernment. It's where reason resides. It's where choice lives. Its erasure isn't innovation—it's strategy.

The subscription model exemplifies this perfectly. From digital streaming and recipe boxes to razors and mindfulness apps, the shift from ownership to ongoing payment has redefined the consumer relationship. But make no mistake: it isn't about convenience alone. It's about *slippage*—the profit generated from the unnoticed, the unreviewed, the forgotten. You didn't mean to spend £7.99 this month on that meditation app. But you did. And so did a million others. And that collective forgetfulness? That's a billion-pound industry.

Nowhere is this apparatus more refined than in Amazon's empire. Through unnerving precision, logistical speed, and algorithmic persuasion, it has transformed consumption into reflex. Not impulse—reflex. Shopping is no longer an action. It's a default setting. Amazon doesn't merely remove the friction from buying. It removes the contemplation. You're not choosing. You're responding. You're not browsing. You're confirming. And in the process, something vital is lost—not just money or time, but sovereignty. When every delay is framed as dysfunction, to pause becomes a kind of rebellion.

Beneath this convenience lies a darker bargain. We imagine that these platforms serve us, that they are streamlined tools responding to our needs. But what they actually harvest is us. Our clicks, our pauses, our preferences. All of it hoovered into vast data mines, to be monetised in real time. You are not simply a customer. You are a behavioural asset—measured, modelled, and sold. Free will exists, yes—but it has been surrounded.

And so, in a landscape engineered for maximal consumption, minimalism—real minimalism, not the hashtag variety—emerges not as aesthetic but as resistance. It's not about white walls and artisanal storage solutions. It's about authorship. It's about refusing to outsource your sense of value to an algorithm. To choose less, not as a sacrifice, but as an act of redefinition.

Don't mistake this for asceticism. It is not a call to reject pleasure or live with monkish austerity. It is an argument for discernment. Minimalism, properly understood, is not about deprivation. It is about clarity. About pruning the mental and emotional clutter that so often masquerades as opportunity. When you no longer chase every impulse, when you stop equating acquisition with affirmation, a peculiar thing happens: your sense of internal abundance returns. You begin to measure wealth not in objects owned, but in needs overcome. And that kind of power? It isn't for sale.

The purpose of this chapter is not to issue a shopping list of ethical purchases or preach the gospel of frugality. It is to reawaken your perception—to help you see the systems that sculpt your desire before it even reaches consciousness. To reveal how frictionless convenience drains agency, and how carefully engineered scarcity keeps you hungry for what you don't need.

We will dig into the architecture of aspirational marketing. We will unpick the subtle hooks of subscription logic and automation that siphon money in increments too small to resist but too numerous to ignore. And we will explore strategies—ranging from deliberate digital detoxing to intentional spending—as tools of self-governance in an age of ambient manipulation.

Because until we grasp that in this economy, *we* are the product, we will keep mistaking transactions for choices. And until we start interrogating the difference between what we want and what we've been told to want, we will continue to confuse movement with freedom.

This is not a polemic against wealth or comfort. It is, rather, a call to reframe what constitutes *value*. Not the curated symbols of a borrowed life, but the quiet, resilient things we safeguard when we stop buying on autopilot: time, attention, presence, and the undivided authority to decide—without coercion—what really matters.

Lifestyle Inflation and the Lie of 'Deserving More'

The most seductive financial trap doesn't come in the form of a high-interest loan or a predatory contract. It arrives dressed as progress. A pay rise, a promotion, a profitable year. These milestones are often welcomed with celebration—and rightly so. But what typically follows is not long-term security or financial peace, but something far more insidious: *lifestyle inflation.* The phenomenon where rising income triggers a proportional, and often disproportionate, rise in spending. Not out of necessity, but under the subtle pressure of status, convenience, and an internalised sense of *deserving more.* What makes this dynamic so dangerous is that it masquerades as reward, even as it quietly undermines wealth.

At its core, lifestyle inflation is not a numbers problem—it's a narrative one. It tells us that as we earn more, we should live "better." But this definition of "better" is rarely our own. It is culturally scripted and psychologically reinforced. We upgrade the car, the home, the wardrobe, the holidays. We move into neighbourhoods with higher expectations, send children to schools with implicit costs, start dining where tips are 20% of an already inflated menu. These decisions are framed as natural expressions of success. But often, they represent a shift from financial empowerment to financial performance. The increase in income is quickly neutralised by new commitments—monthly payments, subscriptions, and lifestyle obligations that quietly become fixed.

The behavioural economics behind this trend is both well-documented and deeply human. One key concept is the *hedonic treadmill*: our tendency to quickly return to a baseline level of satisfaction, no matter how much our circumstances improve. When someone's income doubles, the initial excitement may be genuine—but within months, their expectations recalibrate. What was once a luxury becomes normal. What was once enough now feels inadequate. This psychological drift ensures that even significant financial gains often fail to produce long-term contentment. Instead, they generate new desires, many of which are externally manufactured.

This is where marketing steps in—not as a background influence, but as an active architect of our aspirations. We are told, directly and indirectly, that success should be visible. That "treating yourself" is both self-care and moral entitlement. That after years of hard work, we *deserve* the nicer car, the better wine, the upgraded hotel suite. But this rhetoric is not innocent. It is designed to align personal dignity with consumption. To reject the upgrade, then, is to risk appearing either ungrateful or unsuccessful. It's not just about what we can afford—it's about what we *feel justified* in spending.

The lie of "deserving more" capitalises on this emotional ambiguity. It reframes financial prudence as deprivation. In this narrative, saving is seen as small-minded, restraint as outdated, and modesty as mediocrity. The result is a population of earners who are financially stretched not because they don't make enough, but because their spending has been calibrated to impress—others and themselves. And herein lies the trap: as income grows, so too does the illusion of safety. More money in the account feels like security, but if it is tethered to greater obligations, the net effect may be negative. Many professionals earning six figures are less financially stable than they were a decade ago earning half as much.

Consider the real estate example: a couple receives a substantial raise and moves from a modest flat to a large home in a "better" area. Alongside the increased mortgage comes higher council taxes, maintenance costs, private schooling pressures, and social expectations. They now spend more to maintain their position within a new peer group. Even if their income remains stable, they are more vulnerable than before. Any disruption—a job loss, market downturn, health crisis—carries a heavier financial and psychological toll. They've gained square footage but lost flexibility. The home is bigger, but the margin for error is smaller.

This pattern is not limited to housing. It manifests in childcare, transportation, technology, even how we entertain ourselves. The restaurant you now frequent, the gadgets you replace yearly, the holidays you book impulsively—all contribute to a lifestyle calibrated not for resilience, but for appearance. In economic terms, you have not increased your wealth—you've simply increased your *burn rate.* The distance between what you earn and what you spend remains thin, and often imperceptible until a crisis exposes it.

Cultural messaging intensifies the problem. Social media, in particular, has created a perpetual highlight reel of curated lifestyles that skew perceptions of normalcy. When everyone you follow seems to be on a yacht, at a private retreat, or unveiling a new home, restraint starts to feel like failure. It's not just comparison—it's emotional contagion. And unlike advertising, which we can at least identify as persuasion, social media operates under the illusion of peer recommendation. It doesn't feel like a sales pitch. It feels like life catching up to you—and leaving you behind.

From a psychological perspective, this is further complicated by what behavioural scientists call *anchoring bias*. Once we set a new standard for comfort or convenience, it becomes the mental benchmark against which all future experiences are measured. Downgrading—whether it's moving to a smaller place or flying economy—feels like loss, even if it's fiscally wise. This is not rational. It is emotional. And because money decisions are rarely just about arithmetic, understanding these psychological triggers is critical to reclaiming agency.

The lie that more income equals more freedom is dismantled every day by people who earn handsomely yet feel trapped. They are locked into jobs they dislike, schedules they can't adjust, and roles they can't exit—not because they lack money, but because they have structured their lives around spending it. Freedom doesn't come from income. It comes from *surplus*. From margin. From the space between earning and spending that allows for choice, adaptation, and the dignity of saying no.

To challenge lifestyle inflation is not to reject comfort or ambition. It is to question the premise that upgrades are always upgrades. It is to ask: Who benefits when you spend more every time you earn more? Is it truly you—or is it a system that profits from your predictability? Reframing this question is not about austerity. It's about strategy. It's about recognising that the most powerful financial move may not be to earn more, but to need less.

One alternative model is *value-based spending*: a framework that encourages spending not in reaction to income, but in alignment with deeply held priorities. This involves active reflection on what genuinely enriches life versus what merely decorates it. For some, this might mean investing in experiences over possessions. For others, it might mean allocating more to health, education, or time-saving services—and deliberately cutting back elsewhere. The key distinction is intentionality. Spending becomes a conscious act, not a reflex.

Ultimately, the antidote to lifestyle inflation is not minimalism per se, but *congruence*. When your financial behaviours reflect your values, not the expectations of a marketplace that trades in insecurity, you reclaim control. You step off the treadmill. And in doing so, you redefine what it means to deserve more—not in terms of material display, but in terms of freedom, autonomy, and peace of mind.

Because you don't deserve "more." You deserve *enough*. Enough to be secure. Enough to say no. Enough to live on your own terms. And that—despite what the economy wants you to believe—is not bought through upgrades. It's built through awareness.

Influencer Economics and the Aspiration Trap

There is a strange irony in how modern desire is shaped. We have never had more access to information, and yet our wants—what we think we need—have never been more manufactured. At the epicentre of this shift is a new economic force: the influencer. Unlike traditional marketing, which once came with clear boundaries—advertisements placed between the content we actually wanted—influencer marketing *is* the content. It doesn't interrupt your feed; it *is* your feed. And that distinction is not trivial. It represents one of the most subtle and effective financial manipulations of the 21st century.

The influencer economy doesn't just sell products. It sells *aspirations*. Its power lies not in persuading you to buy a particular face cream or trainer brand, but in creating a phantom reality in which owning these things is synonymous with being attractive, productive, healthy, or successful. The danger is not in the individual transaction, but in the larger illusion it supports: that your current life is somehow inadequate, and that fulfilment is always just one purchase away.

What we are witnessing is not simply the rise of a new marketing tactic, but the codification of lifestyle envy into a monetised business model. Influencers, many of whom are not celebrities in the traditional sense but individuals who have built credibility within specific digital niches, present themselves as relatable. They are not airbrushed magazine icons—they are "just like you," only with better lighting, better wardrobes, and curated weekends in Bali. Their influence is built on intimacy and trust, even though that trust is often engineered, packaged, and monetised through sponsorships, affiliate links, and brand deals.

This dynamic turns every scroll into a psychological microtransaction. You aren't paying money, but you are paying attention—and attention is the currency of influence. Every time you see a sponsored skincare routine, a "What I Eat in a Day" video, or a neatly framed home office tour, you're not just consuming content; you're absorbing a template for what your life *should* look like. And crucially, what it's currently lacking.

The most insidious feature of this ecosystem is its ability to generate *phantom needs*: desires that feel urgent but have no basis in actual utility or values. These needs arise not from within, but from exposure. You didn't think you needed a self-cleaning water bottle, LED vanity mirror, or "emotional support" designer hoodie—until you saw someone online using one and looking radiant. Influencer marketing, especially when embedded within lifestyle content, operates below the level of conscious resistance. It doesn't confront—it seduces.

Psychologically, this taps into deeply wired social instincts. Human beings are mimetic: we imitate those we admire, envy, or feel socially proximate to. The influencer model exploits this by collapsing the distinction between peer and celebrity. You're not just watching someone famous from afar—you're watching someone who vlogs their morning coffee, complains about traffic, and shares relationship advice. The parasocial relationship makes their choices seem like recommendations from a friend. But this friend is being paid—often handsomely—by companies who know that trust, once monetised, can outperform even the slickest ad campaign.

The results are evident in our spending habits. Young adults, particularly Gen Z and Millennials, are increasingly making financial decisions influenced more by social media than by professional financial advice. According to a 2022 Credit Karma report, over 40% of Gen Z consumers said their spending was directly influenced by social media platforms—particularly Instagram and TikTok. Yet these platforms are rarely transparent about sponsored content, nor are their creators held to journalistic standards. The product endorsement you see in a 30-second video may have been scripted, heavily edited, and incentivised by performance bonuses. But the illusion of authenticity persists.

This matters because the aspiration trap is not just a cultural annoyance—it is an economic hazard. It drives lifestyle inflation, encourages debt, and erodes the capacity for long-term thinking. When aspiration is externalised—measured by how closely your life matches the curated lives you consume online—then financial decisions become reactive. You're not investing based on goals or values; you're spending to close a perceived gap between yourself and the illusion of "enough."

Even minimal resistance to this system is costly. To opt out of a trend—or worse, to express ambivalence—risks seeming out of touch. For young professionals navigating industries where personal branding and appearance matter, the pressure to perform lifestyle success is real. The car you drive, the devices you own, the places you holiday—all can function as social currency. Opting for simplicity can feel like self-sabotage. In this environment, not spending becomes a form of rebellion.

And yet, the influencer economy has its own vulnerabilities. It depends on your continued belief in the illusion. Once you see the architecture—the deals behind the post, the filters on the face, the scripting behind the vlog—the spell begins to weaken. That's where critical thinking becomes a financial asset. Recognising that much of what passes as "authentic" online is, in fact, curated to create desire is the first step towards reclaiming agency.

This isn't to suggest all influencers are cynical or that every promotion is deceptive. Some creators share valuable content, promote ethical brands, and disclose partnerships transparently. But the broader system is built on asymmetry: viewers rarely know what's real, what's sponsored, and what's orchestrated. That ambiguity benefits platforms and advertisers, not consumers.

One productive way to resist this manipulation is to interrogate your own impulses. Before any non-essential purchase, ask: *Where did this desire come from? Would I have wanted this if I hadn't seen it online? What do I think this item will signal about me—and to whom?* These are not trivial questions. They cut to the heart of whether your financial decisions are internally sourced or externally engineered.

Philosophically, this raises an even deeper question: *Who gets to define what is "enough" in your life?* If your sense of adequacy is continually outsourced to a feed of curated strangers, then your financial agency has been compromised. You're not living—you're performing. The danger of the aspiration trap is not just that it leads to wasteful spending, but that it erodes satisfaction. It transforms contentment into a moving target.

Counteracting this requires more than budgeting apps or digital detoxes. It requires a psychological shift: from performative consumption to reflective living. It involves redefining success not in terms of aesthetics, but alignment. Are you spending in ways that reflect your values, support your priorities, and build resilience? Or are you spending to keep pace with an invisible, ever-changing standard set by people who don't know you—and whose lifestyles may not even be real?

Ultimately, the aspiration trap is not about envy; it's about identity. The influencer economy thrives by offering ready-made identities that can be purchased and performed. But identity that can be bought is fragile. What sustains you financially and emotionally is not the image you project, but the life you actually lead—quietly, without fanfare, in accordance with your own principles.

Resisting influencer economics is not about cynicism. It's about sovereignty. It's the refusal to let curated content dictate your values, define your self-worth, or drain your resources in pursuit of phantoms. Because when the camera is off, and the post has been sponsored, and the story expires in 24 hours, you're left with the only thing that matters: your choices. And the question of whether they were truly yours to begin with.

When Convenience Becomes a Cage

Convenience has become one of the most valuable currencies of the modern economy—but like all currencies, it comes with hidden exchange rates. We are led to believe that the path of least resistance is always the smart one: that quicker is better, that easier is superior, that automation is progress. And while there is no question that modern systems have dramatically reduced friction in our daily lives, what has received far less attention is what we've traded in return: autonomy, discernment, and—increasingly—choice.

In no sector is this more evident than in the rise of platform capitalism. Amazon, the undisputed titan of this new commercial logic, has redefined not just how we buy but *how we think about buying.* Shopping is no longer an act of decision-making—it's a reflex. Need something? Click. Want something? Tap. From groceries to garden tools, batteries to blenders, our consumption has been compressed into milliseconds. But speed distorts perspective. And what feels like control is often carefully choreographed nudging.

Amazon Prime is perhaps the most effective behavioural engineering tool in consumer history. For a modest monthly fee, it eliminates the "cost friction" of shipping and reframes instant gratification as the norm. But Prime's genius lies not in its logistics; it lies in its psychology. By making the customer feel like they're "winning" by using it—saving time, saving money, avoiding effort—it gradually erodes the comparative mindset. Over time, the act of evaluating alternatives diminishes. Other vendors become inconvenient by default, even if they are more ethical, local, or cost-effective. Amazon doesn't just sell products; it *monopolises convenience.*

This dynamic is replicated across countless other platforms. Uber reframed car travel. Deliveroo reframed meals. Netflix reframed entertainment. What unites them is not merely disruption of legacy models, but a deeper economic manipulation: they train users to accept *passivity* in exchange for speed. And passivity, once habituated, becomes dependence.

Consider subscription models—once rare, now ubiquitous. You pay not just for what you use, but for the privilege of *not thinking about it.* Whether it's software, fitness, shaving kits, audiobooks, or organic snacks, subscription services offer an illusion of simplicity. But this illusion has a cost. The average consumer underestimates how much they spend on subscriptions each month, and many remain subscribed to services they no longer use. A 2021 study by West Monroe found that 89% of Americans underestimated their monthly subscription costs—often by hundreds of dollars. This isn't accident; it's design. Auto-renewal, free trials that become paid without notification, and obscure cancellation pathways all work to transform once-voluntary choices into economic inertia.

The result is a slow atrophy of financial agency. When convenience is always available, it becomes difficult to distinguish *ease* from *autonomy*. We stop asking: Is this the best value? Is this aligned with my values? Do I even want or need this anymore? Instead, we fall into default modes, sleepwalking through spending decisions. This is the essence of the cage: not that it restrains us, but that it convinces us we are free.

This is not a Luddite argument against modernity. Time-saving technologies have transformed lives, especially for those juggling multiple roles or living with limitations. But the problem arises when we fail to interrogate the *terms* of that trade. Who benefits from our automation? What happens to decision quality when the process becomes invisible? And what structures are being reinforced when we choose the easiest option again and again?

From a financial standpoint, the erosion of friction has subtle but serious implications. Friction in spending—having to enter your card number, wait in line, make a trip—once acted as a psychological checkpoint. It slowed down impulse, created room for doubt, and allowed space for re-evaluation. Remove these frictions and you remove the natural breaks in the consumption cycle. As a result, instant purchases feel like non-events. They don't register emotionally. And what doesn't register can't be controlled.

The architecture of modern commerce understands this all too well. Platforms optimise not for your long-term wellbeing, but for conversion rates and customer retention. One-click purchase buttons, pre-filled forms, biometric logins—all of these tools serve to compress the decision-making interval. But compressed decisions are often poor decisions. Convenience, in this context, becomes a method of obfuscation—a way to bypass scrutiny.

We also need to reckon with the *cultural narrative* surrounding ease. We are told that busyness is a badge of honour, that productivity is paramount, and that time is the most precious resource. In this context, any service that promises to "give back your time" is cast as inherently good. But this logic is dangerously one-dimensional. What if time saved is not used wisely? What if it just leads to more scrolling, more spending, more noise? Time *reclaimed* is only meaningful if accompanied by intention. Without it, convenience merely becomes a fast track to distraction.

There's a deeper philosophical cost too. When every aspect of life can be optimised—when meals arrive with taps and groceries reappear via algorithm—we risk losing the value of *effort*. Not just in terms of labour, but in terms of *engagement*. Slower modes of consumption—cooking your own food, shopping at a local market, assembling your own furniture—connect us more directly with the process of living. They require participation. And participation fosters meaning.

The rise of convenience culture also affects our sense of time and patience. Platforms that prioritise speed condition us to expect immediacy in all domains. Waiting becomes intolerable. Slowness becomes a problem to solve, rather than an experience to inhabit. But this constant acceleration fractures our attention and narrows our tolerance for ambiguity. The psychological cost is subtle but cumulative: we become less resilient, less reflective, and more reactive.

So how can autonomy be reclaimed in the age of hyper-convenience? The first step is awareness. Track your subscriptions—not just financially, but cognitively. Ask what each one delivers, whether it still serves you, and whether the ease it offers is worth the cost in discernment. Next, consider *strategic friction*: reintroducing small steps that create space for intentionality. This could be disabling one-click purchases, pausing before renewals, or simply asking, "What's the hard way to do this—and why might that be better?"

Another approach is to cultivate alternative sources of satisfaction—ones that are rooted in process rather than output. Cook instead of ordering in. Walk instead of hailing a ride. Read from a book instead of streaming background noise. These acts are not romantic nostalgias; they are *resets*. They remind us that not all convenience is benign and that autonomy often begins with inconvenience.

Ultimately, this is not about rejecting modern systems wholesale. It's about resisting the assumption that convenience is always a net good. Because when the easiest path is also the most manipulated, staying alert becomes a form of financial and personal self-defence. What we surrender in the name of ease is not just money—it is muscle. The muscle of decision-making, discernment, and participation. And like all muscles, it weakens from disuse.

If we want to regain sovereignty over our lives and finances, we must be willing to ask harder questions, take slower paths, and reclaim the discomfort of choosing deliberately. Because the real cost of convenience is not always what we pay at checkout. It is what we stop noticing, questioning, and ultimately, controlling.

Minimalism as Rebellion

Minimalism, in its commodified form, has been reduced to a sleek lifestyle trend: white walls, artisanal soap, and the promise of inner peace via decluttering. But this aesthetic interpretation obscures its most potent dimension—minimalism as economic defiance. In a global system engineered to keep people consuming, accumulating, and ultimately indebted, the deliberate refusal to participate in perpetual acquisition is not merely a personal preference. It is a quiet but radical act of resistance. This chapter reclaims minimalism from the Instagram flat-lay and restores it as a tool of financial sovereignty, a practical rejection of the economic mechanisms that exploit human psychology for profit.

To understand the insurgent potential of minimalism, we must first recognise the invisible scaffolding that upholds the consumption machine. Consumer capitalism relies on a set of interlocking narratives: that happiness can be bought, that success must be signalled, and that new is inherently better than enough. These stories are embedded in advertising, social media, even workplace culture, all serving the same goal—to keep individuals in a constant state of low-grade dissatisfaction and aspirational striving. This manufactured hunger is not an incidental byproduct of economic activity; it is the business model. Minimalism, reframed as intentional non-consumption, directly undermines that model.

Consider the psychological architecture of the consumer. Behavioural economists have shown that much of our financial decision-making is not rational, but emotional—driven by social comparison, fear of missing out, and the dopamine spike of acquisition. The average person scrolls through hundreds of algorithmically curated images daily, each one subtly reinforcing the belief that self-worth is tethered to ownership. The minimalist stance—*I do not need this to be enough*—is, in this context, a neurological reprogramming. It is not merely self-control; it is cognitive disobedience.

The financial implications are profound. Every act of deliberate non-spending weakens the grip of systems designed to convert labour into lifelong liability. Subscription models, retail therapy, influencer economies—all lose their grip when their core promise is exposed as hollow. The minimalist does not merely reduce expenses; they change the fundamental equation by which value is measured. Where conventional finance asks, "What can you afford?", minimalism asks, "What truly adds value to your life?" This is not semantics—it is a reframing that shifts the individual from a passive consumer to an active sovereign over their resources.

Take, for instance, the structural differences between voluntary simplicity and forced austerity. A financially stressed individual may appear minimalist—delaying purchases, limiting consumption—but the underlying psychology is scarcity. True minimalism, by contrast, is rooted in sufficiency. It emerges from a place of *enoughness*, a consciously chosen boundary that prioritises autonomy over accumulation. This distinction matters. One is imposed by circumstance; the other is an act of authorship.

Minimalism as rebellion also calls into question the legitimacy of a system that equates economic health with ever-increasing consumption. When GDP rises because people are buying more antidepressants, replacing appliances sooner, or financing luxury cars they can't afford, we must ask: who benefits? The answer is rarely the consumer. It is corporations, data brokers, and financiers who profit from the churn. The minimalist, by stepping outside of this loop, disrupts the metrics of success that keep the treadmill spinning.

But this disruption is not easy. Minimalism in the modern context requires both awareness and resistance—two faculties that are deliberately dulled by mainstream culture. Awareness means recognising the psychological hooks: how scarcity is fabricated, how self-image is co-opted, how convenience becomes compulsion. Resistance means setting boundaries that often feel socially awkward: declining gifts, resisting "free" upgrades, wearing the same clothes repeatedly without apology. These acts may seem small, but in aggregate, they amount to a redefinition of status and success on one's own terms.

We must also confront the cultural scripts that minimalism threatens. Many societies associate material possession with moral virtue—diligence, success, responsibility. To opt out of this semiotic code is to risk being perceived as lazy, unambitious, even antisocial. This is not an accidental consequence. The myth of the productive consumer is what keeps wage labourers compliant and aspirants striving. Minimalism as rebellion dismantles this myth by redefining productivity as living in alignment with one's values, not one's purchases.

One might argue that minimalism is a privilege—that only those with financial safety can afford to opt out of consumption. There is partial truth here. But minimalism does not require deprivation; it requires discernment. Some of the most powerful minimalist practices cost nothing: deleting shopping apps, unplugging from curated advertising, learning to repair rather than replace. These acts are not about rejecting comfort but about reclaiming agency from a system that profits when people abdicate it.

Moreover, minimalism exposes a dangerous asymmetry in the financial system. While individuals are nudged to spend constantly, large institutions hoard, speculate, and exploit scale. Governments measure consumer confidence not by savings but by spending. Corporate tax breaks incentivise expansion, not ethical stewardship. In this context, the minimalist becomes the ethical investor—not in financial instruments, but in their own clarity, time, and sovereignty.

There is a deeper philosophical current running through this as well. In a world of engineered excess, restraint becomes a form of clarity. The decision to own less, want less, need less is not asceticism—it is strategic liberation. It frees attention, reduces decision fatigue, and makes space for priorities that capitalism cannot commodify: health, presence, connection, purpose. These gains are invisible on spreadsheets but transformative in lived experience.

As with any rebellion, minimalism invites risk. To live with less in a society that equates more with better is to invite misunderstanding. But the reward is profound: the ability to define wealth not by accumulation but by intentionality. This is financial self-defence at its most elegant—not hoarding, not hustling, but disengaging from the game entirely.

The consumption engine runs on obedience: to trends, to debt, to the idea that more will finally make us whole. Minimalism breaks that spell. Not by denial, but by redesign. Not by guilt, but by grace. To live minimally is not to have less—it is to need less. And that, in a system built on craving, may be the most subversive act of all.

Chapter 5
Debt – The Modern Serfdom

Debt, once an occasional burden or calculated risk, has quietly become a cornerstone of modern life—so ordinary in its ubiquity that we barely flinch at its presence. We borrow to study, to buy homes we rarely inhabit fully, to lease vehicles we don't quite own, and to acquire objects so forgettable we often can't recall ordering them. From the eager graduate to the weary pensioner, there exists a financial product tailored to ensure solvency remains forever just out of reach. What this normalisation obscures, however, is a more primal dynamic: debt, stripped of its spreadsheets and softened language, is fundamentally a mechanism of control. When harnessed by power, it does not simply constrain our spending. It disciplines our lives.

That's where this chapter begins—not with budgets or interest rates, but with the unspoken architecture of control masquerading as personal finance. Debt today is less about responding to misfortune or investing in opportunity, and more about maintaining a system of managed dependence. It shifts liability away from institutions, commodifies aspiration, and reshapes behaviour in ways that rarely favour the debtor. Its psychological grip is not a by-product—it is the entire point. The more indebted you are, the less inclined you'll be to resist, to demand better, to walk away from a job that depletes you. The indebted parent swallows dreams. The indebted worker settles. The indebted mind—disoriented, overstimulated, quietly panicked—is easier to corral, to persuade, and yes, to sell to.

To call this a new form of serfdom may sound provocative. In truth, it's merely accurate. Feudalism never required chains. It thrived on obligation—on the inescapable dues paid to a landowning elite. That dynamic hasn't vanished; it has been digitised. Today, the baron is a student loan provider, a mortgage lender, a "buy now, pay later" platform. And the tithe? A monthly direct debit. The binding is no longer physical, but psychological—rooted in self-doubt, misdirection, and quiet resignation.

What follows is not a familiar catalogue of debt's burdens. That ground has been well trodden. This is an excavation of its deeper anatomy—how it shapes identity, distorts time, and enforces compliance so effectively that many don't realise they're ensnared until they've internalised the chains. Debt shrinks not just your balance sheet, but your sense of what's possible.

Let's start with the emotional terrain. Unlike a one-off loss, which is typically external and finite, debt seeps inward. It embeds itself into self-perception. You don't just *have* debt. You become, in your own eyes, someone who *is* in debt. This fusion of numbers and self-worth corrodes confidence and clouds decision-making. Studies across psychology and behavioural economics draw clear lines between chronic indebtedness and mental health decline—depression, paralysis, tunnel vision. The future becomes a blur, long-term plans recede into fog, and survival replaces strategy.

But this emotional toll does not fall evenly. Those most bruised by debt-related shame are often those most invested in the myth of meritocracy—the belief that effort and intelligence alone ensure financial stability. When the lived reality fails to align with that ideology, the result is self-reproach. The system, cleverly, has taught us to blame ourselves. You didn't save enough. You should've known better. You failed at adulthood. And so, the machine profits not just from the repayments, but from the silence bred by shame.

The next layer requires an unflinching look at the substance of debt itself. Not all debt is created equal. Here, we draw a hard distinction between strategic debt—used with intent, leveraged towards a clear outcome—and what might be more accurately labelled slave debt. The latter isn't about growth or investment. It's about treading water. It funds subsistence, not expansion. It sustains the illusion of access while quietly tightening the noose.

The difference is structural, not moral. A company borrowing to upgrade machinery operates in a different universe from a family using credit to bridge the gap between wages and inflation. One assumes risk with agency. The other absorbs risk with no viable escape route. Many consumer financial tools blur these lines under the guise of convenience. Payday loans, deferred payment schemes, and subprime car leases all parade as opportunities. But behind the friendly interfaces lie coercive contracts, information asymmetry, and default settings that trap rather than empower.

And once trapped, behaviour changes. There's now ample research across cognitive science showing that persistent scarcity doesn't merely stress people out—it warps decision-making. The brain under chronic financial strain begins to favour short-term relief over long-term gain. People delay doctor's visits, ignore red flags in contracts, settle for worse conditions. These aren't signs of weakness. They're signs of adaptation. But adaptation, while useful in the moment, rarely leads to freedom.

Which brings us to a necessary shift: from guilt to strategy. Escaping the debt cycle requires more than discipline or sacrifice. It demands a reconfiguration of perspective. Toward that end, this chapter offers a set of countermeasures—not financial hacks, but deeper frameworks for what might be called economic disobedience. We begin with a method of debt auditing that looks beyond APRs and payment schedules. It asks: what is the *true* cost of this debt? In autonomy, in mental bandwidth, in freedom of movement?

From there, we explore a concept called "liberation metrics"—alternative indicators that assess whether your repayment plan is actually delivering freedom, or merely maintaining the illusion of progress. Is the strategy sustainable? Does it align with your values? Does it enhance your capacity to act with agency, or does it reinforce dependence? We also examine how values-based budgeting—grounded in behavioural psychology, trauma studies, and mindfulness—can displace the shame-laced, spreadsheet-driven model most people abandon within weeks.

But perhaps the most urgent task is dismantling the moral fog that surrounds debt. You are not your overdraft. You are not your late fees. You are not the decimal points on a credit report that updates without context. These are not indictments. They are artefacts—

signals of a system that extracts first and explains later. Shame is debt's most reliable ally. Clarity, on the other hand, begins to strip it of its mystique.

So if you've ever felt like you're running just to stay in place, if every modest pay rise seems to dissolve into thin air, if joy has become something you defer to the future for fear of disrupting repayment plans—this chapter is yours. Not as a pep talk, but as a confrontation with reality. Because the first step toward freedom is not austerity. It's vision. To see the structure clearly. To name what it is. And then, to begin—quietly, deliberately—to outgrow it. With new strategies, new allegiances, and a renewed sense of what life outside the ledger might finally feel like.

Debt as a Business Model

Debt is often presented as a bridge—something to help individuals cross over from need to fulfilment, from aspiration to attainment. Credit, we are told, is a tool of empowerment. Mortgages are marketed as a gateway to property ownership. Student loans are framed as "investments in your future." But a deeper, more honest appraisal reveals that these instruments are not designed primarily to support people—they are engineered to extract from them. Debt, in the modern financial system, is not an unfortunate necessity; it is a product. And like all good products, it is most profitable when it becomes habitual, opaque, and difficult to opt out of.

To understand the true nature of debt today, one must stop seeing it as a public service or even a neutral transaction. It is a business model—one that relies on long-term dependency, not resolution.

This business model did not emerge overnight. It is the outcome of a decades-long shift in how economies allocate risk, regulate capital, and interpret personal responsibility. In earlier eras, debt was seen with moral suspicion—something to be avoided if possible. Today, it is not only normalised; it is expected. It has been woven so tightly into the fabric of modern life that avoiding debt altogether is now a form of economic deviance. Try to attend university, buy a home, start a business, or handle a medical emergency without debt, and you quickly discover how little infrastructure exists for the debt-averse.

The transformation of debt from social stigma to social default was not accidental. It was cultivated—through advertising, lobbying, deregulation, and the financialisation of basic life necessities. The result is a system in which *your need becomes someone else's asset class.*

Consider student loans. Once conceived as public investments in human capital, they have become vehicles for profit, managed by private servicing companies, backed by government guarantees, and structured in ways that make early repayment difficult and complete discharge nearly impossible. In the United States alone, outstanding student loan debt has surpassed $1.7 trillion. But the magnitude of the number tells only part of the story. More important is the model behind it: the longer you take to repay, the more profitable you are. Interest accrual, penalty fees, loan servicing—these are not unfortunate by-products; they are the revenue mechanisms.

Or take the mortgage industry. Most people believe that taking out a mortgage is a step toward ownership. And technically, it is. But the reality is that most mortgage holders spend the majority of their repayment term servicing interest, not reducing principal. A 30-year fixed-rate mortgage, standard in many countries, is structured so that in the first decade, the bulk of your payment goes to interest. This structure benefits lenders and institutional investors who have turned residential mortgages into bundled financial products—mortgage-backed securities traded on global markets. Your home loan, in this context, is less a path to ownership than a yield-generating instrument. The house is not just yours; it is monetised far beyond your doorstep.

Credit cards are perhaps the most naked example of debt-as-business. Their primary function is not to facilitate temporary liquidity but to sustain a revolving balance from which the issuer can extract high interest. The average credit card interest rate exceeds 20%—a rate that would be considered usurious in other contexts.

But regulation has softened, consumer protections have weakened, and behavioural design has become more manipulative. *Minimum payments, reward points, and "pay later" features are not consumer benefits; they are psychological levers to keep debt in play without activating alarm.*

Financial institutions are keenly aware that indebtedness is not just an outcome—it is a behavioural state. Indebted consumers are more likely to accept poor terms, less likely to switch providers, and more vulnerable to upselling. In this sense, debt functions not merely as a profit stream, but as a form of *behavioural anchoring*. Once in debt, your capacity for negotiation weakens. Your decisions narrow. Your tolerance for exploitation rises.

This logic extends into every corner of modern finance. Car loans, medical payment plans, in-app purchases with deferred billing, payday loans rebranded as fintech "advances"—all share the same DNA. They are not neutral tools. They are engineered dependencies. And like any good dependency, they are profitable precisely because they are hard to exit.

What makes this ecosystem so durable is its veneer of empowerment. Credit is sold to us as freedom: the freedom to choose now, to have now, to do now. But this freedom is conditional. The terms are rarely written with the borrower's long-term autonomy in mind. They are written to maximise extraction over time, ideally without triggering defaults or rebellion. Hence the complexity, the jargon, the fees hidden in footnotes, the seduction of pre-approval. *A good debtor is someone who pays reliably but never escapes entirely.*

We must also confront the ideological scaffolding that props up this model. Neoliberal economics, with its emphasis on individual responsibility and market primacy, has recast systemic indebtedness as a series of personal choices. If you are overleveraged, you must be living beyond your means. If you default, you must have failed to plan. This framing is not just inaccurate—it is politically convenient. It obscures how wage stagnation, housing inflation, and austerity have made debt the only viable route to basic social mobility. It also erases how the very institutions profiting from this debt have influenced the policies that made it necessary.

Some defenders of the current system argue that credit expands access. And in narrow terms, it does. But access without stability is not empowerment—it is entrapment. A student can "access" higher education through loans but may spend decades in repayment. A young family can "access" a home through a mortgage but may find themselves one interest hike away from foreclosure. *Access must not be conflated with justice.*

So what is the alternative? Not a return to debt-shaming, nor an unrealistic fantasy of a debt-free economy. Debt can, in some cases, be strategic. But only if it is understood, transparent, and accompanied by genuine upward mobility. The problem is not debt itself. The problem is that we have constructed a civilisation where *debt is the primary business model*—not a support mechanism, not a safety net, but the foundational revenue engine of banking, education, healthcare, and housing.

This chapter's purpose is to equip you not only with understanding, but with discernment. When presented with credit, ask not merely what the terms are, but what the structure assumes. Who profits if I pay slowly? What behaviours are being nudged? What incentives are invisible? Who benefits if I am confused, compliant, or ashamed?

The only antidote to weaponised debt is financial literacy sharpened into financial resistance. That means recognising when support is really surveillance. When access is really entrapment. And when "choice" is being manipulated to serve a model that profits only when your obligations outlast your options.

The Psychological Toll of Indebtedness

Debt is rarely just about money. It is about meaning—what we make of our obligations, what they say about us, and what they silently steal. The financial dimension may be measurable, calculated in interest rates and repayment terms. But the psychological toll is often harder to quantify and far more corrosive. Shame, paralysis, secrecy, compulsive spending, chronic under-earning—these are not simply by-products of poor budgeting. They are trauma responses in disguise.

Modern economies normalise debt, but the human nervous system does not. The feeling of owing more than one can repay—even temporarily—activates the same threat detection systems that evolved for physical survival. The amygdala cannot distinguish between a sabre-toothed predator and a persistent collections notice. *Debt, especially when chronic, is experienced not as a ledger entry but as a constant ambient danger.* It imposes vigilance, triggers cortisol, erodes sleep, shortens patience, and slowly warps one's sense of safety.

It also breeds shame—an emotion so potent that many would rather lie, deflect, or hide than face it. Unlike guilt, which is tied to specific behaviours ("I spent irresponsibly"), shame attacks identity ("I am irresponsible"). Research in affective neuroscience confirms that shame shuts down the executive functions required for problem-solving. The result is paradoxical: the more ashamed a person feels about their debt, the less capable they become of addressing it. They may stop opening statements, avoid discussing money with partners, or push away financial help. *Shame doesn't incentivise repair—it freezes cognition and corrodes trust, especially self-trust.*

Cultural narratives compound this internalised judgment. In societies saturated by meritocratic ideology, debt is easily framed as a personal failing rather than a structural trap. If you're in debt, it must be because you're lazy, entitled, or undisciplined. Never mind the stagnant wages, the inflated cost of living, the rising cost of education, the ubiquity of predatory lending, or the industries built on financial illiteracy. When the systems are rigged but the rhetoric is individualised, people suffer twice: once economically, and again emotionally, under the illusion that it is their fault alone.

Avoidance becomes a natural defence. Psychologists have documented a behavioural phenomenon known as "debt denial," where individuals deliberately avoid looking at their bank balances, bills, or credit reports. They postpone decisions, miss payment deadlines, or refuse to open important letters. On the surface, it appears irrational. But from the brain's perspective, it is logical: *if the data confirms danger and one has no emotional capacity to change it, the most adaptive strategy is to look away.*

This avoidance, of course, deepens the problem. Late fees accumulate. Credit scores drop. Anxiety swells in the background, unspoken but omnipresent. And so the spiral continues: worry fuels avoidance, avoidance fuels deterioration, deterioration fuels shame, and shame locks the system. People find themselves stuck—not just financially, but emotionally and neurologically.

This is where the toll becomes existential. Debt begins to distort self-perception. People report feeling undeserving, fraudulent, or permanently behind. Even moments of pleasure or progress—an earned holiday, a professional achievement—can be tainted by the thought: *I haven't really earned this. I'm still in debt.* This mindset doesn't just damage morale—it can sabotage recovery. If you believe you are someone who always struggles, you are less likely to engage in behaviours that lead to stability.

There is also a profound social cost. Debt isolates. In cultures where financial success is tied to identity and status, few people admit financial distress. Friends aren't told the real reason a dinner invitation is declined. Children are shielded from the tension at home. Spouses often lie to one another, not out of malice, but to protect themselves from judgment or conflict. The longer this secrecy persists, the more entrenched the patterns become. *Debt does not merely impact your credit score; it rewires your relational circuitry.*

Moreover, debt is unevenly distributed—and so is its psychological weight. Women, for example, are more likely to carry debt related to caregiving, education, or part-time employment, and yet are also more likely to feel shame about it. Black and minority borrowers face systemic barriers that inflate the cost and consequences of borrowing, all while being more likely to be portrayed as financially irresponsible by dominant media narratives. Thus, the psychological toll of debt is magnified by the weight of *intersectional injustice*—where economic anxiety intersects with racial, gendered, or class-based narratives of worth.

Despite the darkness of this terrain, not all debt experiences result in paralysis. The difference often lies not in the size of the debt, but in the framework used to interpret it. Research from behavioural economics and clinical psychology has shown that people who view debt as a solvable problem—rather than a personal indictment—are more likely to engage in proactive behaviours. They create repayment plans, seek financial advice, and develop healthier coping strategies. These outcomes are not merely economic—they are cognitive and emotional victories.

This distinction leads us to a critical insight: *the first step out of debt is not financial; it is psychological.* Before one can tackle interest rates or payment schedules, one must untangle the deeper narratives of shame, avoidance, and learned helplessness. Doing so requires support—sometimes from financial coaches, sometimes from therapists, often from both. It also requires reframing.

One powerful reframing technique is to externalise the debt narrative. Rather than saying "I am bad with money," say "I was never taught how to navigate a debt-based economy designed to confuse me." This may sound semantic, but it has profound neurological effects. It shifts the frame from identity to environment, from helplessness to strategy. Another method is to decouple debt from morality. Borrowing is not a sin; it is a transaction. And when that transaction becomes exploitative, the blame lies not with the borrower but with the structure.

Mindfulness-based cognitive approaches have shown particular promise here. Techniques that strengthen present-moment awareness—such as breathwork, non-judgemental observation, and compassion exercises—can reduce the overwhelm triggered by financial stress. Over time, they create the emotional space required for deliberate action. *Debt shrinks the psychological field; mindfulness widens it again.*

Ultimately, we must recognise that the true cost of debt cannot be calculated in pounds or percentages. It is measured in hours of lost sleep, in conversations avoided, in opportunities passed over, in diminished self-regard. It is paid in silence and shame, and—perhaps most damagingly—in the surrender of hope. Reclaiming agency begins not with spreadsheets, but with rehumanisation. By acknowledging that chronic debt is not a failure but a wound, we open the door not only to financial recovery, but to emotional and relational repair.

The systems may not be fixed overnight. But the narrative we carry about our place within them can be rewritten. The debt may still exist—but its power to define us need not.

Strategic Debt vs. Slave Debt: Understanding Leverage, Entrapment, and the Cost of Borrowing

Not all debt is created equal. This is not a moral claim—it is a structural truth. And yet, across financial discourse, personal development rhetoric, and even government messaging, debt is often treated monolithically. Borrowing, we are told, is either wholly dangerous or entirely necessary. This binary framing is misleading at best and financially disabling at worst. To navigate the modern economy with agency, one must understand a critical distinction: the difference between *strategic debt* and *slave debt.*

At its core, strategic debt is a deliberate financial instrument—used by individuals, corporations, and even nations to create value beyond the cost of borrowing. It is debt with a purpose, a plan, and a positive spread. Slave debt, by contrast, is debt that owns the debtor. It generates no long-term return, erodes optionality, and keeps the borrower in a cycle of dependency, often under the illusion of progress. *Strategic debt expands freedom; slave debt contracts it.*

But how does one distinguish between the two in real life? The answer is not in interest rates alone. It lies in understanding *intent, context, structure,* and *exit strategy*—and perhaps more importantly, the *psychological posture* one adopts in entering the obligation.

Take, for instance, a mortgage. A first-time buyer might assume that a mortgage is inherently "good debt"—it builds equity, enables homeownership, and may even offer tax advantages. But this blanket logic is flawed. If the house is purchased at the top of an inflated market, with minimal deposit, high interest, and no flexibility for income fluctuation, the mortgage may in fact be *slave debt* disguised as middle-class aspiration. It drains liquidity, restricts mobility, and often leads to financial fragility. The same product—used in a different context—carries entirely different consequences.

Strategic debt is characterised by alignment. The terms align with one's financial goals, the repayment structure aligns with expected income flows, and the risks are understood, not ignored. A business loan that funds scalable operations, or a student loan taken on with a clear cost-benefit analysis and high earnings trajectory, may qualify. *Strategic debt is never casual—it is calculated.*

Slave debt, on the other hand, thrives on misalignment. It is debt incurred without a path to recovery—used to soothe emotional needs, signal status, or simply survive within an economic architecture that penalises the poor for being poor. High-interest credit cards used to cover basic expenses, payday loans issued with triple-digit APRs, or education loans tied to degrees with little labour market demand are modern instruments of bondage. They exploit vulnerability, not opportunity.

The psychology here is crucial. Slave debt often emerges from emotional decision-making. The borrower may feel backed into a corner—pressured by timelines, expectations, or shame. There is often an absence of informed consent; the borrower signs without fully understanding compound interest, wage garnishment, or the long-term implications of default. The illusion of quick relief masks the reality of long-term extraction. *It is not that the debtor is foolish; it is that the system is predatory by design.*

To see this clearly, one must understand how profit is engineered. Banks and lenders thrive on prolonged indebtedness, not swift repayment. The credit card industry alone generates billions annually through minimum payments that ensure interest continues compounding indefinitely. In this model, the most lucrative customer is not the one who repays quickly—it's the one who can just barely manage to stay afloat. Debt becomes not a bridge, but a business model. *And the debtor is the asset.*

This reality becomes starker when viewed across socio-economic lines. Strategic debt is most often accessible to those who already have assets, education, and safety nets. They can negotiate better terms, leverage collateral, and recover from risk. Slave debt disproportionately targets those without such buffers. Consider how subprime auto loans and exploitative rent-to-own schemes are marketed in low-income neighbourhoods. The same credit score gap that justifies higher interest rates also deepens inequality over time. *Debt, in this light, is not just personal finance—it is a mechanism of social stratification.*

Even the language of "creditworthiness" masks this dynamic. A high credit score does not measure character; it measures one's compliance with the rules of financial institutions. Those rules are neither neutral nor equitable. They reward access, not ethics. They punish volatility, even when that volatility is due to illness, caregiving, or systemic barriers. To be "worthy" of better debt, you must first not need it. That is the paradox.

The implications for the individual are profound. To avoid slave debt, one must learn to interrogate not just the terms of a loan, but its *true cost*—financially, psychologically, and in terms of life trajectory. Questions worth asking include:

Will this debt generate more value than it costs?

Is the repayment plan compatible with my income reality?

Am I borrowing from a place of agency or desperation?

Do I understand the worst-case scenario, and could I survive it?

These are not questions of optimism or ambition—they are exercises in *sovereignty*. To borrow strategically is to enter into a contract with eyes wide open. To fall into slave debt is often to be pulled in blindfolded, misled by advertising, social pressure, or systemic misinformation.

Even more insidious is the way some debts mutate over time. A debt that begins as strategic—a student loan, say—can become slave debt if the borrower's employment prospects fail to materialise. Conversely, what appears to be slave debt—a high-interest business loan—can become strategic if it catalyses a successful, self-sustaining enterprise. *Debt classification is not static; it evolves with context and execution.*

Thus, one must revisit their debt portfolio regularly, not just to manage payments but to re-assess strategic alignment. Refinancing, restructuring, or even default (in rare, considered cases) may be the most strategic move available. What matters is not moral purity, but *conscious engagement.*

None of this is to suggest that all debt can or should be avoided. In fact, a purist stance against debt can itself be a trap, leading to missed opportunities or underinvestment in one's own potential. But the wisdom lies in discernment. *Debt, when used with intention, can be a ladder. When accepted passively, it becomes a leash.*

The true education here is not merely financial literacy—it is critical financial consciousness. The ability to decode offers, assess risk, resist emotional manipulation, and prioritise long-term freedom over short-term comfort. This is not taught in schools. It is rarely taught at home. And yet it is essential if we are to resist an economy that increasingly depends on financial ignorance for its profit margins.

To reclaim our autonomy, we must become students not just of money, but of power—how it moves, who designs its flows, and how we either leverage or become leveraged. The question is not "Should I borrow?" but *"Who benefits if I do—and on what terms?"* If the answer is unclear, it is worth pausing. Because once you sign, the cost begins—not just in currency, but in clarity.

Breaking the Cycle: Reclaiming Autonomy from Debt-Based Living

Debt, when it becomes chronic, is rarely just about numbers. It is a condition of mind as much as of money—one that embeds itself into daily choices, emotional wellbeing, and long-term possibility. To escape its grip is not merely a financial act but a comprehensive reorientation of how we relate to risk, reward, and identity. And yet, many frameworks offered to "get out of debt" collapse into oversimplified lists, punitive budgeting, or moralistic shame. These are insufficient. To break the cycle, we must look deeper—at the architecture of belief, the traps of modern finance, and the kind of decision-making that leads not only to debt exit, but to *debt immunity*.

Let us start with the truth: the system is designed to keep you tethered. From student loans that shadow early adulthood to buy-now-pay-later platforms that sanitise indulgence into friendly monthly bites, the default assumption of contemporary life is not financial agency but perpetual liability. Debt is the engine of consumption and the leash of compliance. It numbs the population, fattens institutional profits, and constrains protest. To break from this requires more than repayment—it requires an unlearning.

The first misstep in most debt narratives is framing the issue as a purely behavioural problem. As if spending less or cutting lattes were adequate responses to systemic overpricing, wage stagnation, and predatory interest models. While personal discipline plays a role, we must also acknowledge the landscape: education costs have outpaced inflation by multiples; housing markets reward speculation, not shelter; and financial products are engineered for opacity. *You are not in debt because you failed—you are in debt because the default settings are rigged.*

That said, opting out is possible. But it must begin with a mindset shift: away from guilt and towards *governance*. Debt is not a moral stain; it is a contract—one that can be renegotiated, restructured, or refused. The starting point is not panic; it is clarity.

Step one is diagnostic, not reactive. Before any action plan, one must establish a *comprehensive inventory* of obligations. This is not about listing balances alone, but mapping the nature, terms, and psychological weight of each debt. What is the interest rate? What is the monthly minimum? Is this debt increasing or decreasing over time? Is it secured or unsecured? Most importantly, *what was the original purpose of this debt—and does that purpose still serve you?* Treat each debt not just as a sum, but as a story. Some stories must be ended; others, rewritten.

From there, we move to *triage*. The dominant advice here is to pay off the highest interest debt first (the "avalanche" method) or the smallest debt (the "snowball" method, for motivation). Both can be useful—but a more nuanced approach considers *flexibility*. Which debts restrict your cash flow the most? Which carry penalties for early repayment? Which have consequences beyond finance—such as student loans tied to professional licensing? A surgical strategy outperforms a generic one.

Next comes *containment*. It is difficult to exit debt while continuing to accumulate it. This requires a firm boundary: no new consumer debt while exiting existing obligations. For some, this means cutting up cards. For others, it means freezing spending patterns, delaying gratification, or rethinking the social environments that normalise overspending. This is not austerity for its own sake—it is *temporary insulation* to allow for financial recalibration.

That recalibration involves *earning power*. Too often, debt recovery plans fixate on cost-cutting. But there are limits to how much you can save—while income has the potential for greater scalability. Whether through negotiation, skill development, side ventures, or a shift in employment model, growing one's income accelerates escape velocity. *Austerity alone does not build wealth; surplus does.*

Yet even a surplus is useless if misallocated. Which brings us to perhaps the most neglected phase: *value-based planning*. Why are you getting out of debt? What will freedom allow you to do? What lifestyle aligns with sustainability rather than spectacle? Without anchoring new behaviour in personal values, one merely replicates old patterns with new money. *Debt freedom without vision becomes another void to fill.* You must pre-empt that vacuum by designing a life that thrives on intentional limits, not imposed ones.

This is where emotional work re-enters. Most chronic debt is reinforced by unconscious scripts: "I deserve this after what I've been through," "I'll never really be ahead anyway," or "This is how people like me live." These are not trivial beliefs. They are coded identities—formed through family, culture, advertising, and trauma. Rewriting them requires more than willpower; it often demands therapeutic insight, community support, and ongoing reflection. Financial literacy without psychological literacy is incomplete.

Let's be clear: breaking the cycle is not the same as erasing hardship. You may still face housing costs that outstrip wages. You may still live in a city where affluence is mistaken for virtue. And you will still be marketed to—relentlessly. The goal is not to create an illusion of control, but to cultivate resilience. You cannot stop the storm, but you can waterproof your thinking.

To that end, long-term freedom is achieved not by perfection, but by *policy*. Think of your household as a micro-economy. What are your fiscal rules? What are your emergency protocols? Do you build in redundancy? Do you audit yourself regularly? Most people resist this formality, imagining it cold or restrictive. In truth, it is liberating. *Structure creates space for creativity—and safety for risk.*

Another key principle is *automation*. Debt thrives on entropy: late fees, missed payments, compounding costs. Automation—of minimums, savings, even charitable giving—removes friction from good habits. Just as institutions use algorithms to extract, you can use systems to protect. Make the ethical use of tech part of your strategy.

Lastly, a word on shame. Debt often breeds secrecy, which magnifies the burden. One of the most radical acts in debt liberation is *disclosure.* Whether to a trusted friend, a partner, or a mentor, saying "I am in this situation" breaks the internal narrative of failure. It converts guilt into accountability. And it opens the door to resources, referrals, and relief. *Silence is expensive.*

Breaking the cycle, then, is not a single act—it is a sequence. Assessment. Triage. Containment. Growth. Integration. Protection. Each stage demands not just knowledge but *conscious participation*. The goal is not just solvency—it is sovereignty. Debt-free living is not merely a number on a balance sheet. It is the regained ability to choose, to move, to build—and most of all, to sleep at night without the weight of invisible creditors pressing on your chest.

You do not escape debt by accident. You do it through strategy, integrity, and emotional clarity. And once free, your task is to remain vigilant—not paranoid, but informed. You will be courted again. You will be tempted again. But this time, you'll recognise the offer for what it is: a contract. And you'll know, finally, that you are allowed to say no.

Chapter 6
Financial Self-Sabotage and Inner Predators

Few betrayals cut deeper—or leave one more disoriented—than the kind we commit against ourselves. Especially when it comes to money, where what looks like a rational decision—*just this once, I've earned it, next month I'll get on track*—masks patterns rooted in something far more ancient, and more difficult to name. For many, the primary threat to financial wellbeing isn't external at all. It's internal. Not the economy or tax codes, but the subtle, relentless undertow of self-sabotage—driven by inherited beliefs, emotional wounds never quite healed, and unconscious allegiances that quietly sabotage our capacity to flourish. This chapter isn't about numbers. It's about the inner landscape—the quiet saboteurs within us and the discipline it takes to face them.

We're too quick to reduce financial missteps to laziness or a lack of willpower. *The spreadsheet doesn't lie*, they say—*just follow the budget.* But under the surface of missed payments, compulsive purchases, and chaotic accounts often lies something else entirely: shame, unresolved identity conflicts, trauma, grief. The compulsive shopper may not be indulging—they may be self-soothing. The chronic under-earner might not lack ambition—they might carry a story that says success alienates. And the one who hoards cash isn't greedy, but paralysed—trapped in fear by losses that time hasn't dimmed. These aren't financial behaviours. They're emotional strategies dressed up as fiscal choices.

Strangely, we rarely speak of money in emotional terms, though it sits at the core of our adult lives saturated with meaning, contradiction, and history. It is never *just* currency. It is love, power, proof, rebellion, safety, shame. It is how we give, how we withhold, how we measure our worth. It is also, more often than we realise, where the ghosts of our upbringing battle our adult aspirations. To understand why we self-sabotage financially is to look not at the numbers, but at the scripts—quietly inherited, never consented to—that drive us.

One of the most insidious scripts? Guilt around wealth. Many religious and cultural traditions carry deep suspicion of money's accumulation. Riches are linked to moral decay, spiritual compromise, or social betrayal. Phrases like "money is the root of all evil" or "it's easier for a camel to pass through the eye of a needle…" don't just vanish when faith fades. Their residue lingers. The result? A subtle aversion to prosperity. Success begins to feel like a moral failing. And financial modesty becomes a marker of virtue—however quietly, however irrationally.

Now picture this: gifted professionals, deeply generous souls, chronically undercharging not because they doubt their skill, but because deep down they fear that financial gain equates to selling out. Or that to rise economically is to risk exile from their community. These are not abstract anxieties. They are social ones. Money becomes a threat to belonging. And so we quietly choose smaller lives—not because we lack ambition, but out of fidelity to the unspoken contracts of the group.

Then there are those whose money scripts are forged not by philosophy, but by pain. Trauma distorts the sense of agency—and money, being perhaps the most direct form of adult power, becomes a hotspot for that distortion. Those raised amid financial chaos or neglect often experience money as volatile, elusive, even dangerous. Some react with avoidance: unopened letters, ignored statements, financial self-neglect. Others respond with hyper-control: obsessive tracking, an almost religious refusal to spend or invest. Neither is logical. Both are survival responses—attempts to manage the unmanageable.

Trauma-fuelled spending, in particular, is grotesquely misunderstood. Mainstream narratives dismiss it as impulsivity or indulgence. But more often, it's regulation. A way to feel *something*—safety, excitement, significance—in moments when the emotional terrain feels barren. One person, raised in a household where love was conditional, learns that buying gifts earns affection. Another, raised amid instability, comes to equate a full shopping bag with security. These are not "bad habits." They are emotional feedback loops, hardwired into memory.

Escaping these loops requires more than willpower or apps. It demands the cultivation of what this chapter calls the Inner Guardian—not a disciplinarian, but a custodian of value. This internal figure does not scold or control. It protects. It knows your worth, and it can distinguish between spending that nourishes and spending that numbs. Building this Guardian is not easy. It calls for introspection, discomfort, and a kind of grief—grief for the years spent in patterns that no longer serve. But it's the only reliable route to financial self-trust.

This Guardian is not the accountant of your inner world. It is the wise strategist. It understands your emotional architecture and sees beyond immediate gratification to long-term coherence. In this chapter, you'll be invited to give this inner figure voice—to practise pausing before a transaction and asking, with honest intent: *What am I seeking in this moment? Safety? Validation? Escape?* Not just *what does this cost in pounds*, but *what does it cost in dignity, alignment, time?*

Because this isn't about shaming the impulse. It's about decoding it. The overspender may be avoiding shame. The habitual borrower may be soothing loneliness. The person who consistently "forgets" to invoice might actually fear visibility. These are not failures. They are attempts—flawed but sincere—to meet emotional needs. And once seen clearly, they become moveable.

Self-sabotage loses its grip when it is met not with punishment but with precision. This chapter leads you through that precision. You'll map behavioural patterns to emotional needs. You'll trace triggers to origin stories. You'll replace judgment with strategy—not to control yourself, but to act in conscious alignment with what actually matters.

If the earlier sections of this book dismantled the external systems that extract and confuse, this chapter turns the light inward. Because even when the structures are unjust, the stories we carry can bind us more tightly than any contract. Financial literacy must expand to include emotional fluency. And wealth—if it is to be ethical, if it is to last—must begin with self-understanding.

There are no silver bullets here. What follows is not a hack, but an invitation: to reparent the parts of you that were financially abandoned; to question the stories you absorbed before you had the capacity to disagree; and to write a new agreement—not with creditors, but with your own unfolding life.

The opposite of financial sabotage isn't austerity. It's integrated agency. The quiet power that comes from knowing you are no longer playing out someone else's fear. That your decisions reflect care, not compulsion. That money, finally, is being placed back in its rightful role: a tool to serve your life—not the other way around.

This chapter offers no shame. What it offers is sovereignty.

The Inner Critic and the Saboteur

We like to believe that our failures—especially financial ones—are the result of external constraints or unfortunate timing. But in many cases, the most persistent obstacles to progress are not systemic or circumstantial. They are internal. They wear familiar voices. They sound like self-discipline, caution, modesty. They insist they are trying to protect us. Yet what they reliably produce is self-limitation, missed opportunity, and a fractured sense of financial self-worth.

These are not random neuroses. They are *subconscious roles*—scripts that individuals unconsciously adopt in response to early life dynamics, internalised expectations, and unresolved emotional wounds. In the realm of money, these roles are especially potent. Because money isn't just a tool. It is also a mirror. And for many people, the reflection it offers is distorted by inner actors who quietly sabotage progress under the guise of loyalty, survival, or control.

This subchapter explores three such roles in detail: *the Spender*, *the Avoider*, and *the Martyr*. Each functions as a kind of financial saboteur, but not in the sense of overt destruction. Their sabotage is more subtle—embedded in emotional logic. These roles were not chosen deliberately. They were formed over time, shaped by relational environments and reinforced by repetition. And until they are named, understood, and re-scripted, they operate with quiet efficiency in the background of our lives.

Let us begin with the most culturally recognisable figure: **the Spender**. This is not merely someone who enjoys luxury or occasionally buys impulsively. The Spender, as an internalised archetype, uses money as a means of self-regulation—emotionally, socially, or existentially. It is a coping role. For some, spending is about affirmation: *"I buy, therefore I matter."* For others, it's rebellion: *"I never had control growing up—now I choose what I want."* Often, it's a temporary balm for emptiness, sadness, or unarticulated grief. Buying something becomes a way of asserting control in the face of internal chaos. But the relief is short-lived, and often followed by guilt—fuel for the next cycle of avoidance or overcorrection.

In clinical terms, this behaviour can be understood as a form of affect regulation—managing unmanageable emotion through tangible action. But what's critical to understand is that the Spender doesn't arise from greed. It arises from *need*. From unresolved emotional hunger. From a history in which needs were unmet, unspoken, or punished. The Spender, therefore, deserves not contempt but curiosity. The way forward is not austerity. It is integration—learning to meet emotional needs through conscious choices, not compulsive transactions.

Then we have **the Avoider**—the saboteur who works not through excess, but evasion. The Avoider often presents as passive, vague, or perpetually unprepared. Bills go unopened. Budgets remain theoretical. Income gets deposited but not tracked. This isn't laziness. It is often *dissociation*. A nervous system that has learned, through early experiences, that money equals danger—conflict, instability, criticism, or shame. Avoidance, in this context, is not irresponsibility. It is self-protection. But over time, the act of looking away becomes its own source of suffering.

Financial avoiders frequently carry a deep ambivalence: they desire security, but fear what facing reality will demand of them. The ledger becomes an emotional minefield. To engage with it feels like inviting judgment or triggering an identity crisis. So they delay. Postpone. Rationalise. And the longer they do, the more monstrous the truth becomes in their imagination. Ironically, it is the avoidance itself—not the actual numbers—that corrodes peace of mind. *Avoidance is rarely about the content. It is about the emotional meaning we assign to the content.*

Finally, there is **the Martyr**—a less visible but equally destructive role. The Martyr does not overspend or avoid. They overgive. They sacrifice. They pride themselves on financial self-denial in the name of service to others. On the surface, this appears noble. But dig deeper, and one often finds unspoken resentment, burnout, and a self-worth tethered to being needed rather than nourished. The Martyr rarely invests in themselves. They refuse rest. They dismiss personal desires as "indulgent" or "selfish." And in doing so, they train others to devalue their labour—professionally, emotionally, and financially.

Martyrdom in money often emerges from early caregiving roles, religious conditioning, or gendered expectations. It is deeply moralised. But the morality is lopsided: the Martyr expects themselves to suffer for the benefit of others, but rarely holds others to reciprocal standards of care. Over time, this creates a dynamic in which their financial depletion is framed as virtue, rather than violence. They starve themselves—and call it service.

What unites these three saboteurs—Spender, Avoider, Martyr—is that each arose to protect something vulnerable. A wound. A fear. A longing for love, safety, or approval. And because they were often effective in the past (or necessary for survival), they resist retirement. They operate reflexively, even when they no longer serve our present goals. *These saboteurs are outdated strategies masquerading as personality traits.*

To change financial behaviour, then, we must do more than adopt better tools. We must understand the internal actors who are using those tools. Left unexamined, these roles form what psychologists call *parts*—sub-personalities with their own motivations, fears, and logic. Modern therapeutic modalities such as Internal Family Systems (IFS) offer a compelling framework for working with these roles, not through suppression, but through relationship. The goal is not to "eliminate" the Saboteur, but to unburden it. To help it evolve.

For instance, the Spender may be invited to relinquish its role once the person has other ways to access pleasure and self-worth. The Avoider may begin to engage with financial tasks once they are framed not as punishment, but as empowerment. The Martyr may learn to redirect their generosity toward self-investment, understanding that *serving from depletion is not sustainable service.*

This chapter provides exercises to help readers identify their dominant saboteur roles and trace them back to origin stories. But recognition is only the first step. The deeper work is integration—building an internal system in which all parts are seen, valued, and guided by a clear, self-led authority. That authority—the Inner Guardian introduced in the previous section—must lead not with shame, but with structure and compassion. It is the part of us that can honour the survival strategies of the past without allowing them to dictate the future.

Let us be clear: financial sabotage is not a character flaw. It is the echo of a time when we didn't have options. But we do now. And with the right frameworks, we can move from fragmentation to coherence. From compulsion to clarity. From inherited scripts to conscious authorship.

The Spender, the Avoider, the Martyr—they are not enemies. They are messengers. And their messages, once decoded, become maps.

What remains is the will to read them.

Money and Moral Guilt

There is a peculiar contradiction embedded in the collective psyche of many modern societies: wealth is simultaneously desired and distrusted, envied and condemned, pursued and yet subconsciously repelled. For all the sophisticated tools we use to accumulate and manage money, a significant portion of the population still harbours deeply internalised guilt about possessing it. This guilt is not purely psychological. It is cultural, spiritual, and systemic. It is the residue of moral codes that, across centuries, have cast wealth as a corrupting force—and poverty, in turn, as a proxy for virtue. In this chapter, we examine the origins of this guilt, its manifestations in self-sabotaging behaviours, and the philosophical question of whether money can ever be morally neutral.

To grasp the depth of money-related guilt, we must start by recognising that financial shame is rarely about numbers. It is a mirror reflecting our unresolved beliefs about fairness, identity, and worth. Cultural scripts—often inherited unconsciously—can instil the idea that *earning too much* is selfish, or that *spending on oneself* is indulgent, or that *not sharing* is a moral failure. In certain religious traditions, these beliefs are doctrinally encoded: the Christian valorisation of humility and sacrifice; the Buddhist renunciation of attachment; the Islamic call for zakat (charitable giving). In and of themselves, these values are not problematic. They promote compassion and justice. But when internalised rigidly or distorted by guilt, they can manifest in an unconscious rejection of financial stability or abundance.

Consider a professional who consistently undercharges for their services—not due to market conditions or strategic pricing, but out of an inner discomfort with "taking too much." Or the person who compulsively donates money they don't have, not as an act of generosity but as a way to neutralise their own perceived privilege. Or the entrepreneur who achieves financial success but then sabotages it through reckless spending, rationalised by the idea that they don't "deserve" to keep what others lack. These are not eccentric anomalies. They are patterned behaviours, deeply shaped by the narratives we inherit about what money represents and who is allowed to have it.

The notion that wealth is morally suspicious is not new. Throughout history, societies have oscillated between reverence for affluence and scorn for its accumulation. In Ancient Greece, Aristotle distinguished between "oikonomia"—the household management of resources for a good life—and "chrematistics," the pursuit of wealth for its own sake, which he regarded as unnatural and degrading. In medieval Europe, the Church forbade usury (charging interest) as a sin, rooted in the belief that money should not reproduce itself without labour. Even in contemporary political discourse, terms like "late capitalism" and "wealth hoarding" carry with them a moral indictment of financial success—particularly when it is seen as unearned, extractive, or exploitative.

But these critiques, valid though they may be in systemic contexts, often become confused at the individual level. We begin to apply collective guilt to personal experience. A salaried employee, born into modest means, may still feel conflicted about a promotion. A first-generation wealth builder may hesitate to invest or save, afraid that to do so is to abandon their community or betray their roots. In some cases, people fear that success will isolate them, severing emotional bonds with loved ones who remain in financial precarity. *In this way, money becomes not just a tool, but a test of loyalty, identity, and virtue.*

Psychology reinforces this dynamic. Studies in behavioural economics and psychodynamics suggest that many people hold "money scripts"—deeply ingrained beliefs about money, often shaped in childhood, that influence adult financial behaviours. A 2011 study by Klontz et al. identified four dominant types of money scripts: money avoidance, money worship, money status, and money vigilance. Of these, *money avoidance*—the belief that money is bad or that people with money are inherently greedy—has the strongest correlation with chronic financial self-sabotage, under-earning, and compulsive giving. Notably, money avoiders may also resent those who are wealthy, creating a double-bind of envy and guilt that corrodes both aspiration and self-esteem.

What makes this guilt so insidious is that it often masquerades as virtue. Unlike envy, which is socially condemned, guilt cloaks itself in righteousness. To feel guilty about money is, in some circles, a mark of being morally awake. It signals that one is not complicit in a corrupt system, not blind to inequality, not greedy. But the effect is paralysing. When guilt overrides agency, it becomes a form of self-censorship. It constrains not just how we spend, but how we think, dream, and contribute. And ironically, it can prevent the very redistributive actions—such as ethical entrepreneurship, philanthropy, or systemic reform—that might meaningfully address inequality.

The moralisation of money is further complicated by cultural narratives that position suffering as a prerequisite for legitimacy. In artistic, academic, or non-profit spaces, for instance, there can be an implicit hierarchy where financial struggle is seen as proof of authenticity. The starving artist is noble. The well-paid one has "sold out." Within such frameworks, accepting money—especially large amounts—is not just a financial act but a betrayal of values. This creates a paradox for mission-driven individuals: they are expected to do meaningful work, but not to prosper from it.

Undoing money guilt, then, is not about denying moral complexity. It is about discerning the difference between ethics and shame. Ethics asks: what is the just use of money? Shame whispers: you are bad for having it. Ethics empowers action; shame inhibits it. The challenge is to replace inherited dogma with intentionality—to shift from unconscious aversion to conscious stewardship.

There are practical ways to begin this reframing. Journaling exercises can help identify and interrogate inherited beliefs: What did your family teach you about money? What messages did your culture or religion send? Whose approval are you unconsciously seeking—or avoiding—through your financial behaviour? Mindfulness-based financial therapy has also shown promise in helping individuals build somatic awareness of money-related anxiety, allowing them to respond with clarity rather than compulsion. Philosophically, adopting a values-based lens—one that aligns spending, saving, and earning with articulated personal values—can transform money from a source of guilt into a vehicle for integrity.

None of this is about glorifying wealth for its own sake. It is about freeing individuals from narratives that equate wealth with moral failure. Just as poverty is not inherently virtuous, neither is prosperity inherently corrupt. What matters is intentionality: what one does with money, how one earns it, and whether one's relationship with it reflects freedom or fear.

To cultivate financial maturity in the modern world, we must confront not only our budgeting tools and income streams but also the internalised scripts that shape our sense of deserving. Guilt, when left unexamined, binds. But when exposed to light—critically, compassionately—it can be transmuted into discernment. It is only through this psychological reckoning that financial sovereignty becomes possible.

And that, perhaps, is the deeper imperative of this subchapter: not just to understand money as currency, but to reclaim it as a site of psychological autonomy—free from inherited shame, and rooted in ethical clarity.

Trauma-Driven Spending and Hoarding – Money Behaviours as Survival Responses, Not Flaws

The way we relate to money is rarely rational, and even more rarely conscious. While economic theory imagines a world of logical actors maximising utility, real-world financial behaviour is tangled in memory, fear, longing, and loss. For many, patterns like compulsive spending, chronic under-saving, or obsessive hoarding are not signs of financial illiteracy or moral failing. They are *trauma responses*—adaptive mechanisms developed in environments where safety, control, or love were uncertain. The sooner we recognise this, the more humane and effective our financial frameworks become. Shame obscures; understanding liberates.

To frame self-defeating money habits purely as poor discipline or faulty character is not only unhelpful—it is intellectually dishonest. Neuroscience, psychotraumatology, and behavioural economics all point to the same core insight: *repetitive, irrational financial decisions often originate in the limbic system, not the spreadsheet.* In other words, people are not just being "bad with money"; they are navigating invisible emotional terrain where money stands in for security, power, belonging, or identity.

Consider the compulsive spender. They may shop not for status, but for self-regulation. Each purchase delivers a short-lived dopamine spike—calming anxiety, numbing pain, or filling an internal void. Shopping becomes a strategy to soothe disorganised attachment, not a pursuit of luxury. Likewise, the chronic hoarder may not be greedy, but terrified. Accumulating money or objects offers a bulwark against the chaos they once endured. To them, every saved pound is a brick in the wall that separates them from past helplessness.

This is not abstract theory. Trauma-based money patterns show up across income levels, professions, and cultures. A child who grew up in a home where eviction was always a possibility may develop a deep-seated fear of financial ruin, regardless of actual income later in life. Even in high-paying roles, such individuals may hoard money to the point of social isolation, or alternately, burn through it in panic-fuelled spurts. Similarly, someone who was made to feel unworthy of care may develop a pattern of spending excessively on others as a way to earn affection. These behaviours are not driven by greed or ignorance, but by *implicit memory*—a psychological imprint from earlier, unresolved pain.

The work of psychologist Bessel van der Kolk, author of *The Body Keeps the Score*, is foundational in understanding how trauma shapes behaviour long after the triggering event. Traumatic memory is stored not just cognitively, but somatically—in the nervous system, muscle memory, and hormonal feedback loops. When financial stress triggers a threat response, the prefrontal cortex (responsible for planning, logic, and regulation) is often bypassed. Instead, the amygdala takes over, scanning for danger and defaulting to survival strategies. *Overspending, avoidance, or hoarding are not choices in the conventional sense; they are attempts at self-preservation through familiar pathways.*

Importantly, trauma-driven behaviours often persist even when the external threat is gone. A person raised in scarcity may feel intense guilt for buying something enjoyable, even when they are financially secure. Another may avoid opening bills not because they lack the funds, but because the act triggers a cascade of panic linked to childhood experiences of parental conflict or instability. When we see such behaviours, we are not witnessing a lack of willpower. We are witnessing the echo of a past that is still present in the body.

To break these patterns, we must first reframe them. Financial behaviours shaped by trauma are *intelligent adaptations*—just misapplied to a new context. Understanding this does not absolve us of responsibility, but it shifts the focus from blame to inquiry. Instead of asking, "What's wrong with me?" a more productive question is, "What happened to me that made this feel necessary?"

This distinction is crucial in both therapeutic and practical terms. Healing trauma-informed financial behaviours requires more than budgeting apps or shame-based incentives. It calls for trauma-aware financial education—programmes that acknowledge emotional literacy as foundational to economic agency. Some emerging interventions in this space include:

Somatic finance practices, which integrate body awareness into money decision-making, helping individuals notice physical cues of dysregulation and pause before reacting impulsively.

Narrative money mapping, where individuals reconstruct their money biography—identifying key formative experiences, inherited beliefs, and emotional turning points.

Parts work, such as Internal Family Systems (IFS) therapy, which identifies the "inner spender," "inner hoarder," or "inner avoider" not as enemies, but as protective sub-personalities trying to help, often through outdated means.

None of these approaches aim to pathologise the individual. Instead, they restore complexity to a domain that is too often reduced to simplistic moral binaries. Spend less, save more, invest wisely—these are valid guidelines, but they presuppose that people are operating in a vacuum of emotion. They are not. *Until the emotional drivers behind behaviour are named, no amount of advice will stick.*

This insight also has implications for how we talk about financial literacy. Too often, educational resources treat financial knowledge as purely cognitive—an issue of information access or numeracy. But financial literacy without emotional literacy is like handing someone a car without teaching them how to steer in a storm. We need frameworks that treat trauma recovery and economic empowerment as interconnected.

It is worth noting, too, that trauma-informed financial behaviours are not always visible as dysfunction. Some individuals become hyper-functional, appearing extremely "good with money" while driven by compulsive anxiety. They save diligently, invest aggressively, and avoid debt—but not out of confidence. Rather, they are driven by fear, perfectionism, or the need to control an unpredictable world. Their spreadsheets are immaculate; their sleep is not. *Financial competence does not always equate to financial peace.*

This raises the larger philosophical question: *What does it mean to be financially well?* Not just solvent or successful, but *well* in the sense of whole, aligned, and unburdened? True financial wellness involves recognising when our money habits serve us—and when they are the residue of past harm. It involves replacing fear-based patterns with values-based choices. And above all, it involves granting ourselves the compassion to evolve.

That evolution is not linear. Trauma work is recursive, and money habits will relapse under stress. But the presence of a relapse is not evidence of failure. It is a prompt for deeper inquiry. What am I really trying to protect right now? What fear am I responding to? Whose voice am I hearing when I feel guilty for spending or saving?

The answers to these questions are not always comfortable, but they are generative. They help shift the locus of control from unconscious survival to conscious strategy. And they remind us that our relationship to money is not fixed. It can be unlearned, rewired, reclaimed.

In short, trauma-driven money behaviours are not a pathology to be eradicated. They are an intelligence to be honoured and then redirected. Through that process—courageous, non-linear, and deeply personal—we move from financial reactivity to financial agency. Not perfectly. But progressively.

And that shift, more than any budgeting trick or investment tactic, is what builds true economic resilience.

Building the Inner Guardian – Cultivating Your Financial Protector Persona

A remarkable paradox sits at the heart of modern financial life: we live in an age of near-limitless information, yet millions make money decisions that actively undermine their long-term stability. The problem isn't knowledge scarcity; it's *internal governance.* People know they should save, avoid high-interest debt, question unnecessary purchases—but that knowing is frequently overridden by inner impulses, anxieties, or habits rooted in past wounds. The question is not simply "What should I do with my money?" but "*Who within me is making this decision—and why?*" Enter the concept of the Inner Guardian: a conscious, cultivated persona that acts as a financial protector, strategist, and truth-teller within the psyche.

Unlike most financial advice, which focuses on external systems—budgets, markets, interest rates—this approach begins within. It draws from disciplines including depth psychology, behavioural economics, Internal Family Systems therapy, and contemplative neuroscience to propose something deeply pragmatic: that the most important financial ally you'll ever have is the *version of yourself that knows how to protect you from harm—especially self-inflicted harm.*

In contrast to the inner critic, who shames and paralyses, or the inner saboteur, who justifies reckless indulgence, the Inner Guardian functions as a steady, measured voice of discernment. This persona is not a fantasy or an abstraction; it can be *built*—through introspection, structured mental rehearsal, and consistent practice. And once developed, it becomes a critical anchor in moments of financial uncertainty or emotional turbulence.

Why is this necessary? Because money is rarely about money. It is a proxy for survival, status, safety, and sometimes love. Financial behaviours are often decisions made under emotional duress or subconscious scripting. Whether it's the compulsive spender who "deserves a reward" or the hoarder who "must never be vulnerable again," these impulses are not character flaws—they are orphaned strategies for coping. The Inner Guardian is not at war with these parts of the self. Rather, it is tasked with negotiating between short-term urges and long-term welfare—*not from a place of suppression, but integration.*

Consider this: when faced with a significant financial decision—whether to accept a lucrative job that compromises your values, whether to buy something expensive to soothe a deep ache, whether to loan money to someone who repeatedly fails to repay—most people default to internal monologues shaped by fear, fantasy, or guilt. Very few are trained to pause and *consult an internal board of directors*, let alone invite their Guardian to take the floor.

Let's look at how this Guardian is formed.

Step One: Identify the Financial Subpersonalities

Every person houses multiple internal voices, many of which were forged in specific relational or developmental contexts. These

include:
– *The Spender*, who seeks pleasure or escape.
– *The Avoider*, who hopes problems will resolve themselves.
– *The Martyr*, who sacrifices for others at personal cost.
– *The Depriver*, who withholds joy for fear of future scarcity.
– *The Justifier*, who rationalises poor decisions under a veneer of logic.
None of these voices is inherently bad. Each emerged to serve a need. The task is to *listen without giving them full control.* Naming them reduces their power and allows for dialogue rather than domination.

Step Two: Articulate the Guardian's Voice
This is the voice that combines:
– Strategic foresight (What are the second-order consequences?),
– Emotional wisdom (What am I feeling, and is that driving the decision?), and
– Self-protection (Does this move preserve or erode my stability and dignity?).

To begin, it's often helpful to *write a letter from your Inner Guardian to yourself.* This might include phrases such as:
– "I know you feel pressure to say yes, but let's pause."
– "It's okay to want that, but we need to check if this aligns with what matters most."
– "You've worked hard to get here. Let's not destabilise what you've built on impulse."

The tone of the Guardian is firm, not punitive; compassionate, not indulgent. This voice earns authority not through domination but through demonstrated care and truth.

Step Three: Rehearse the Guardian in Real Scenarios
Theory becomes practice when it is stress-tested. Before making a purchase, agreeing to a loan, or signing a contract, insert a pause. Imagine inviting your Guardian into the room. What would they ask? What would they caution against or support? Over time, this

becomes instinctive—*a reliable internal pattern interrupt in high-stakes situations.*

Neuroscientific studies on mindfulness and metacognition show that *building an observing self*—a part of consciousness that watches thoughts without being consumed by them—strengthens the prefrontal cortex, the part of the brain responsible for impulse control and rational decision-making. The Inner Guardian, while metaphorical, reflects this exact faculty: awareness without reactivity.

Step Four: Cultivate Daily Micro-Practices

Financial resilience isn't built in single, dramatic decisions but in micro-choices repeated over time. The Guardian thrives in habits such as:
– Reviewing transactions weekly with curiosity, not judgement.
– Asking "What am I trying to feel or avoid with this purchase?"
– Checking in with long-term goals before saying yes to short-term urges.
These moments, though small, *compound into a fortified psychological structure.* The Guardian becomes a lived presence, not just a concept.

Step Five: Evolve the Guardian Over Time

Just as life changes, so must the Guardian. A protector for a newly employed graduate will speak differently from one advising a parent with financial dependents, or someone navigating the final years before retirement. The Guardian must be updated regularly—*like a software patch—so that it serves current needs rather than outdated fears.*

This evolution also involves grief. Many people maintain self-defeating behaviours not out of ignorance, but because change means letting go of familiar identities. A spender might have to mourn the self-image of being generous and spontaneous. A hoarder may have to face the fear of letting go. The Guardian supports this mourning process, offering structure during emotional withdrawal.

Why It Works: Psychological and Behavioural Evidence
The concept of developing an internal persona with regulatory authority is supported by diverse disciplines:
– *Internal Family Systems* therapy shows how giving voice to internal parts reduces their grip.
– *Cognitive Behavioural Therapy* demonstrates that structured self-dialogue can rewire maladaptive thoughts.
– *Neuroscience* validates that conscious reflection alters synaptic plasticity, enabling habit transformation.
What this amounts to is a practical truth: *the Guardian is not wishful thinking—it is mental architecture with neural legitimacy.*

The Broader Implication
In a culture that celebrates autonomy but rarely teaches inner leadership, the Guardian represents an antidote. It embodies both personal responsibility and emotional sophistication. It reframes financial self-defence as not only a matter of external vigilance against predatory systems, but *internal vigilance against impulsive or inherited behaviours that silently erode agency.*

This subchapter's role within the broader architecture of the book is to offer not just insight, but integration. We cannot merely understand our financial patterns; we must be equipped to interrupt them. The Guardian is that equipment—a living strategy, not a slogan.

To build it is to honour every version of yourself that tried to survive. To listen to it is to honour the version of yourself you are becoming.

Chapter 7
Wealth Without Capture – Defining True Freedom

If we insist on measuring wealth purely by what piles up in the ledger, freedom keeps slipping into tomorrow. Hidden in that arithmetic is a stubborn fiction: that the next bump in salary, the larger house, the bulkier portfolio will finally unlock autonomy. Yet genuine latitude— the kind that stands independent of titles, algorithms, or the mood swings of markets— seldom arrives with surplus. It arrives with vision. Vision of what is enough, where you are headed, and how the pieces fit together. This chapter is a quiet mutiny against the gospel of endless accumulation. It sets out not to teach you how to hoard capital, but how to step off the treadmill that capital often powers.

To chart a course towards wealth minus captivity, we must first recognise captivity itself. Not just the corporate variety, woven from lobbying and closed-door deals, but the subtler, more intimate sort. A six-figure pay-packet can still be a collar if it demands chronic exhaustion. A seven-digit balance sheet built on sleepless nights is no triumph—merely a gilded cell. Captivity wears many disguises: an income stream that cannot pause without panic, a lifestyle forever scaling with earnings, a dependence on employers or platforms whose interests diverge from your own. Most pernicious of all, captivity is fuelled by the promise that freedom waits patiently on the far side of decades' worth of deferral.

This chapter declines that proposition. In its place, it offers a design for wealth structurally averse to cages.

First, escape velocity. Borrowed from physics and repurposed with intent, the term describes the point at which your assets, cash flows, and boundaries combine to free you from compulsory labour and consumer choreography. It is not retirement in the brochure sense; it is sovereignty. That threshold might sit at £28,000 a year or £2.8

million—context dictates. What matters is that beyond it, choices answer to internal guidance rather than financial dread. You do not serve the engine; the engine serves you.

Second, sovereign earning. Conventional employment—however well-heeled—entangles you in hierarchies, time-for-money swaps, and raises approved by committee. Contrast that with income designs rooted in autonomy: modular online ventures, royalties from intellectual property, decentralised finance plays, or freelance constellations that travel with you rather than pin you down. None are risk-free, but here risk aligns with reward—and crucially, with control. The modern economy hands us unprecedented tools for self-direction, provided we abandon 20th-century assumptions about "a good job".

This is not a manifesto urging everyone to become wandering crypto-savants. It is an insistence that you own the scaffolding of your income, not merely the digits it spits out.

Third comes the anti-consumer blueprint: part philosophy, part practical engineering. Anti-consumerism, in this context, is neither hair-shirt minimalism nor curated austerity for Instagram. It is economic resilience by design. The questions shift: What do I genuinely need? What can be automated once, then left to run? Which dependencies can I prune without courting needless scarcity? Intentional simplicity isn't deprivation; it is armour against manufactured craving and shock-tested supply chains alike.

Along the way we'll probe what financial independence must be inoculated against. Tools today arrive bundled with cunning traps—subscriptions wearing the costume of freedom, "passive" income schemes demanding round-the-clock hustle, platforms that gate-keep visibility unless you pay tribute. The essential discipline is discernment. You will learn to audit not just inflows and outflows but the silent psychological contracts attached to them.

None of this rejects ambition. It simply redraws the map of a life well lived. The objective is wealth that is portable, modular, and difficult to capture.

Every idea that follows serves a single end: to build an economic architecture that lets you walk away from whatever no longer serves. Employers, fads, even entire sectors if need be.

This chapter cannot sell you freedom. What it can do is help you cease purchasing your own captivity.

The Redefinition of Wealth

Ask most people what it means to be wealthy, and you'll hear variations of the same answer: high income, substantial savings, real estate portfolios, luxury possessions, or a specific net worth figure. But when you look past the surface of that culturally reinforced definition, something crucial emerges—*many of the people who possess those things do not feel wealthy at all.* They may feel exhausted, time-poor, overcommitted, or trapped by the very assets they've accumulated.

This dissonance is not a fluke. It is a clue that the prevailing concept of wealth is incomplete—perhaps even defective. To rectify this, we must engage in what this chapter calls a *redefinition of wealth*: a rigorous re-examination of what it actually means to be rich in ways that money alone cannot measure.

Financial capital, while important, is only one layer in a multidimensional framework. Wealth must be viewed as *an ecosystem*, not a single currency. It is entirely possible to be poor in time, peace, autonomy, or adaptability—even while being technically rich in income. Conversely, it is possible to have relatively modest means and yet possess *a deep surplus of functional wealth* in the form of optionality, skills, networks, and inner equanimity.

This redefinition is not about romanticising poverty. Nor is it an exercise in semantic gymnastics. It is about recognising the full architecture of human flourishing—what allows individuals not just to survive but to *operate freely and intelligently* within the constraints of the real world.

Let's begin with the most overlooked—and arguably most vital—dimension of non-financial wealth: **time**.

Time is the only asset that is perfectly non-renewable. You cannot borrow it, invest it, or reclaim it once lost. Yet paradoxically, people sacrifice vast swathes of time in pursuit of money, imagining they can redeem it later through retirement or leisure. What this logic fails to grasp is that *not all time is equally valuable*. Time when you are young, healthy, creative, and mentally agile is not the same as time when you are depleted or constrained. What we ought to ask is not just "How much do I earn?" but "How much *sovereign time* do I control—and at what psychological cost?"

Seen through this lens, someone working eighty-hour weeks to maintain a high-income lifestyle may be far less wealthy than someone with half their income but double their autonomy. To control your time is to control your bandwidth, your attention, your ability to respond—qualities that compound in value far beyond what a payslip can reveal.

Closely related is the concept of **optionality**. Derived from financial theory but increasingly used in life design, optionality refers to the *range of viable choices* available to you at any given moment. Optionality is what allows you to walk away from a toxic employer, relocate on short notice, pursue an opportunity without asking permission, or shift strategies without collapsing your foundations.

Importantly, optionality isn't just about having money—it's about having *agility*. A well-paid specialist locked into one profession with golden handcuffs may be less wealthy in optionality than a generalist with diverse skills, a mobile income stream, and minimal debt. The greater your optionality, the harder you are to control—and the more resilient you become in volatile conditions. *True wealth, therefore, includes the ability to pivot without implosion.*

Another underappreciated form of wealth is **peace of mind**. This is not a euphemism for passivity or spiritual bypassing. It refers to the inner stillness that arises when your external life is aligned with your values, and your internal world is not at war with itself. Chronic financial anxiety, comparison-driven consumption, and achievement addiction all corrode this peace—even when money is abundant.

Peace of mind is an operational advantage. It improves cognitive function, decision-making, and relational depth. It makes you harder to manipulate and less susceptible to coercive marketing or political fear. Yet it is routinely sacrificed in pursuit of ill-defined success metrics that often deliver status but no serenity.

In tandem with this is the often invisible currency of **access**. Access means more than wealth of contacts—it includes access to quality information, to mentorship, to medical care, to safe housing, to fresh air, to meaningful education, to digital infrastructure, to legal support. Access multiplies opportunity. It is what allows some individuals to recover from setbacks swiftly, while others are dragged down for decades by a single misstep.

Access is a form of systemic wealth: it is unevenly distributed, but its impact is profound. And unlike mere consumption, which depletes resources, access often amplifies capacity. For instance, access to one hour with a brilliant mentor can outperform years of self-education. Having access to a supportive community during crisis is more valuable than any emergency fund. *In a world where inequality increasingly operates through information silos and gatekeeping, access is often more powerful than income alone.*

Lastly, and perhaps most robustly, there is the enduring value of **skill**. Unlike money, which can be lost to inflation, fraud, or poor decisions, skill is internally compounding. It travels with you, adapts across contexts, and builds trust-based capital wherever applied. Skill creates leverage—especially when deployed in ways machines cannot easily replicate: emotional intelligence, synthesis, storytelling, strategic thinking, and craft.

Skills grant independence. A skilled individual can enter markets, create value, and sustain autonomy even when systems collapse or economies shift. In uncertain futures, skill *is* the currency of adaptability. And yet, many people spend decades acquiring credentials instead of skills—mistaking certificates for competence, and mistaking competence for security.

The redefinition of wealth, then, requires an expanded balance sheet—one that includes time freedom, psychological integrity, adaptability, mobility, community, and access alongside financial metrics. This is not theory—it is *functional finance for intelligent living*. It urges readers to stop measuring life solely in income or assets and begin measuring it in *degrees of flexibility, mental quiet, self-direction, and surplus capacity*.

The dominant economic narrative insists that success is a singular ladder, with the top reserved for those who sacrifice the most in the name of more. But this framework is obsolete. In its place, we need a latticework model of wealth: one that supports flourishing across multiple domains, and one where money is a servant, not a sovereign.

This article does not ask you to abandon financial goals. It asks you to *reframe them*. To pursue money as a means, not a master. To pursue accumulation only when it enables the deeper wealths that define a rich and sovereign life.

If we fail to redefine wealth, we risk spending decades accumulating assets that cost us the very things we sought freedom for. If we succeed, we gain something rarer than riches: *a life that is structurally aligned with clarity, autonomy, and inner surplus*.

That, by any rational definition, is true wealth.

Escape Velocity: When Enough Is Truly Enough

The dominant myth of modern economics is this: that more is always better. More money, more scale, more productivity, more accumulation. Growth has become the unquestioned organising principle—not just for businesses and nations, but for individuals trying to "improve" their lives. It is easy to forget that the very word *enough* used to be a destination. Now it is merely a rest stop on the way to *more.*

But the question no longer being asked—and the one this subchapter insists we confront—is: *what is your point of liberation?* Not the point of maximum wealth or status, but the moment at which additional income ceases to meaningfully increase freedom, autonomy, or peace. That moment is your *escape velocity*—the point at which you have enough to break free from the gravitational pull of dependency, social comparison, and the industrialised fear of "not keeping up".

Escape velocity is a concept borrowed from astrophysics. It is the precise threshold of energy required for an object to overcome the gravitational force of the planet it's leaving. Anything less, and you fall back into orbit. Anything more, and you're wasting fuel. Transposed into financial and psychological terms, it becomes a radical reframing of success: *you don't need to out-earn the world—you just need to earn enough to escape being controlled by it.*

This shift in framing is essential. The endless growth mindset is not only unsustainable; it is often deeply misaligned with personal wellbeing. Chasing more without ever defining enough is not ambition—it is entrapment disguised as progress.

To locate your personal escape velocity, you must understand the gravitational fields currently holding you down. These fall into three categories: economic, psychological, and social.

The **economic gravitational field** is most visible. It includes your baseline cost of living, your debt load, your geographic constraints, your income-to-expense ratio, and your financial obligations to others. This is where most people stop their analysis. But what they often miss is that this field is elastic. You can reduce its force—not just by earning more, but by radically altering its structure. Living costs, for instance, are not fixed facts. They are choices embedded in cultural assumptions: the size of your home, the type of education you pursue, the car you drive, the city you inhabit. Every line item is a vote for your own gravity or your own escape.

The **psychological gravitational field** is subtler but more powerful. It includes fear of scarcity, shame around "not being enough", internalised worth tied to productivity, and the unconscious belief that struggle is the price of virtue. Many people reject simplicity because it feels like failure. They overwork, not because they need more, but because *they don't know who they are without the chase.* As psychologist Carl Jung noted, "Until you make the unconscious conscious, it will direct your life—and you will call it fate."

This psychological gravity also explains why so many high earners remain trapped. Their lifestyle inflates alongside their income. Their peer group recalibrates. Their identity calcifies around being "the successful one." And soon, they are no freer than they were at half their salary—just wearing better clothes.

The third field is **social gravity**: the subtle coercion of expectations. This includes familial pressure, cultural scripts, corporate narratives, and the social media feedback loop. A six-figure salary, two international holidays, private school for the kids, a side hustle, and property ownership are often considered *normal*, not because they are optimal or necessary—but because they are standardised templates in the success script of your class or culture. Deviating from this script is often interpreted as failure or eccentricity, even if it leads to vastly more autonomy.

To break free from these gravitational pulls, one must define *enough*—not abstractly, but concretely, with real numbers, boundaries, and thresholds.

Consider a case study: A 35-year-old freelance designer living in Manchester earns £80,000 per year. His lifestyle costs him roughly £55,000 annually—including rent, travel, and discretionary spending. With no dependents and minimal debt, he could comfortably reduce his client load, relocate to a less expensive city, and reclaim hundreds of hours per year for learning, health, or creative projects. But he doesn't. He continues to push for more clients, more exposure, and more accolades—because he's been conditioned to believe that stepping off the treadmill is a kind of death. He has already achieved escape velocity. But he doesn't know how to stop accelerating.

This is not rare. Many people could downshift tomorrow and still be secure. The real challenge is not mathematical—it is *existential.* It requires a complete realignment of how you measure progress. It means replacing growth with sovereignty as your central metric. It means choosing the "boring enough" over the "impressive more".

Let's be clear: this is not a call to complacency. It is a call to clarity. Escaping the need for more does not mean rejecting ambition. It means decoupling ambition from perpetual scale. It means building lives that prioritise quality over quantity, and resilience over performance.

This kind of ambition is not just personal—it is political. A society of individuals who know their enough is far harder to manipulate. They consume less, fear less, and panic less. They become structurally resistant to marketing, to overwork cultures, and to authoritarian control. *Knowing your enough is a form of civil disobedience against systems that profit from your restlessness.*

There is also a deep ecological argument here. If everyone pursues exponential growth indefinitely, collapse is inevitable—planetary, emotional, or both. But if enough becomes the cultural aspiration—not in a Luddite, anti-tech sense, but in a grounded, system-aware way—we stand a chance of designing economies that serve life, not the other way around.

To begin this reorientation, ask:

What's my real monthly cost to live well—not luxuriously, but with dignity, health, and mobility?

What would I do with my time if work was optional?

What am I afraid would happen if I stopped growing my income?

Whose approval am I still chasing, and why?

These are not surface-level budgeting questions. They are design prompts for a life that prioritises sovereignty over status.

Escape velocity is not about austerity or minimalism for its own sake. It is about having enough control over your economic reality that your time, energy, and decision-making are no longer captive to a system you didn't design. It is about reaching *escape from dependency*—not escape from effort.

In closing, the modern economy has no built-in stop condition. It is a treadmill engineered to escalate. If you do not define your enough, the system will do it for you—and it will never declare you free.

But when you do define it—rigorously, thoughtfully, and unapologetically—you gain something rare: *the right to stop running without falling behind.* That is the beginning of real wealth. That is the beginning of actual freedom.

Sovereign Earning Models – Paths to Income Without Dependency

The modern labour market has taught us to be grateful for a paycheque, even when it comes tethered to burnout, surveillance, and dependency. We are trained, often from adolescence, to pursue "stable" employment within institutional frameworks—be it the corporation, the university, or the government bureau. But stability, in the 21st century, has become a euphemism for control. The paycheck that arrives predictably on the 28th is not just a transaction;

it is an anchor. It dictates where you live, how you speak, what you do with your time, and—critically—who you answer to.

Sovereign earning models are not about entrepreneurship in the self-congratulatory sense. Nor are they about tech utopianism or naïve "passive income" dreams. They are, at their core, about one thing: *earning a living on terms that minimise dependency, maximise agency, and decouple income from institutional obedience.* This subchapter will explore how new technologies, decentralised platforms, and psychological reframing are converging to make this increasingly possible—*not easy*, but possible.

Let's begin by naming the problem clearly: traditional employment concentrates power. When income, healthcare, and social validation are all locked into one institutional source, the employer becomes not a partner—but a gatekeeper. This is not merely a structural critique. It is a psychological one. A person whose economic survival depends on external validation is rarely free to speak, create, or walk away.

Sovereign earning, by contrast, asks a different question: *How can I create value in the world that is hard to censor, hard to replace, and under my control?*

This question has no single answer. But today, there are several viable domains where sovereignty is not just theoretical—it is actionable.

1. Freelancing and Contract Autonomy

The freelance economy is often dismissed as precarious or temporary—a stepping stone to a "real job". But when structured correctly, freelancing is a form of sovereign labour. The key distinction lies in *client diversification.* A freelancer with one client is still dependent. But one with five clients, three income streams, and a financial cushion has optionality. Optionality is not just economic—it is psychological. It means the ability to say *no* without catastrophe.

The most successful freelancers build *reputation capital* rather than resume lines. They cultivate niche expertise, own their audience, and systematise their delivery. What looks like instability from the outside is, in fact, *distributed resilience.*

Take the example of independent consultants who operate under retainer models. They move beyond project-by-project scrambling and instead become strategic allies. Their income is not just reactive—it's relational. This changes the power dynamic. They are no longer "hired hands" but *nodes of value* in a broader network.

2. Creator Economies and Intellectual Property

Platforms like Substack, Patreon, Gumroad, and YouTube are reshaping how knowledge, art, and expertise are monetised. The creator economy, when wielded intentionally, is not just about virality or influence—it is about *owning the means of production and distribution.* It's not that you write articles. It's that you *own your mailing list.* It's not that you make videos. It's that *you own your content archive and analytics.*

The fundamental shift here is from audience *rented* (through platforms like Instagram or TikTok) to audience *owned.* That is the difference between exposure and sovereignty. An influencer with 200,000 Instagram followers has reach—but is entirely at the mercy of the algorithm. A creator with 10,000 email subscribers and a paid newsletter has *control.*

Crucially, creators are learning to *productise insight.* This could mean an ebook, a workshop, a course, a membership, or a toolkit. Each of these, when built once and sold repeatedly, acts as a *time-multiplier.* They convert attention into equity.

However, creators must also navigate the *temptation of platform dependency.* Many build audiences on borrowed land, never establishing true independence. The sovereign creator builds portable assets—*audiences, products, and processes* that are not platform-bound.

3. Crypto-Native Income and Decentralised Work

Cryptocurrency and decentralised finance (DeFi) are often discussed in speculative terms. But their true innovation is *permissionless value exchange*. For the first time, individuals can store, earn, and transfer value without needing a central authority's blessing. This has profound implications for sovereign earning.

Consider the rise of DAOs (Decentralised Autonomous Organisations). These are internet-native entities where contributors can earn tokens for work, vote on governance, and often *own equity* in the projects they build. Unlike traditional firms, DAOs do not require residency, credentials, or even real names. *Value is decoupled from geography and gatekeeping.*

There are now writers, designers, developers, and strategists earning full-time income via DAO contributions—sometimes across multiple communities. Payments are instant. Ownership is real. Portfolios are on-chain.

Critically, crypto also allows for *pseudonymous earning*. A developer in a politically unstable country can contribute to open-source projects, earn tokens, and convert to stablecoins—all without revealing their identity or relying on a national bank.

But this path is not without risks: regulatory volatility, token price fluctuations, and the psychological disorientation of operating in emergent systems. Sovereignty requires *literacy*. Those who thrive in this domain are not just tech-savvy—they are structurally observant, ethically grounded, and capable of rapid self-education.

4. Remote-First Microbusinesses

Remote work exploded during the pandemic, but what matters now is *remote ownership*. Anyone can log into Slack from Bali. That is not sovereignty. What matters is *designing an operation that does not collapse without you.*

This is where microbusinesses—small, lean, location-independent operations—come in. Think: a copywriter with productised services, a web developer with automated client funnels, a coaching business with group cohorts, or an ecommerce brand fulfilled via third-party logistics.

The sovereign entrepreneur does not need venture capital. They need *margin*. Margin in time, in cash flow, and in stress. The goal is not to build the next Airbnb. It is to build an entity that funds your life *without hijacking it.*

Sovereignty also requires saying *no* to scale when scale would erode autonomy. Many founders pursue growth reflexively, only to become employees of their own creation. A sovereign business optimises for *sufficiency* + *autonomy*, not maximum revenue.

5. The Psychological Infrastructure of Sovereign Work

No amount of tactical advice matters without addressing the internal dimension. Sovereign earning requires a particular psychological stance: *comfort with uncertainty, tolerance for solitude, and immunity to external validation cycles.* These are not native traits—they are cultivated capacities.

Dependency often masquerades as security. To opt out of dependency is to choose *exposure.* This means no boss to blame, no HR to hide behind, no institutional prestige to carry your credibility. It requires building your *own scaffolding of worth*—not in arrogance, but in resilience.

You must also confront *your own internal gatekeepers*: the inner critic, the imposter complex, the perfectionist. These voices grow loudest when you work alone. But over time, as you build evidence of value creation and income generation on your terms, they quieten. *Confidence is a trailing indicator of repeated sovereignty.*

Conclusion Without Saying 'In Conclusion'

Sovereign earning is not a fantasy. It is a strategic, often difficult, but utterly viable approach to modern work. It is for those who refuse to trade all their time for borrowed stability. It is for those who understand that real wealth is not just about income—but about *control, dignity, and freedom from coercion.*

Each path—freelancing, creating, decentralised work, microbusinesses—has its own map and minefield. But what they share is this: *a transfer of power back to the individual.* Not the myth of the lone wolf genius, but the reality of the self-responsible, system-literate, strategically autonomous person.

In the chapters that follow, we will explore how to build resilience into these paths: how to create buffer, reduce fragility, and convert optionality into enduring independence. But remember: the first move is not technical—it is philosophical. It is to ask: *What does a free life actually look like—and am I willing to build it from the outside of the system inward?*

The Anti-Consumer Blueprint – Life Design for Anti-Fragility, Sufficiency, and Autonomy

Consumerism is not merely an economic system—it is a psychological operating system. It dictates our defaults: what we admire, what we fear, what we believe will solve our problems. It shapes desire in ways that feel natural but are profoundly engineered. When someone says they "need" the latest phone, the second car, or the seventh pair of nearly identical shoes, they are not just expressing preference. They are reciting programming. *Anti-consumerism, then, is not about asceticism—it is about awareness. It is not deprivation; it is design.*

The most powerful form of resistance in a consumption-based economy is not protest. It is *non-participation.* To consciously exit the game—at least partially—is to reclaim the ability to think, act, and spend from a place of clarity rather than compulsion. This subchapter explores what it means to build an *anti-consumer life blueprint*—one that prioritises *anti-fragility*, *sufficiency*, and *unshakeable autonomy*. These are not abstract ideals; they are measurable, observable, and—critically—achievable.

Let us begin by confronting the false foundation of consumer logic: *that more is better*. This belief underpins nearly every sector of modern life—from education to housing, fitness to finance. But endless accumulation creates a paradox: the more you own, the more you are owned by what you accumulate. Each new object requires storage, maintenance, mental bandwidth. Each new subscription adds another drain on attention and agency. What begins as convenience often ends as captivity.

An anti-consumer blueprint rejects accumulation for its own sake and instead asks three decisive questions before any economic or life choice:

1. *Does this make me more fragile or more resilient?*
2. *Does this serve a real need or a manufactured desire?*
3. *Will this increase my autonomy or deepen my dependency?*

Anti-Fragility: Systems That Benefit from Stress

The term "anti-fragility" was coined by Nassim Nicholas Taleb to describe entities that *improve* when exposed to volatility, randomness, or stress. Muscles are anti-fragile. So are decentralised networks, evolutionary systems, and high-trust communities. By contrast, most consumer behaviours create *fragility*. The person with an expensive lifestyle, high fixed costs, and zero redundancy is exquisitely vulnerable—to job loss, interest rate hikes, or even a delayed invoice.

To build an anti-fragile life, one must design for stress—not against it. This might mean:

– Having multiple income streams instead of relying on a single employer.
– Living beneath your means even when you could afford more.

– Maintaining a habit of skill acquisition, even when not immediately profitable.

One potent example comes from the 2008 financial crisis. Those with high-status jobs, large mortgages, and no financial cushion were devastated. Meanwhile, those with modest but flexible setups—like freelance coders living in low-cost cities—saw little disruption and often capitalised on the chaos. They were not just resilient. They were anti-fragile.

The anti-consumer blueprint *welcomes volatility*—because it has nothing essential to lose. If your sense of worth is not tied to your latest purchase, your image, or your car, then marketing loses its grip. You become, in a very real sense, economically ungovernable.

Sufficiency: Knowing When Enough Is Enough

Consumer culture depends on dissatisfaction. If you ever genuinely believed you had "enough," the entire engine would sputter. Advertisers rely on the manipulation of aspiration—pushing the horizon just far enough that you'll spend today chasing a better tomorrow. Sufficiency is the radical act of saying *"This is enough."* Not because you've given up—but because you've *woken up.*

Sufficiency is not static; it is situational. For one person, "enough" may mean a one-bedroom flat, a bicycle, and a part-time income. For another, it may mean running a small enterprise, working 20 hours a week, and being able to take two months off per year. There is no moral high ground in one version over another. What matters is that the line is *conscious*. Not inherited. Not mimicked. *Claimed.*

Psychologically, sufficiency rewires the compulsion to compare. You are no longer benchmarking your life against the upgraded version of someone else's highlight reel. You are instead asking: *Can I meet my core needs—financial, social, creative, emotional—without sacrificing integrity or autonomy?* If yes, then more becomes optional, not mandatory.

This is the death knell for consumerism, because it breaks the cycle of *perpetual insufficiency.* When you no longer need to prove your worth through material signals, you are free to pursue deeper forms of wealth: time, attention, mastery, and peace of mind.

Autonomy: Exit Over Voice

Most systems of power want you to complain loudly but remain obedient. They will let you rant on social media, march in the streets, write angry reviews—as long as you keep paying, subscribing, and showing up on Monday. The true threat is not critique. It is *exit.*

Autonomy is the ability to *walk away without losing your footing.* Financially, that might mean having six months' runway, multiple income sources, or a low-cost lifestyle. Socially, it might mean cultivating a community that doesn't depend on status signalling. Logistically, it might mean designing your work around mobility, not location.

Importantly, autonomy is not just about the *ability* to walk away—it's about the *willingness.* That takes courage. Most people are terrified of non-conformity because their identities are tangled in collective norms. The anti-consumer blueprint, by contrast, views self-direction not as a risk, but as a skill. One that can be cultivated through repeated acts of clarity.

For example, the decision to not upgrade your phone, even when it's affordable, sharpens autonomy. The decision to leave a high-status job for a lower-paying but freer life is autonomy in action. The willingness to live in a smaller flat to reclaim time from commuting is not sacrifice. *It's sovereignty.*

Blueprint in Practice: Constructing a Life Around These Values

Let us now synthesise these ideas into an actionable lens. What does a life built around anti-fragility, sufficiency, and autonomy actually look like?

– *Housing*: You choose a home that supports flexibility—not just comfort. That may mean renting in a high-cost area while building portable income, or owning in a low-cost town to maximise cash flow and time.
– *Income*: You structure work around optionality. Not necessarily maximising income, but *de-risking dependency*. This may involve freelancing, remote microbusinesses, or hybrid creator models.
– *Consumption*: You create spending rituals—not restrictions—that align with values. For instance, a "48-hour pause rule" before any non-essential purchase. Or budgeting for books, courses, and high-quality tools—but not for status goods.
– *Social environment*: You invest in relationships not based on lifestyle similarity but value alignment. You spend more time with people who are curious, creative, and content—not chronically comparative.
– *Time use*: You eliminate pointless obligations masked as productivity. You replace them with capacity-building activities: reading, making, training, and resting.

None of these actions are extreme. What they require is *intentionality*. The average consumer blueprint is *defaulted*. The anti-consumer blueprint is *designed*.

A Final Note Without Summing Up

Anti-consumerism is not about frugality for its own sake. It is not a rejection of beauty, quality, or celebration. It is a redefinition of *value*—one where your worth is not measured by how much you can buy, but by how little you need to feel secure, expressed, and free.

It is also a philosophical position. It is the recognition that in a world engineered to monetise distraction, *attention is capital*. That in a system built to reward scale, *small is sovereign*. That in a culture fuelled by debt, *sufficiency is subversion*.

Those who live by this blueprint may not look impressive to the algorithm. They may not flash credentials or chase followers. But beneath the surface, their lives are built like oak—slow-growing, deeply rooted, and capable of weathering the storms to come.

Chapter 8
The Language of Power – Financial Literacy, Redefined

Power is not always grabbed by force; more often, it is wielded through language. It is woven into legalese, folded into tax policy, etched into the terms of contracts, and—most insidiously—disguised in the fine print we nod along with but do not truly grasp. If money is the tool, then language is the grip. And to be truly financially literate is not to parrot terminology but to understand which words move capital, which ones guard it, and which quietly hand it away.

Today's citizen is expected to make irreversible financial choices—signing mortgages, investing for retirement, navigating employment clauses, filing taxes—all while remaining barely literate in the systems that shape these decisions. This is not an unfortunate oversight. It is a feature, not a bug. Complexity feeds compliance. Ambiguity ensures submission. And our collective reticence to speak frankly about money? That's not cultural humility—it's inherited obedience.

This chapter will not insult your intelligence with a pastel-coloured guide to budgeting, nor will it recycle the tired refrain of "save more, spend less." That's available in abundance—and often, let's be honest, served with a patronising undertone. What this chapter offers instead is something starker: an invitation to become financially multilingual. Not fluent in jargon for its own sake, but fluent as a means of resistance, self-protection, and authorship over your economic narrative. It begins from the assumption that you are sharp, inquisitive, and perhaps tired of being patted on the head by well-meaning experts who offer answers without translating the questions.

To be literate in modern finance is not to memorise acronyms or chase the latest asset class. It is to recognise how systems of power are dressed up as neutral procedures. It is to spot that the ability to say "no" to a deal can carry more economic weight than an impulsive "yes." It is to understand that leverage in a negotiation doesn't hinge on aggression, but preparation. And it is to realise that the mechanics of wealth are rarely rooted in luck—though those who benefit from them often enjoy dressing them up that way, particularly in language foreign to outsiders.

Let's consider a small but telling imbalance. Miss a credit card payment by a day, and the penalties come swift and automated. Yet if your employer delays your salary, the road to redress is slow, bureaucratic, and frequently fruitless. What's at play here? Not simply policy, but fluency. Institutions speak enforcement fluently. Individuals, meanwhile, are typically versed only in submission. We are taught to ask politely, not to assert rights. We are encouraged to trust systems we don't understand, while quietly absorbing the consequences when they fail us.

The solution isn't outrage, though that has its place. The antidote is fluency—measured, grounded, unapologetic fluency.

Becoming Financially Multilingual

Imagine if every person leaving school had basic operational fluency in four domains: taxes, credit, investing, and legal tools. Not abstract theory, but the kind of practical literacy that demystifies contracts, audits, compound interest, and equity dilution. This would not guarantee prosperity—but it would disarm predation. The reason predatory loans thrive, the reason many renters don't challenge illegal lease clauses, the reason people lose equity in their own ventures, is not stupidity. It is illiteracy—engineered, not innate.

In this chapter, we will decode these domains in real terms. We will show how tax law, often treated as a fearsome beast, is in fact a system of incentives disguised as penalties. We will examine credit not merely as a score but as a proxy for trustworthiness—manipulable, measurable, and weaponised. We will outline how to read an investment pitch or a term sheet with a protective lens. And we will equip readers with the interpretive skills to scrutinise legal fine print—where power is most quietly claimed.

To become fluent in these areas is not to master all the technicalities. It is to *know which questions to ask, which professionals to consult, and which assumptions to challenge.* Financial fluency, like language fluency, is less about perfection and more about *participation with confidence.*

The Power of Saying No

In capitalist societies, power is too often confused with acquisition. But real power begins with *refusal.* The ability to decline a contract, to walk away from an exploitative employer, to say no to a "once-in-a-lifetime" investment opportunity—these are not acts of passivity. They are assertions of agency.

Yet from an early age, most people are conditioned to associate "no" with rudeness, risk, or loss. They learn to say yes to bad deals because the fear of exclusion outweighs the discomfort of exploitation. This is not accidental—it is social conditioning with economic consequences.

Saying no is not just a financial tactic; it is a *political gesture.* It is what allows one to avoid debt traps, resist lifestyle inflation, and retain negotiating power. The person who can say no without panic has far more leverage than the person who says yes out of desperation. *Economic independence begins not with having more money, but with needing less compliance.*

Consider, for example, the difference between someone who accepts a high-paying job with toxic hours and one who chooses a lower-income role with freedom and mobility. The first may appear more successful on paper. But the second may have more actual power—because they can say no to soul erosion, to burnout, to debt-financed lifestyles. Refusal, when exercised consciously, is not abstention from power. *It is its exercise.*

Negotiation as Self-Defence

Negotiation is commonly portrayed as a high-stakes skill for executives and entrepreneurs. But this is a misconception that weakens the average person's position in everyday life. *Negotiation is not advanced. It is basic.* It governs how much you are paid, how much you pay, and what terms you accept in nearly every aspect of modern adulthood—jobs, leases, fees, contracts, divorces.

Yet those taught to be polite, agreeable, or non-confrontational—especially women and people from historically marginalised backgrounds—are often denied the very frameworks that would empower them to protect their interests. This is not just cultural; it is structural. The less someone believes they can ask for more, the more extractive the system becomes.

This chapter will recast negotiation not as confrontation, but as *navigation*. We will cover the architecture of a fair agreement, the power of silence, the strategic use of alternatives, and the emotional stamina to handle discomfort without collapse. These are not tactics for the boardroom. They are lifelines for freelancers, renters, gig workers, small business owners, and anyone whose value is routinely undervalued or misclassified.

Moreover, we will challenge the idea that negotiation is inherently adversarial. At its best, negotiation is collaborative boundary-setting. It is the process by which people clarify mutual value, prevent resentment, and signal self-respect.

What Readers Will Gain

By the end of this chapter, the reader will not walk away with a perfectly optimised financial plan. That is not the point. They will, however, walk away *more dangerous*—to those who prey on ignorance, who rely on confusion, and who benefit from quiet compliance.

They will have:

– A grounded understanding of key financial systems and how to interact with them tactically.
– A renewed confidence in their ability to question, refuse, and renegotiate.
– A set of mental models for recognising coercion disguised as opportunity.
– The conceptual and emotional vocabulary to speak the *language of power*—with clarity, not shame.

This is not financial literacy in the traditional sense. It is not a list of dos and don'ts. It is a philosophical reorientation—a shift from passive recipient to active interpreter. From consumer to participant. From anxious survivalist to deliberate operator.

We do not promise control over the system. But we do promise one thing: *fluency in its language.* And from that fluency comes choice. And from choice, power.

Words That Bind: Contract Language 101

No one reads the terms and conditions. But everyone lives under their weight. Every time we click "I agree," sign a rental lease, accept a loan, or register for a service, we bind ourselves—often irreversibly—not to the spirit of a deal, but to the letter of it. That letter is not written to illuminate. It is written to *protect the drafter.* Not all contracts are traps. But many are engineered not to be read, let alone questioned. *They are meant to be endured.*

This chapter is not about turning readers into contract lawyers. It is about something more urgent: *demystifying the strategic use of language in contracts, advertising, and fine print.* At the core of most financial disempowerment is an asymmetry not just of money, but of meaning. One side has legal teams and templated clauses. The other has consent shaped by fatigue, trust, or necessity.

The modern citizen is bombarded daily with linguistic sleights of hand. A "free trial" that auto-renews. An "introductory APR" that quietly expires. A "lifetime warranty" that applies only under

Byzantine conditions. These phrases are not accidental. *They are tools of behavioural engineering.* Contracts—broadly understood—are how power moves through language, and understanding their structure is how individuals begin to reclaim it.

The Architecture of Ambiguity

Legal language is often framed as dense because the concepts are complex. That's partially true. But complexity also serves another function: to *discourage scrutiny*. When a mobile phone contract stretches to 30 pages, when a user agreement runs longer than Shakespeare's *Macbeth*, the message is clear—"Don't bother." This is not merely inefficient; it's *strategic opacity*.

Take, for example, the word *may*. In common speech, it signals possibility. In contract law, it signals *permission without obligation*. A clause that says the lender *may* charge a late fee doesn't mean they *will*—but it grants them full discretion to do so without further notice. The word *shall*, by contrast, is legally binding. These subtle linguistic distinctions are not trivia. They are tools. *They are how institutions keep their options open while closing yours.*

Another classic technique is the *sandwich strategy*: burying a controversial or onerous clause between two mundane ones, hoping the reader will scan, skim, and sign. Cancellation policies, liability waivers, forced arbitration clauses—they are all placed precisely where attention is least likely to land.

Language also hides behind definitions. A contract might state that "user data" excludes personally identifiable information (PII), while later redefining what constitutes PII in a conveniently narrow way. The trick is simple: redefine the problem so it legally ceases to exist.

Every term in a contract is a negotiation, even when it pretends not to be.

Contracts as Unilateral Instruments

Most contracts are not negotiated. They are *offered.* What's presented is a take-it-or-leave-it document—clickwraps, standard leases, employment agreements. These are known as *contracts of adhesion*—where one party holds the pen and the other holds nothing. Legally, they are enforceable. Ethically, they are asymmetric.

This is where most people mistakenly abdicate agency. Just because a contract is "standard" does not mean it is sacrosanct. Even consumer contracts—those with landlords, lenders, or insurers—often have modifiable clauses, if challenged before signing. But challenge rarely happens because people assume (and are conditioned to believe) they have no leverage.

Here is a critical insight: *you have more leverage before signing than at any other time.* After signature, the terms crystallise. Before signature, the possibility of withdrawal—*even if theoretical*—grants you negotiating power. Asking for clarification, edits, or legal review is not a nuisance. It is prudence. And if the other party is evasive or hostile to scrutiny, that is not a red flag—it is a klaxon.

Advertising as Pre-Contractual Framing

Contracts don't begin when the pen hits paper. They begin in the subconscious, seeded by advertising. The language of marketing is the language of expectation management. And what's promised in an advert often subtly diverges from what's delivered in a contract.

A classic example is the phrase *"starting from"* in pricing. A product advertised as "starting from £29" primes the customer to expect affordability. In the fine print, the base model may be functionally unusable without costly add-ons. Or the rate may be restricted to impossible-to-access conditions.

Another familiar manipulation is the guarantee that "your call is important to us"—while keeping you on hold for 45 minutes. This phrase isn't designed to be true. It's designed to *frame the delay as benign*—to prevent rage from transforming into complaint.

Language in advertising isn't just hyperbole—it's behavioural design. The words used to describe a product create a pre-contractual narrative that consumers internalise. When the actual contract contradicts the narrative, most individuals override their scepticism because the emotional frame has already been set.

How Legal Fine Print Exploits Cognitive Limits

Behavioural economists have long studied what is now called *bounded rationality*: the idea that humans, constrained by time, attention, and energy, make decisions based on limited information. Fine print exploits these cognitive boundaries by overloading, not informing.

Consider an airline that offers "priority boarding" as part of a paid upgrade, while boarding all customers in near-identical groups regardless. Or a bank that lists a promotional interest rate without clearly disclosing the revert rate after the offer expires. These are not lies. They are *truths in camouflage*—truths technically disclosed, but functionally concealed.

Even basic formatting matters. Fine print uses dense paragraphs, small fonts, and legalese for a reason: it reduces comprehension and encourages passive agreement. Psychological studies show that information presented in harder-to-read fonts is more likely to be skimmed and skipped. In other words, *obscurity has a design logic.*

From Victimhood to Vigilance: Building a Contractual Defence Ethic

So how does one respond—without becoming paranoid, cynical, or litigation-obsessed?

First, *understand the role of contracts as tools of asymmetry.* When reading one, ask not just what the terms say, but *who benefits if you misunderstand them*. Read slowly. Annotate liberally. And never confuse legalese with legitimacy.

Second, *spot coercive language*. Any contract that imposes high penalties for early exit, restricts recourse to arbitration only (thereby removing your right to sue), or includes automatic renewals without opt-out reminders, should raise suspicion. These features are not benign. They are *designed to bind you without engagement.*

Third, *normalise consultation*. If a contract is significant—employment, intellectual property, leasing, investment—treat it like a surgery plan: get a second opinion. Paying for a legal review may cost £100. Not doing so may cost your autonomy.

Fourth, *recognise your right to ask*. "Could you walk me through this clause?" "What does this phrase mean in practice?" "Is this negotiable?" These are not confrontational questions. They are signals of literacy. And if asking them makes the other party uneasy, *you're learning who you're dealing with*.

Final Reflections: Contracts as Mirrors of Culture

Ultimately, the way contracts are written—and the way we are taught to respond to them—reflects something deeper: *how societies distribute trust and agency*. A population fluent in contract language is harder to manipulate. A workforce that reads its employment agreements closely is harder to exploit. A renter who questions their lease is less likely to be evicted illegally. *Literacy is not just a skill. It is a shield.*

The goal is not to read every contract with suspicion. It is to read every contract *with clarity*. To stop interpreting "standard" as "safe," or "legal" as "fair." Words bind when they are not understood. But once illuminated, those same words can be tools of liberation.

This chapter doesn't aim to make you a legal technician. It aims to make you *dangerously attentive*. To read not just between the lines, but beneath them. Because in a world where most people are taught to click and comply, *the ability to pause, read, and ask*—that is power.

Becoming Financially Multilingual

Why mastering money's dialects—tax, credit, investing, and legal tools—is no longer optional

Fluency in money is not the same as having it. That distinction is critical. One can have wealth without understanding how to protect it. And just as often, one can understand money's rules fluently—yet still be excluded from its benefits. What separates financial survivors from the financially sovereign is *fluency across domains*: tax, credit, investment, and the legal frameworks that govern all three. This is not optional knowledge for professionals or the elite. It is now basic literacy for anyone who wants to function freely inside systems that are designed—intentionally—to be obscure.

To be financially illiterate in today's world is to be structurally vulnerable. Not stupid, not lazy—*vulnerable.* The language of money is fragmented across disciplines and delivered through silos. Tax law is written in loopholes and thresholds. Credit systems operate like private rating agencies with opaque algorithms. Investing is wrapped in jargon that intimidates the uninitiated. And legal tools—from contracts to corporate structures—are cloaked in a rhetoric of complexity that dissuades scrutiny.

This is not an accident. It is a feature. *Power preserves itself by hiding in process.*

What this subchapter offers is not encyclopaedic knowledge, but something more useful: a lens. A way of seeing through the abstraction. To become financially multilingual is to learn not only the content of these systems, but *the mindset behind them.* The objective is not fluency for its own sake—it is to reclaim *interpretive agency.* To understand what is being done *to you, with your data, with your consent,* and ultimately *with your capital.*

Let's explore what fluency really entails—and why it must begin with unlearning.

1. Tax: Not Just What You Owe, But How the System Is Built

Most people experience taxes only at the point of payment: the deduction on the payslip, the VAT added at checkout, or the stress of annual returns. But to be financially literate in tax is not just to know how to comply—it is to understand *design*. Tax systems are not neutral instruments of contribution. They are *behavioural frameworks*. Every deduction, exemption, and deferral option is a clue about the behaviour the government wants to incentivise—property ownership, retirement saving, charitable giving, corporate formation.

The financially fluent don't just ask, *"How much do I owe?"* They ask, *"How is this system steering me?"*

For example, in the UK, tax relief on pension contributions isn't merely a perk. It's a long-term nudge—an encouragement to delay gratification and outsource future income to regulated funds. Similarly, the capital gains tax exemption on a primary residence isn't just a break for homeowners—it's a systemic reward for those participating in the property-owning class.

Understanding tax fluency means knowing not just your marginal rate, but how your *life design* intersects with the tax code. It means learning to interpret *structure*, not just numbers.

2. Credit: The Price of Trust in a Digitised Reputation Economy

Credit scoring is one of the most consequential—and least understood—mechanisms in personal finance. To the average consumer, a credit score feels like a mysterious number issued by a hidden tribunal. But at its core, credit is simply the *quantification of trust*. The problem is that the metrics are opaque, and the consequences are asymmetrical.

A missed phone bill might lower your score more than years of responsible rent payments will raise it. A hard inquiry could harm your rating, even if the loan is never taken. These are not anomalies. *They are engineered outcomes in a risk-based pricing economy.*

To be fluent in credit is to understand that you are not the customer—you are the *product.* Credit bureaus sell your behavioural profile to lenders. Their incentive is not to help you succeed, but to help banks extract risk-adjusted returns. This doesn't mean credit is inherently evil. It means *you must use it with intention.* Responsible leverage (e.g., for real estate, business, or education) can build wealth. But unconscious dependency—credit card churn, "buy now, pay later" schemes, refinancing as default—is how consumers are converted into annuities for lenders.

Credit fluency means knowing what data is tracked, how to contest errors, when to use credit strategically—and when to walk away entirely.

3. Investing: Not Just Growth, But Ownership and Optionality

Investing is often framed as a vehicle for growth—compound interest, dividend income, appreciation over time. But this framing conceals a deeper reality: investing is about *ownership.* It is a shift from earning through labour to earning through capital. And capital plays by different rules.

To be financially fluent in investing is not to memorise tickers or worship at the altar of "passive income." It is to understand the *architecture of markets.* That every share of stock is a claim on future earnings. That every fund is a bundle of voting rights, risk exposures, and systemic correlations. That "diversification" is not a buzzword but a governance strategy.

Real investment literacy involves understanding not only instruments (stocks, bonds, REITs, crypto) but *infrastructure*: who issues these products, who benefits, and how fees erode returns. It means knowing that "past performance is no guarantee of future results" is not just a disclaimer—it's *an indictment of backward-looking strategy.*

Perhaps most importantly, investment fluency demands *clarity of purpose.* Are you investing for autonomy? For income? For retirement? For legacy? Because the strategy shifts radically depending on the answer.

4. Legal Tools: The Invisible Grammar of Financial Sovereignty

Financial knowledge without legal literacy is like knowing how to cook but not how to own a kitchen. Contracts, entities, and legal instruments are how financial intent is structured—and protected.

Basic fluency should include understanding:

What a contract really commits you to (and how to spot coercive clauses)

The difference between sole trader, partnership, and limited company structures

What an NDA protects (and what it doesn't)

The function of trusts, wills, and power of attorney in long-term financial planning

This is not the realm of the elite. It is the grammar of survival. Without these tools, your wealth remains vulnerable to litigation, taxation, misinterpretation, or even familial conflict. *Legal literacy is not a luxury. It is how freedom is formalised.*

Why "BS-Free" Matters More Than Ever

A growing movement of financial educators is reclaiming this knowledge from jargon and distortion. What they have in common is a refusal to patronise. The best ones do not ask you to memorise acronyms. They ask you to *see the incentives*. They expose not just how things work, but *for whom they were built*. This is the essence of real-world financial literacy: *interpreting systems through the lens of power, not just protocol*.

That's why the idea of becoming financially "multilingual" is more than metaphor. It signals that each discipline—tax, credit, investing, law—has its own syntax, its own logic. Fluency means knowing how to *switch contexts*, how to *translate concepts*, and how to *spot contradictions* across domains.

The Endgame: Financial Sovereignty, Not Just Competence

Competence is the ability to function in a system. Sovereignty is the ability to opt out, renegotiate, or rebuild it. Becoming financially multilingual is a step toward that sovereignty. It enables individuals to move from compliance to strategic navigation. To stop reacting and start designing.

For the professional, it means negotiating contracts with confidence. For the freelancer, it means building pricing models that account for tax and risk. For the single parent, it means using available credit without becoming beholden. For the graduate, it means investing early—not aggressively, but *intelligently*.

This is not about being perfect. It is about *refusing ignorance as default*. It is about making financial decisions as a conscious act of self-authorship—not as a default response to opaque incentives.

Because in a system built on asymmetries of knowledge, *literacy is liberation*. And when you speak the language of money fluently, you stop being a passive recipient of its consequences—and become an active shaper of your financial future.

The Power of Saying No

Why refusal—not consumption—is a radical economic act

There is a curious paradox at the heart of modern capitalism: while we are surrounded by choice, we are discouraged from exercising refusal. Every swipe, click, tap, or purchase affirms a system built not on sufficiency but on escalation. You are taught to equate freedom with options—but not with boundaries. You are told that empowerment lies in your capacity to say "yes": to a new product, a better job, a faster upgrade. But the deeper truth is this—*real power lies in the ability to say "no."*

Not "no" as self-denial, but "no" as sovereignty.

In a culture that prizes consumption, "no" is seen as friction, resistance, even ingratitude. But within systems designed to extract attention, data, and money, the refusal to participate—or to participate unconsciously—has profound implications. It is a declaration of authorship over one's decisions. It interrupts the compulsive circuitry of scarcity and says: *"I decide what is enough. I choose when I engage. I am not for sale."*

This subchapter explores what saying no means in a capitalist society where every surface has become an invitation to transact. From behavioural psychology to market design, from digital monetisation to social norms, we will uncover why resistance to automatic consumption is no longer a lifestyle preference—it is a political and economic act of self-defence.

The Myth of Infinite Yes

Capitalism doesn't just sell products; it sells an ideology: that fulfilment lies just one purchase away, and that your next yes might unlock status, convenience, or peace of mind. But implicit in this worldview is a sleight of hand: saying "yes" is framed as active, progressive, modern—while saying "no" is coded as regressive, fearful, or lacking ambition.

This is not accidental. The "infinite yes" is profitable. Subscription models are built on the inertia of auto-renewals. Targeted advertising depends on micro-frictions being removed. Buy-now-pay-later schemes flourish by collapsing the psychological distance between desire and acquisition. The less time you spend deliberating—*the less space you have to say no*—the more efficiently you can be converted into revenue.

From this vantage point, "no" is costly. It breaks momentum. It forces reconsideration. It introduces friction. Yet precisely because it is disruptive, "no" is powerful. It creates a space in which autonomy can reassert itself.

No Is Not Negativity. It's Design.

Refusal does not mean austerity. It is not about living in scarcity or retreating from ambition. *Saying no is design-thinking for your life.* It is the deliberate subtraction of what doesn't serve you—so what remains can be chosen, owned, and aligned with your values.

This kind of design-thinking manifests in multiple financial domains:

Saying no to predatory financial products that promise convenience but mask dependence

Saying no to work that expands income at the expense of health, relationships, or autonomy

Saying no to social pressure that ties self-worth to branded expression

Saying no to over-optimisation, where every minute must be monetised

Each of these "no's" reclaims space for a deeper yes—yes to time, clarity, relationships, recovery, peace.

This is not rejection for its own sake. It is *discernment.* And discernment is a higher cognitive function than desire.

Capitalism's Weaponisation of Shame

Refusal becomes harder in systems that associate saying no with failure. In many corporate or entrepreneurial contexts, declining an opportunity is interpreted as a lack of hustle. Opting out of a trend is viewed as falling behind. Even minimalist or frugal choices are often treated with subtle condescension—as though less consumption reflects a deficiency, not a strategy.

This weaponisation of shame reinforces the compulsive yes. Financial independence movements like FIRE (Financial Independence, Retire Early) have popularised the counter-narrative, but even these are frequently reabsorbed into performative consumption—trackers, merchandise, apps, conferences—ironically monetising the very mindset they claim to challenge.

To truly resist requires *emotional sovereignty*. A willingness to sit with discomfort while others equate maximalism with success. It demands that you rewrite your metrics—not just for success, but for *sufficiency*.

The Neurology of No

There is a neurological component to this as well. Decision fatigue—the depletion of willpower across repeated micro-decisions—weakens your ability to resist. In environments designed to trigger impulse, your capacity to say no is literally under siege. Supermarkets, newsfeeds, streaming platforms—all deploy infinite scroll, variable rewards, and cognitive overload.

Saying no becomes an act of pre-emptive architecture. It's not just a one-time decision; it's a system of boundaries. For example:

Unsubscribing from marketing emails to reduce temptation

Pre-setting spending limits on debit cards or apps

Blocking or filtering digital ads

Automating ethical investment choices so you don't have to constantly monitor them

In each case, "no" is embedded *upstream*—not as a reactive decision, but as an intentional filter. This is where refusal evolves into infrastructure.

Refusal as a Statement of Values

What you refuse is as revealing as what you pursue. In economic terms, refusal has opportunity cost. You are, in effect, sacrificing potential utility. But in ethical terms, refusal is *value expression.* You are stating, often implicitly, *"This trade-off does not serve my definition of a good life."*

Historically, some of the most powerful social movements have been built not around demands for more, but around principled refusal: civil disobedience, boycotts, conscientious objection. In each case, saying "no" to participation in a given system forced a confrontation with its values.

Refusal is not passivity—it is *repositioning.* In your personal financial life, this might mean refusing:

To upgrade your phone annually when your current one works fine

To join workplace culture built on overwork and performative exhaustion

To accept "prestige" debt (e.g., luxury cars, status-based real estate) as normal

These are not small choices. They reshape your cost structure, time use, and emotional bandwidth. They allow you to build from sufficiency, rather than debt, pressure, or signalling.

The Economic Multiplier of No

There's also a practical dimension: every unnecessary yes incurs a future tax. Every subscription you didn't cancel, every purchase made to alleviate a momentary discomfort, every upgrade done for status—each carries a downstream consequence. Some erode your savings. Others compound your workload. Many simply dilute your attention.

The discipline of no is not frugality for its own sake. It is *resource efficiency*. Saying no to the unnecessary extends the life of your assets, lowers your dependency on debt, and protects your bandwidth for truly strategic opportunities.

In a broader sense, saying no is how you *regain margin*. Margin is space—time, liquidity, energy—from which better decisions can be made. Without it, even the best knowledge becomes inaccessible under pressure.

Reframing Identity: From Consumer to Architect

You are not merely a consumer of products. You are the architect of your systems. That shift in identity is central to understanding the role of refusal. To be a consumer is to receive what is offered. To be an architect is to design what is needed.

This means that your financial systems should be shaped not around what's available, but around what's *essential*. The architecture of no includes:

Designing a minimalist budget that reflects your values, not your peer group

Structuring time blocks that defend your attention from unnecessary meetings or platforms

Practising "buying delays" as a default filter to reduce emotional purchases

In each instance, no becomes the guardrail. Not against joy or abundance—but against dilution and entropy.

Conclusion Without Concluding

We won't close this chapter with a rallying cry or a poetic summary. That would dilute the point. This isn't about crafting a tidy philosophy of refusal. It is about reclaiming the power to design your life—not as a reaction to capitalism, but as a decision to live within your own thresholds.

Saying no is not about minimalism or stoicism or contrarian virtue. It is about reclaiming the one asset that underwrites all others: *agency.*

Because in a system that monetises your attention, your data, your labour, and your future earnings, *no* is not resistance. It's *reclamation.*

Negotiation as Self-Defence

The unspoken power skill for those who were taught to stay small

It is often said that negotiation is a business skill. Something for boardrooms, brokers, and high-stakes deals. This framing is not only incomplete—it is dangerous. It conceals a more profound truth: *negotiation is a life skill.* One that determines your income, your rent, your schedule, your peace of mind—and your ability to exist on your own terms.

Yet millions of people—especially women, migrants, people of colour, and those raised in conservative or collectivist cultures—have been taught to avoid asking, to minimise discomfort, to say yes quickly and quietly. They are instructed, sometimes subtly and sometimes explicitly, that to be good is to be agreeable. That to ask for more is greedy. That silence ensures safety.

This is not etiquette. It is conditioning. And it is precisely what predatory systems rely upon.

In a world of contracts, terms, fees, and asymmetrical power, *not knowing how to negotiate is like walking into battle without armour.* This subchapter reframes negotiation not as a strategy for gain, but as a framework for *self-defence.* The goal is not manipulation or conquest. It is clarity. Dignity. And consent.

The Hidden Cost of Compliance

Every year, billions are lost not through scams or theft, but through quiet compliance: salaries left unchallenged, fees unquestioned, lease terms unreviewed, time volunteered unpaid. The cost is not just financial—it is existential. It shapes a life in which one is perpetually over-obligated, under-compensated, and privately resentful.

Consider the following everyday negotiations:

A job offer, where the candidate accepts the first number out of fear it will be withdrawn

A freelance contract, where the scope creeps endlessly because the client "thought it was included"

A tenancy agreement, where penalty clauses or repair responsibilities are quietly one-sided

A family arrangement, where caregiving labour is assumed, not discussed

These are not anomalies. They are outcomes of imbalance—between the party who is comfortable asserting needs and the party who has been conditioned not to.

To understand negotiation as self-defence is to recognise this imbalance and to take steps to neutralise it—not through aggression, but through clarity, language, and calm repetition.

Negotiation Is Not Conflict

The aversion many people have to negotiation stems from the belief that it is inherently adversarial. That to negotiate is to create tension. But this reflects a fundamental misunderstanding.

Negotiation is not conflict. It is boundary setting under uncertainty. It is the process of aligning expectations in contexts where power, needs, or stakes differ. And in most domains of life—work, finance, even relationships—this is the norm, not the exception.

Refusing to negotiate does not create harmony. It creates opacity. When you don't negotiate, you don't avoid discomfort—you *defer it.* And it often returns in the form of burnout, broken trust, or resentment.

A well-structured negotiation, by contrast, prevents escalation. It invites specificity. And when framed collaboratively, it builds trust by making the invisible visible.

Why So Many Were Taught Not to Negotiate

To dismantle negotiation aversion, we must examine its roots. Across cultures and social classes, the following narratives are common:

"If you're grateful, you won't ask for more."

"If you push, they'll think you're difficult."

"If you're good enough, they'll just offer it."

These beliefs are particularly embedded in groups taught to derive security from acceptance. For example, many women are socialised to maintain harmony, while marginalised workers often fear retribution for "rocking the boat." Even high-achieving professionals can internalise the myth of meritocracy—that if they simply keep performing, recognition will follow.

These mindsets, while emotionally understandable, are strategically hazardous. They externalise agency and allow systems to define your worth.

Negotiation, properly understood, is not about proving worth. *It is about declaring your terms.* Not as ultimatums, but as proposals. Proposals that reflect your preparation, your boundaries, and your long view of what a sustainable arrangement looks like.

The Psychology of Ask Aversion

Research in behavioural science confirms what experience suggests: people are often more afraid of asking than of rejection. This phenomenon—ask aversion—is driven by several forces:

1. **Fear of being seen as greedy or pushy**
2. **Overestimation of the likelihood of rejection**
3. **Underestimation of the power of preparation**
4. **Cognitive fatigue from unclear goals or messy information**

In a now-famous 2015 study published in *Psychological Science*, participants significantly underestimated how willing others were to help or accommodate them—even in low-stakes contexts. The insight? *People are more receptive than we assume—but only if we ask with clarity and respect.*

Negotiation is not about "talking them into it." It is about *framing your value, your conditions, and your limits* in a language that reduces ambiguity.

Rehearsal as a Tool of Resistance

For those raised to stay small, preparation is not just logistics—it is emotional inoculation. A well-prepared script or outline becomes your scaffold in moments where nerves rise or tone is misread. For example:

"I appreciate the offer. Based on the role's scope and industry benchmarks, I was expecting something closer to £X. Is there room to revisit that?"

"I'd like to be clear that my availability includes X hours per week. If the project expands, let's re-discuss scope and compensation."

"Before I sign, can you walk me through how disputes are resolved under this agreement?"

These phrases are not magical. They are *transitional bridges*—simple, neutral openings that buy time and reduce emotional overload.

Every negotiation requires its own vocabulary. But once a few core phrases are rehearsed, your nervous system starts to recalibrate. What once felt dangerous becomes navigable.

Negotiation as Pattern Interrupt

In exploitative systems, silence is operationalised. Consider unpaid internships, vague project scopes, or job offers below market rate. These persist not because they are defensible—but because they are unchallenged.

Negotiation breaks that pattern.

When someone asks, "Is there any flexibility on that figure?" it forces the other party to *explain*, not just assert. That single moment—the request for clarity—shifts the power balance. Even if the answer is no, the act of asking elevates the discourse.

This is especially critical in cultures where financial terms are treated as taboo. The taboo exists to protect asymmetry. *Negotiation breaks the spell of presumed consent.*

Teaching the Next Generation to Ask

The failure to teach negotiation is not neutral. It perpetuates generational inequality. Those whose families, schools, or communities frame negotiation as normal gain compound advantage. They ask earlier. They ask often. And they are not deterred by discomfort.

By contrast, those who internalise negotiation as conflict defer their needs, settle too soon, or frame self-advocacy as aggression.

If negotiation were taught like a language—gradually, contextually, with feedback—millions could escape exploitative dynamics. Children could learn to say, "That doesn't feel fair, can we talk about it?" without fear. Teenagers could practice salary conversations or rental disputes in safe contexts. And adults, long silenced by habit, could finally begin to edit the scripts that have cost them so much.

Negotiation Is a Muscle, Not a Personality

Perhaps the most dangerous myth is that negotiation is a talent—something innate to salespeople or extroverts. This is false. *Negotiation is a muscle.* It is strengthened through use, and weakened through avoidance.

The most powerful negotiators are often not the loudest, but the clearest. They know what matters. They stay anchored when emotions rise. And they do not confuse discomfort with failure.

Negotiation does not require domination. It requires *posture*—a sense of internal alignment that says: *"I am willing to collaborate, but I am not willing to disappear."*

Final Thought

If you were raised to be small, silent, or sacrificial, negotiation may feel like a betrayal of your conditioning. But that feeling is not evidence of wrongness. It is evidence of *growth friction.* You are interrupting a script that was never designed to serve your autonomy.

Negotiation is not about getting everything. It is about refusing to absorb the cost of imbalance in silence.

It is the quiet art of stating your terms—before someone else writes them for you.

Chapter 9
Decentralising Your Life

The more centralised a system grows, the more susceptible it becomes to collapse. Banks, governments, digital infrastructure—even food distribution—once lauded for their scale and reliability, now expose a different truth: the larger the hub, the more catastrophic the failure when it breaks. And break they do, with increasing regularity. Financial implosions, mass data breaches, political overreach—these are no longer freak anomalies but the pulse of the present. Millions are learning, often too late, that access does not equal ownership, and that convenience can be the velvet glove of control.

This chapter does not aim to provoke fear. What it offers is strategic clarity. Choosing to decentralise is not a retreat from society, nor is it a fringe survivalist fantasy. It is a pragmatic response to a world where fragility hides behind polish. To live fully dependent on external systems—be it for your money, identity, security, or livelihood—is to accept that your autonomy hangs on the benevolence of institutions that may not know you, and certainly don't answer to you. You may borrow from these systems. But your sovereignty should never be mortgaged to them.

Let's be clear: "decentralisation" has become something of a buzzword—overused, occasionally misused, and often evangelised without substance. But strip away the hype and you'll find an ancient, robust idea: resilience through dispersion. Whether it's the logic behind keeping a second set of house keys, maintaining an emergency stash of water, or spreading investments across asset classes, the underlying instinct is the same—never be beholden to a single point of failure.

Now, imagine applying that instinct not just to your portfolio, but to your entire architecture of autonomy—your digital presence, your financial structure, your geographic base. This chapter lays out a framework for doing precisely that, divided into three interlocking strategies:

1. Crypto, Gold, and the Post-Bank Reality

Cryptocurrency has been praised as a financial revolution and dismissed as a speculative fever dream—often in the same breath. This section takes neither view. Instead, it offers a grounded exploration of what decentralised digital assets are, how they actually function, and how they can be used without dogma. The focus here is not on get-rich-quick schemes, but on infrastructure: what digital assets might offer in a future where institutional trust continues to erode. Alongside this sits a renewed look at gold—not as a relic, but as a form of unencumbered value in regions where fiat currency has decayed or where the rule of law bends to power. What emerges is a distinction between liquidity for speculation and liquidity for sovereignty—a distinction likely to define the next financial era.

2. Building Invisible Fortresses

You needn't vanish to reclaim privacy. You simply need to become less legible. This section is about operational discretion—not secrecy for its own sake, but the ability to reduce unwanted exposure. It's about smart layering: encrypted communication, decentralised cloud storage, legal vehicles for asset protection, and digital hygiene practices that sever your footprint from your identity. These aren't toys for the paranoid or luxuries for the elite. They're tools of modern agency. In a world where data is both currency and vulnerability, learning how to disappear from certain maps is not misanthropic—it's wise. Power, after all, is not just about visibility. It's also about choosing when—and whether—you wish to be seen.

3. The New Exile: Strategic Withdrawal from Dysfunction

Not every system is salvageable. Some must be exited. This final section deals with what was once an unspoken strategy reserved for oligarchs and ideologues: geopolitical self-realignment. Call it what you will—geoarbitrage, relocation, legal repositioning—the principle is simple: move yourself, your capital, or your enterprise to jurisdictions where the trade-offs suit your values. Whether that's pursuing a second passport, establishing a more rational tax domicile, or building a life where the rules aren't stacked against autonomy, the mechanisms are now accessible to a much broader tier of individuals. Thanks to digital work, international legal frameworks, and shifts in global mobility, freedom has—quite literally—more addresses than it used to.

Taken together, these three strategies don't promise invincibility. But they do offer a new kind of freedom—one rooted in design, not reaction. What unites them is the act of rebalancing power. Not accumulating it, but reclaiming it from systems that assume your dependence.

Where institutions are vulnerable—or outright predatory—decentralisation acts as quiet resistance. It doesn't require slogans or confrontation. What it demands is preparation. To stop relying on goodwill where architecture would do. To replace trust with structure. It is, in essence, the shift from renting peace of mind to owning it.

This chapter won't tell you precisely what to do. It will do something more enduring: it will show you how to think systemically. How to design a life that cannot be revoked by policy changes or platform bans. How to build escape hatches before you need them.

Because in an era where permissions are increasingly provisional, waiting for someone else to give you the green light may be the costliest decision of all.

Owning Your Ecosystem

The quiet revolution of decentralised self-reliance

No one will announce the collapse of a system. It simply stops working. One day, your bank imposes a 72-hour freeze on transfers "for your security." A payment processor unilaterally blocks funds because your industry is flagged as high risk. A government issues capital controls that convert your freedom of movement into a footnote. In these moments, theory becomes reality. And those who assumed stability—those who built their entire lives within institutional rails—suddenly find themselves negotiating from zero.

To own your ecosystem is not to abandon society. It is to understand that resilience does not scale top-down. It is designed, deliberately, bottom-up. The concept refers to the creation of personal or micro-collective systems—of income, value exchange, shelter, energy, and security—that are *optionally independent* from failing or captured structures. The operative word is *optionally*. You do not need to withdraw from the modern world. But if you cannot *exit* a system, you are beholden to it.

This chapter explores three interlocking pillars of autonomous design: off-grid income, decentralised currencies, and parallel systems. Each is not only a tactical hedge against economic instability, but a philosophical stance: **to reclaim your inputs, reduce your dependencies, and restore your agency in a world increasingly structured around extraction rather than contribution**.

Off-Grid Income: Turning Skills Into Sovereignty

Off-grid income is not limited to homesteading or barter economies. It refers to the cultivation of income streams that *do not depend on a single employer, a national financial system, or the goodwill of a centralised authority*. These streams are portable, uncorrelated with national economies, and shielded from institutional disruption. Freelance work across borders, crypto-native consulting, micro-businesses selling via privacy-preserving payment rails, even low-tech value creation like skilled craftsmanship, tutoring, or permaculture systems—all qualify when structured deliberately.

Consider this: most people's livelihoods are not only centralised, but *fragilely singular*. The average professional's income is routed through one jurisdiction, one payroll system, one tax apparatus, and one currency. By contrast, a person earning in three currencies via remote freelance platforms, partially reinvested into staked digital assets and local physical goods, is operating with *built-in resilience.* A government freeze, policy change, or institutional collapse in one vector does not destroy their capacity to earn or operate.

Off-grid income is not about secrecy. It's about redundancy. It is the financial equivalent of a diversified immune system.

But this cannot be achieved passively. It demands a new kind of economic literacy—one rooted not in traditional career paths, but in entrepreneurial dexterity. *Can you identify high-trust, low-dependence opportunities? Can you market your skills globally while minimising your digital footprint? Can you structure contracts and payouts in legally sound yet jurisdictionally diversified ways?* These are no longer fringe questions. They are the frontline of financial sovereignty.

Decentralised Currencies: Access, Autonomy, and the End of Permission

Most people still think of cryptocurrency as speculative assets—something one trades, gambles with, or watches swing wildly in value. This is not financial literacy; it is media caricature. The deeper truth is that decentralised currencies, when used correctly, **represent programmable access to trustless infrastructure**. Not just "money you own," but *money that doesn't ask for permission.*

In practical terms, decentralised currencies allow you to store, send, and receive value outside of traditional gatekeepers. There is no need to wait for banking hours, justify your income source to a risk officer, or beg a financial institution to release your own capital. Combined with privacy-preserving tools—such as mixers, multisig wallets, and decentralised exchanges—crypto becomes not just a hedge against volatility, but a foundation for *uncorrelated liquidity.*

But decentralisation is not magic. It is design. Which is why most users fail to realise its power. The average person holds their crypto on a centralised exchange, linked to their identity, subject to the same

KYC/AML laws and surveillance logic as any bank. That's not decentralisation; it's decoration.

True ownership requires deeper fluency: understanding cold storage, navigating stablecoins pegged to real-world value, selecting networks with security track records, and most importantly, knowing how to transact privately, legally, and ethically. Crypto, when properly used, can shield against institutional overreach, capital controls, and surveillance. When misused, it's just another brittle node.

Decentralised currencies are not about getting rich. They're about staying *free.* And freedom, in financial terms, begins with control over one's medium of exchange.

Parallel Systems: Building Quiet Alternatives Before They're Needed

When central systems work, parallel systems look redundant. When they fail, they become lifelines. The tragedy is that most people realise this *too late.* Whether it's a power outage, internet censorship, legal entrapment, or inflation spiralling out of control, the absence of alternatives renders individuals compliant by necessity, not consent.

The most powerful ecosystems are not loud. They are *quietly functional.* A community mesh network that bypasses ISPs. A private server that hosts your data encrypted and locally. A DAO-managed fund that allocates emergency capital to vetted members. A co-owned piece of rural land with food security and clean water access. None of these require conspiracy thinking. They require *contingency thinking.*

Parallel systems do not need to match the scale of public infrastructure. They only need to function when the latter breaks. That is the genius of micro-resilience. You don't need to control the whole energy grid—just your own access to it. You don't need to replace the global food system—just your week-to-week security. *You do not need to decentralise the world. You need to decentralise your life.*

In this sense, owning your ecosystem is about building "soft exits"—small but decisive moves that reduce your reliance on institutions designed for scale, not care. It's a reorientation toward *horizontal resilience over vertical dependence.* And in times of disruption, that difference is everything.

Final Thought: Sovereignty Is Built Before It's Needed

This chapter is not a manifesto for isolation. It is a call to reclaim personal architecture in an era of institutional decay. The goal is not to reject civilisation, but to stop *outsourcing foundational responsibility* to systems that no longer earn our trust.

To own your ecosystem is not to become a hermit. It is to become ungovernable by dysfunction. It is to cultivate income without compromise, liquidity without gatekeeping, and redundancy without excess. It is to build your own safety net—not just financially, but *structurally, digitally, legally, and communally.*

Because the future doesn't wait for your preparedness. And when systems fail—and they increasingly do—only those who've built their own architecture will still be standing.

Crypto, Gold, and the Post-Bank Future

Reclaiming Wealth in an Age of Institutional Fragility

It no longer takes a revolution or a war to disrupt access to capital. A policy change, an algorithmic error, a misapplied fraud alert—any of these can sever an individual from their own money. Across the globe, we have entered a silent but seismic shift: trust in banks and financial intermediaries is no longer presumed; it is conditional, transactional, and increasingly brittle.

What happens when you no longer control access to your own stored labour? What does wealth mean when it can be *paused, frozen,* or *redefined* at will by external actors? These are not theoretical questions. They are the new financial reality for professionals, entrepreneurs, and families navigating a post-stability world.

This subchapter addresses that reality with clarity, not alarmism. It is not an invitation to abandon institutions entirely, but a rigorous argument for decentralised preparedness. Gold and cryptocurrency, when understood on their merits rather than as ideological tokens or speculative thrills, offer a practical foundation for wealth protection. Not because they are perfect. But because *they are outside the perimeter of institutional control.*

We are not speaking here of profit. We are speaking of access, security, and continuity—*when systems fail or withdraw their favour.*

A Reframing of Risk: Institutional Dependency as a Liability

Before examining crypto or gold, one must first confront a core myth: that institutions are inherently safe. This belief—engrained through decades of consumer banking, regulated finance, and modern risk management—no longer holds under scrutiny.

Bank accounts are not vaults. They are *claims* on a financial institution, which may choose, under government directive or internal discretion, to restrict or delay access. Bail-ins (Cyprus, 2013), bank freezes (Lebanon, 2019–2023), emergency capital controls (Argentina, India), and regulatory seizures (Canada's protest-related asset freezes in 2022) illustrate the point: *your balance does not equal your liquidity.*

A decentralised store of value is not about ideology. It is about *optionality.* The option to transact when banks collapse. The option to move wealth across borders without waiting for approval. The option to preserve value when national currencies implode from inflation, war, or institutional incompetence.

If your entire financial identity is rooted in centrally intermediated systems, you are not wealthy—you are *rented.*

Gold: Stability Through Tangibility

Gold remains the historical benchmark of stored value. Its endurance is not superstition; it reflects unique properties that make it materially unreplicable. Gold is finite, divisible, portable, universally recognisable, and inert. It does not degrade, rust, or corrode. It requires no counterparty to validate its value.

More importantly, gold is *non-digital.* It cannot be de-platformed, hacked, or erased by cyberattack or software failure. In a world increasingly mediated by software-defined trust, physical gold remains the archetype of self-custodied security.

But gold is not frictionless. It is heavy. It requires secure storage. It is awkward for small transactions and nearly useless in a hyper-connected, mobile, service-based economy. Try paying a developer in Krugerrands, and you'll understand its limitations quickly.

The strategic role of gold is *preservation*, not agility. It is ideal for medium- to long-term security, inheritance planning, and cross-border hedge. For those in unstable jurisdictions, physical gold buried, vaulted, or offshore-held can mean the difference between generational loss and dignified continuity.

And yet, despite its millennia of credibility, gold still requires some degree of infrastructure to be functional. This is where digital complements—like crypto—emerge as relevant.

Crypto: Programmable Sovereignty

Cryptocurrency, in its purest form, is not money. It is *infrastructure.* It is an alternative monetary architecture that allows people to hold, transfer, and verify value without relying on banks, governments, or payment processors.

Used correctly, crypto allows anyone to:

Store value without intermediaries

Transact globally in minutes

Control access without identity-based authorisation

Engage in smart contracts that self-enforce

This is not theory. Ukrainian refugees used USDT (a stablecoin) to exit conflict zones and settle in neighbouring countries without losing access to capital. Iranian dissidents rely on Bitcoin to fund secure servers and VPNs. Argentinian freelancers demand crypto payment from international clients to escape a 100%+ inflationary peso. In each case, crypto is not a speculative asset—it is *permissionless survival.*

However, crypto is also treacherous. It is not regulated for consumer protection. It demands personal responsibility and technical literacy. Custodial exchanges—Coinbase, Binance, etc.—are convenient but ultimately replicating traditional financial gatekeeping. If your funds are held in a password-protected cloud account, they are *not truly yours.*

The transition from ownership to *sovereign custody* involves cold wallets, seed phrases, and security practices that most are unwilling to learn. But that learning curve is the price of financial autonomy. As the adage goes: not your keys, not your coins.

The goal is not to evangelise crypto, but to demystify it. When paired with stablecoins, decentralised finance protocols, and privacy-preserving layers, cryptocurrency becomes *a parallel financial stack*—one that can be activated when the dominant stack malfunctions or turns hostile.

Strategic Integration: Blending Legacy and Alternative Systems

We are not suggesting an all-in bet on crypto or gold. That is another form of fragility. The wise move is *strategic pluralism*: to diversify not merely what assets you hold, but *where, how, and under what rules they exist.*

A resilient individual or family might:

Keep 3–6 months of local fiat in liquid bank accounts for everyday use

Hold physical gold in secure jurisdictions, or via trusted storage agreements with full audit rights

Custody crypto in cold wallets split between multisig safes and trusted geographic locations

Use stablecoins for international payments or freelance income

Structure a portion of assets in vehicles like irrevocable trusts, private foundations, or foreign-held insurance wrappers to avoid unilateral seizure

Each layer is not a rejection of the system—it is a *failover.* You do not unplug from society. You give yourself options to remain functional if society's trust layers break down.

This is not paranoia. It is continuity planning. And in an era of political volatility, digital fragility, and institutional overreach, *continuity is a luxury that must be designed for.*

Closing Insight: Protecting Wealth Means Redefining It

Wealth, in the traditional sense, has been defined as balance sheet accumulation. But post-2008, post-COVID, post-banking collapses and capital freezes, wealth now includes *resilience*, *mobility*, and *retention under pressure.*

The modern store of value must answer this test:

Can I access it without permission?

Can I move it across jurisdictions?

Can I transact in it when institutions fail?

Can I protect it from inflation, seizure, or surveillance?

Gold answers some of these questions. Crypto answers others. Fiat institutions, when stable, offer convenience but not immunity. Your job, as a financially literate actor in a post-trust economy, is to *construct a blend that serves function, not fantasy.*

Do not ask what asset will make you rich. Ask *what configuration of assets will keep you sovereign when the system forgets its promises.*

Building Invisible Fortresses

The Quiet Architecture of Privacy, Security, and True Autonomy

Power, in its modern form, is no longer enforced solely through the barrel of a gun or the iron grip of state bureaucracy. It is enforced quietly—through data trails, opaque algorithms, clickwrap agreements, invisible surveillance, and centralised gatekeepers who shape what you may access, say, or keep. Most people are not surveilled violently. They are surveilled *passively.* And they are not robbed overtly. They are *exposed*, *quantified*, and *left vulnerable.*

In such an environment, wealth is no longer defined solely by what you *have*, but by what you can *protect.* And protection—true, strategic protection—is not about paranoia or fortress bunkers. It's about *design.* Design that is precise, invisible, and legal. It is the architecture of resilience, crafted in plain sight but understood only by those who choose to think beyond compliance.

This subchapter is for those who have realised that privacy is not a luxury—it is a *precondition for freedom.* It is for individuals who understand that wealth, without discretion, becomes a target. That data, if not guarded, becomes leverage. That your family's security is not merely a matter of physical safety, but of *digital, legal, and reputational shielding.*

What follows is not fantasy or theory. It is a strategic blueprint for creating personal and financial infrastructure that remains *invisible to predators*, *resilient to intrusion*, and *legally coherent.* It does not require vast fortunes. It requires precision, intentionality, and a willingness to do what most affluent people neglect until it is too late.

Let us begin with the foundational shift: understanding *what needs protection*, and *why.*

Exposure Is the Default. Privacy Must Be Engineered.

Every digital interaction—searches, purchases, browser tabs, biometric logins—feeds a behavioural profile more valuable than gold to advertisers, insurers, governments, and adversarial actors. This data is not stored in a vault. It is *sold, scraped, and weaponised*—often without your knowledge and always without your control.

Likewise, legal exposure is quietly built into common financial structures. If you operate as an individual—owning property, running a sole proprietorship, or holding direct title—you are offering your assets as collateral in every dispute, divorce, or jurisdictional overreach. Your personal name becomes a single point of failure.

What's needed is not secrecy. Secrecy is brittle. What's needed is *structured opacity*—visibility only where necessary, and design everywhere else.

Principle One: Separate Identity from Ownership

The first step in fortification is legal detachment. Not hiding—*disentangling.* The wealthy do not "own" things in the conventional sense. Their homes are held in trusts. Their companies are managed via nominee directors. Their cars are leased by corporations they control. Their investments flow through tax-neutral structures that divorce control from liability.

This is not about tax evasion. It is about *risk containment.* If your assets are held by you personally, they can be frozen, litigated, or confiscated. If they are held by entities you legally do not "own"—but lawfully *control*—then they exist in a different tier of exposure.

Foundational strategies include:

Holding property via limited liability companies (LLCs) or international trusts

Using holding companies to manage income-generating entities

Establishing privacy-respecting nominee arrangements where legally compliant

Separating online activity from personally identifiable information using digital aliasing and robust encryption

These are not exotic tactics. They are standard operating procedure for global entrepreneurs, legacy families, and sovereign individuals. What is radical is that *so few people* consider them necessary—until exposure arrives.

Principle Two: Privacy Is a Stack, Not a Switch

There is no single "privacy setting" in life. Protection comes from layering. Think of your digital and legal life as having multiple perimeters—each requiring reinforcement.

At the digital level:

Use privacy-centric browsers (Brave, Firefox) and encrypted search (Startpage, DuckDuckGo)

Employ VPNs or decentralised alternatives (e.g. Orchid) for obfuscating IP origin

Replace Gmail with secure email providers (ProtonMail, Tutanota)

Use end-to-end encrypted messengers (Signal, Session) for sensitive communications

Store passwords in offline or zero-knowledge vaults (Bitwarden, KeePassXC)

At the device level:

Use physical security keys (YubiKey, Nitrokey) instead of SMS-based 2FA

Enable full disk encryption on all mobile and laptop devices

Minimise app permissions, block background data harvesting, and audit telemetry settings

At the cloud level:

Avoid default syncs to Google Drive, Dropbox, or iCloud unless end-to-end encrypted

Use zero-trust storage options (Tresorit, Sync.com) or go local with air-gapped backups

Regularly rotate credentials and separate admin access from usage accounts

This is not Luddism. It is digital sovereignty. In an environment where metadata is more revealing than content, controlling your digital fingerprint is *not optional*—especially for those with assets, influence, or dependants.

Principle Three: Legal Fortresses Are Built, Not Bought

Most people assume that privacy begins and ends with software. But without legal structures, privacy collapses under scrutiny. True fortresses are *legally robust.* They withstand court orders, audits, asset discovery, and legacy events.

Start with wills and trusts—not just for estate planning, but for *jurisdictional agility.* A living trust can shield assets from probate. An irrevocable trust, structured correctly, can *remove assets from your estate entirely*—thus shielding them from creditors and political instability.

Family protection doesn't begin with a bank account. It begins with *guardianship directives*, *medical powers of attorney*, and *cross-border continuity plans.* If you cannot speak for yourself, who can access your assets? Your data? Your children?

Consider jurisdictional diversification:

Store title documents, digital keys, and backups in different legal environments

Use data residency laws to your advantage—hosting sensitive data in countries with strong privacy protections (e.g. Switzerland, Iceland)

Maintain multiple residencies or citizenships to avoid becoming hostage to a single nation-state's policies

These are not extreme measures. They are *moderate safeguards for an extreme age.*

Case Study: The High Net-Worth Individual Who Lost Everything—Digitally

In 2021, a successful European entrepreneur found himself the target of a politically motivated investigation. He had no criminal record. His business was legitimate. But a regional tax authority, eager for leverage, issued a freeze on all local bank accounts and demanded asset disclosures within five days.

What they discovered: his properties were in his name, his digital identity was tied to personal email and phone numbers, and his data was hosted in local cloud servers. Within 72 hours, he lost operational control of his business, his liquidity, and his privacy. All because he *owned things visibly* and *lacked legal buffers.*

Contrast that with another individual, a modest but security-conscious investor who used an international trust to hold her real estate, crypto assets stored in air-gapped cold wallets, and data routed through non-jurisdictional channels. Her online identity was a decoy. Her real communications travelled through a parallel ecosystem. When a cyber-extortion group attempted to locate and threaten her assets, they found only *empty shells* and *sealed doors.*

What made the difference? Not wealth. *Design.*

Final Principle: Visibility Is a Liability—Unless You Control It

Everything about modern finance, governance, and advertising is designed to increase your surface area. Social media normalises oversharing. Fintech normalises hyper-disclosure. Cloud software normalises full access. But control over your own visibility—what you show, where, and when—is an *unrecognised superpower.*

You do not need to become invisible. But you must *choose* what remains visible. Not everything you can do should be done in your name. Not every account needs to be tied to your identity. Not every dollar needs to sit inside an institution that can lock it.

To the extent that you design your life around *low-resolution public optics*, and *high-resolution internal structure*, you gain leverage others do not even realise exists.

This is not about hiding. It is about *hardening*. The world rewards visibility, then punishes those who are too visible. What you build quietly is what protects you when noise becomes a threat.

Build it now. Before you need it. Because by the time you *know* you need it, it will already be too late to start.

The New Exile: Exit Strategies from Toxic Economies

Geoarbitrage, Second Residencies, and Sovereign Citizenship as Tools of Strategic Withdrawal

There is a quiet shift taking place—far beneath headlines, beyond immigration queues, and outside the tired narratives of national pride or economic loyalty. A growing number of people are not fleeing war, famine, or environmental catastrophe. They are opting out. Not because they must, but because they *can*. These are the new exiles—not refugees, but rational defectors. Highly mobile, digitally empowered, legally informed individuals and families who are *exiting* toxic economies with precision rather than desperation.

The term "toxic" here is not used rhetorically. It refers to environments where fiscal abuse, political instability, regulatory overreach, unsustainable taxation, or cultural hostility toward independence have rendered participation *costlier than exit*. In these contexts, geoarbitrage, second residencies, and sovereign citizenship are not luxuries. They are *deliberate countermeasures*—life design tools for those unwilling to tie their wellbeing to the failures of a single jurisdiction.

This subchapter explores what it means to leave—not just geographically, but *systemically*. It is about decoupling from economies that no longer serve, protect, or reward rational, sovereign participation. It is about *building optionality as insurance*, not ideology.

Toxicity Defined: When Loyalty Becomes Liability

Not all dysfunction is visible at once. A country may appear democratic but behave autocratically with regard to finances. It may allow free speech, but punish economic dissent. It may champion opportunity while taxing growth out of feasibility.

Indicators of toxicity include:

Confiscatory taxation without proportional benefit (e.g., 50%+ marginal rates with failing infrastructure)

Currency debasement through unchecked inflation or monetary manipulation

Legal unpredictability—where contracts, property rights, or banking access are subject to abrupt override

Capital controls or exit taxes aimed at *trapping* rather than retaining talent and capital

Systemic hostility toward entrepreneurs, wealth builders, or digital nomads

Importantly, none of these are merely financial issues. They are *sovereignty issues*. When a system's default response to prosperity is suspicion, and its core fiscal policy is coercion, leaving becomes less about adventure—and more about protection.

Geoarbitrage: Not Just Cheaper Living, but Smarter Living

Geoarbitrage—the act of earning in one currency or economy and spending in another—has been romanticised in digital nomad circles. But its strategic application extends far beyond tropical escapes or startup enclaves. At its core, geoarbitrage is a *leverage strategy*. It is a way to:

Maintain global income while radically lowering cost of living

Access higher-quality healthcare, education, or legal stability at lower cost

Optimise tax obligations by becoming a non-resident in high-burden jurisdictions

Enhance lifestyle security by living in countries where personal freedoms, safety, or rule of law are more aligned with one's values

For example, a British entrepreneur earning through a global e-commerce business may relocate to Portugal under the Non-Habitual Resident (NHR) regime, reducing their effective tax rate while gaining EU access, temperate climate, and quality public services. Meanwhile, their income—denominated in USD, GBP, or crypto—goes significantly further when spent in a eurozone economy with moderate living costs.

The best geoarbitrage candidates are not necessarily the cheapest countries. They are those where *value*—not just cost—is disproportionately favourable. Georgia, Panama, Malaysia, Uruguay, and even parts of Eastern Europe now compete to attract mobile earners and location-independent professionals with favourable residency programmes and minimal regulatory friction.

Geoarbitrage works best when paired with *strategic detachment*—the deliberate restructuring of personal, financial, and corporate presence to avoid default entrapment by home-country obligations.

Second Residencies: The Legal Architecture of Optionality

Residency, often misunderstood as mere location status, is in fact a *keystone legal category*—it determines which country has first claim on your income, compliance, and civil responsibilities. For those seeking distance from a toxic system, acquiring second (or third) residencies is *not optional.* It is the legal basis upon which freedom of movement and jurisdictional flexibility rest.

Key strategies include:

Residency by investment: e.g., Portugal's Golden Visa, Greece's Property Investment Residency, Panama's Friendly Nations Visa

Residency by income: e.g., countries offering digital nomad visas or independent means residencies (Croatia, Estonia, Costa Rica)

Residency by ancestry: e.g., Ireland, Italy, and Poland offer streamlined routes for those with documented heritage

Residency does not require renunciation of citizenship. It is a legal foothold—allowing presence, bank access, healthcare, and taxation within a new system, often with lower burdens and higher autonomy. In jurisdictions with territorial taxation (where foreign income is not taxed), this can serve as the foundation for highly efficient global lifestyles.

Residency diversification is also the first shield against *policy risk*. When one country restricts movement, enforces financial controls, or collapses into political volatility, residency elsewhere provides not just a plan B—but a *place to land.*

Sovereign Citizenship: The Last Firewall

Where residency is a right to stay, *citizenship* is the right to *belong*. It is the final firewall against displacement, disenfranchisement, or involuntary exclusion from any national economy. It secures full political rights, passport issuance, and the capacity to live, work, and own in a country without permission.

For many, obtaining a second citizenship is a long-term project. But its value cannot be overstated. Sovereign citizenship reduces single-country dependency, enables visa-free travel, and can serve as a *lifeboat jurisdiction* when others sink.

Acquisition routes include:

Citizenship by descent: available in dozens of countries with generous ancestral policies

Citizenship by naturalisation: earned through years of residency, often fast-tracked in strategically welcoming nations

Citizenship by investment: a controversial but legal route in select jurisdictions (e.g., St. Kitts, Antigua, Vanuatu), where citizenship is exchanged for capital contribution, property investment, or donation

What matters is not prestige but *access*. A second citizenship in a stable, low-tax, diplomatically neutral country can offer safety disproportionate to its global profile. In a world of rising authoritarianism and weaponised compliance, *passport diversification* is a serious act of self-defence.

Moral Clarity: Exit Is Not Betrayal

One of the greatest barriers to executing an exit strategy is *moral conditioning*. Many internalise the belief that leaving their country—particularly for financial or legal reasons—is disloyal, unethical, or cowardly. But when loyalty is expected in exchange for abuse, the moral failure lies not with the leaver, but the system demanding sacrifice without fairness.

Choosing to exit is not a rejection of civic responsibility. It is a rejection of *compulsory sacrifice*. It is a refusal to be coerced into subsidising broken systems while being denied protection, prosperity, or basic respect.

And for those with children or dependants, exit is not just a right. It is a duty. Remaining in a failing economy out of fear, habit, or misplaced sentimentality risks anchoring future generations to unnecessary hardship.

Designing Your Exit

A successful exit strategy is not a one-time escape plan. It is a progressive, layered process involving:

Legal relocation of income-generating entities

Domicile change to reset tax residency

Acquisition of second (or multiple) residencies

Opening of international banking and investment accounts

Travel flexibility via multiple passports

Personal and family adaptation to cross-cultural environments

The most resilient individuals are those who decentralise *every layer* of their lives—not just money, but access, identity, mobility, and security.

In doing so, they do not become exiles in the old sense. They become *post-national actors*—untethered from decaying systems and invested in agile, ethical, self-directed futures.

Exit is not escape. It is strategy. It is sovereignty. It is the clearest expression of refusal in an age where silence is consent.

Chapter 10
Teaching the Next Generation to Disobey

How does one raise a child not merely to survive a system, but to see it clearly—and, where necessary, to walk away from it? Most parents, often with the best intentions, prepare their children to function within the world they themselves were shaped by: a world that rewarded compliance, predictability, and incremental advancement. But the scaffolding of that world is rusting. Institutions falter, rules shift without warning, and the once-sturdy path to security—study hard, work hard, retire in peace—has become a fading myth. What does it mean, then, to prepare a young mind for a world so inherently unstable?

The answer is not obedience. In fact, obedience, once a protective instinct, may now be a liability. A child conditioned to defer, to accept, to play by rules never explained—such a child is more vulnerable, not less. Vulnerable to exploitation, to misinformation, to systems designed to benefit from their passivity. What's needed instead is an education in economic agency. Not just how to earn, or save, or invest, but how to think critically in financial terms—how to recognise the hidden scripts beneath the numbers.

To raise a financially autonomous thinker is to start from a radical assumption: that systemic disobedience, when rooted in discernment, is not rebellion for its own sake—it is self-defence. It means cultivating not just the ability to question authority, but to spot the structures behind the authority. To ask: Who profits from this rule? What assumptions does this system make about me? Where is the exit, and who controls it?

This chapter, then, is not a guide to teaching children budgeting tips or how to open their first account. There's plenty of that elsewhere. This is something more subversive: a manifesto for raising children who are not economically docile. Children who do not mistake access for freedom, or branding for truth. Children who understand that banks are not benevolent, that taxes are political, and that financial literacy is often taught just far enough to keep people compliant.

A financially autonomous child is one who understands not just money, but power. Who knows that a job offer is a negotiation, not a favour. That debt can be a tool—but also a trap. That ownership matters more than appearances, and that economic systems are designed by people, not gods.

Parents must be willing, then, to question their own conditioning. To say, out loud, "This is how I was taught—but I'm not sure it still works." To speak candidly about financial mistakes, missed opportunities, and the myths they once believed. Not from a place of shame, but from honesty. Children don't need perfect models. They need transparent ones.

And the home, if reimagined, can become a sort of shadow school. A place where children learn to read between the lines of advertising. Where they see how decisions are made—not just what is bought, but why. Where they are invited into conversations about trade-offs, priorities, and long-term consequences. Not as bystanders, but as contributors. The goal is not to turn a child into a miniature capitalist. It is to raise someone who knows how to spot a lie dressed in economic logic.

Part of this training involves re-framing failure. Financial systems punish risk with shame. But children raised with the permission to experiment—to build, to break, to rebuild—will grow up less afraid of the unknown. They'll understand that mistakes are data, not verdicts. That recovery is a skill. That the ability to pivot is as valuable as the ability to persist.

There is also the matter of language. Children inherit not just their parents' assets and liabilities, but their metaphors. So when parents speak about money with fear, or resentment, or vague guilt, that atmosphere is absorbed. But if money is spoken of as energy, as strategy, as a design element—then it becomes something to be shaped, not endured. The shift is subtle, but transformative.

Finally, to raise financially autonomous thinkers, we must resist the urge to protect them from discomfort. To shield them from complexity is to deny them the very skills they'll need to navigate it. Teach them how systems fail. Teach them how inflation erodes value, how governments rewrite rules, how platforms can vanish overnight. Not to scare them, but to empower them. Because resilience is not the absence of fear—it is the presence of preparation.

In an era when so much feels engineered to keep people financially reactive, raising a child to be economically sovereign is not simply a parenting choice. It is an act of quiet revolution. And it begins with a question every family should dare to ask: What kind of mind are we building here? One that obeys? Or one that sees?

Obedience as Risk: Why Compliance Can No Longer Be the Default

Modern economic systems reward obedience only when it serves the system's growth, not the individual's wellbeing. The entire pipeline—schooling, debt-driven higher education, wage dependency, consumerism—is optimised for *predictability*, not empowerment. A child who learns to follow the rules unquestioningly is, by design, easier to manage as a worker, consumer, and debtor—but infinitely more vulnerable to manipulation, burnout, and financial exploitation.

Teaching kids to obey is no longer a neutral act. It is *risk transference.* We are asking them to place their future in the hands of systems we ourselves know are untrustworthy.

What's needed is not an alternative ideology to indoctrinate them with, but a deeper kind of fluency. Children must learn to ask: *Who benefits from this structure? What is the cost of compliance? What options exist outside this frame?* These are not just financial questions—they are existential ones. And we must teach them as early, honestly, and rigorously as possible.

Raising Financial Rebels: Skill-Building Beyond the Curriculum

A truly financially sovereign person does not merely know how money works. They understand how *systems* work—how laws are written, how taxes are structured, how language is weaponised in contracts and advertising, how value is extracted by platforms while cloaked in convenience. Teaching children to navigate this terrain means demystifying power early. It also means resisting the urge to moralise wealth, shame autonomy, or idealise sacrifice.

This requires deliberate, multi-dimensional parenting:

Teach negotiation, not just manners. A child who can push back against unfairness in a school rule is developing the same muscle they'll need to question exploitative workplace policies or misleading loan agreements.

Frame refusal as strategy, not rebellion. Saying "no" to a trend, a fee, a default path must be celebrated as discernment, not defiance.

Introduce money as language. Explain that every financial system is just a set of human-made agreements—some ethical, some predatory. Teach them to *read those agreements*, not just participate in them.

More than any curriculum, *modelling matters*. A child who sees their parent question a norm with grace and precision learns that dissent is not dangerous—it's intelligent.

Inheritance Without Chains: Wealth That Liberates, Not Controls

Families often conflate legacy with control. Money passed down from one generation to the next becomes a tether: to specific life choices, to unsaid expectations, to buried resentments. In traditional family wealth transfers, *the assets arrive heavy with narrative*—who deserves what, who disappointed whom, what strings are quietly attached.

But to raise truly free thinkers, we must rethink inheritance not as a transfer of assets, but a transfer of *agency*. That means:

Sharing the logic behind decisions, not just the results

Creating structures that enable autonomy (e.g., trusts with built-in optionality, not rigid directives)

Being transparent about both abundance and its ethical use

It also means letting go of guilt as currency. A child should not have to perform gratitude to access their own legacy. Nor should they fear stepping off the expected path because of imagined consequences.

Multigenerational wealth, when designed well, is not just capital. It is cultural. It is a transmission of *tools, context, and trust*—the things that let someone move through the world with clarity and conviction, not hidden pressure.

Home as a Cultural Counterforce: Rewriting Norms at the Source

Most financial conditioning happens at home. Not because of explicit lectures, but through repetition, silence, and observed behaviours. When a parent stresses about bills but never explains the cause, the child learns that money is both central and mysterious. When shopping is used to soothe emotions, they learn that consumption equals relief. When career choices are framed as respectable or not, they absorb class scripts without ever naming them.

To teach a child to disobey, we must *first disobey the culture ourselves.* That means interrogating family myths like:

"Debt is normal."

"Hard work always pays off."

"Talking about money is rude."

"Better safe than sorry."

It also means actively designing family life around *anti-fragile values*: time sovereignty, low-overhead living, mutual aid, decentralised income streams. When children grow up seeing parents *choose autonomy over prestige, enough over more*, and ethics over optics, they internalise the possibility of building lives on their own terms.

Home becomes the first ecosystem of rebellion—not loud or reckless, but *principled, strategic, and rooted.*

Conclusion Without Conclusion

This chapter is an invitation, not a lecture. It is for those raising children not to replicate themselves, but to surpass them—not in status or accumulation, but in *clarity, autonomy, and courage.*

To teach the next generation to disobey is not an act of disloyalty. It is a final act of love. It says: *I do not need you to fit in. I need you to see clearly, choose wisely, and build bravely.*

The rest of this chapter offers concrete tools to do just that. From designing family economies that reflect post-consumerist values, to crafting intergenerational legacies free from manipulation, to raising children fluent in systems thinking and financial language—what follows is not just a parenting strategy. It's a cultural intervention.

Because the world your children inherit will not reward obedience. It will reward *discernment.*

Why Financial Education is Intentionally Broken

Dissecting the Institutional Gaps That Cost Children Their Autonomy

A child can graduate from school able to recite the parts of a plant, describe the periodic table, or quote Shakespeare, yet have no understanding of what interest on a credit card means, how taxes actually work, or how to read a rental contract. This is not an oversight. It is a design. And it's costing generations not just money, but power.

In a society where financial infrastructure shapes nearly every aspect of adult life—housing, healthcare, work, marriage, mental health—it is conspicuous that schools omit the very knowledge that might make the next generation resilient, literate, and difficult to exploit. The average teenager is more likely to be taught trigonometry than how compound interest can trap them in debt. Why?

Because the current education system is not broken—it is functioning precisely as intended. And what it is designed to produce is not financially sovereign individuals, but compliant economic participants: dependable consumers, obedient workers, predictable borrowers.

This chapter peels back the curtain on what financial literacy *should* include, why it's been kept out of reach, and how we must intervene if we're to raise children who can outsmart—rather than be outpaced by—the systems they inherit.

Financial Illiteracy is Policy, Not Accident

The first lie we must abandon is that the lack of financial education in schools is due to time constraints, curriculum overload, or simple bureaucratic inertia. These excuses do not withstand scrutiny. Topics central to adult survival—how taxes function, how credit is scored, how contracts are enforced—are excluded not because they're too complex, but because they threaten the passive trust on which extractive economies depend.

Teach a 16-year-old how compounding interest works, and they may question the student loan offers they're handed at university orientation. Show them the fine print on a lease or mobile phone plan, and they may learn to say no. Explain how advertising manipulates scarcity and shame, and they may consume less. In short, *they may become economically inconvenient.*

There is a difference between education that informs and education that prepares. Most schools do the former—dispensing facts, encouraging memorisation—but stop short of teaching the analysis and scepticism needed to navigate power. Nowhere is this more stark than in the absence of meaningful financial instruction.

Consider what is typically left out:

How debt is sold, structured, and enforced

How the tax code rewards certain asset classes over others

How to recognise psychological tactics in consumer marketing

The legal implications of signing a contract

The difference between income and wealth

How to think critically about financial "advice" from institutions that profit from your ignorance

These are not advanced adult topics. They are *foundational civic knowledge.* Yet their omission remains near-universal.

Who Benefits from a Financially Passive Population?

We must ask a difficult but necessary question: *who profits from a population that lacks financial fluency?* The answer is neither subtle nor speculative.

Banks benefit from uninformed borrowers who don't fully grasp interest terms or penalty clauses. Employers benefit from workers who don't understand wage negotiation, equity compensation, or retirement vehicles. Governments benefit from citizens who don't challenge regressive tax codes or opaque fiscal policies. Advertisers benefit from consumers who conflate spending with identity, and who never pause to ask who designed that desire in the first place.

To be clear: this isn't a conspiracy of shadowy figures in a boardroom. It's a system-wide convergence of incentives. The more inert and financially insecure the population, the more dependent it becomes on the very institutions profiting from its dependence.

Financial illiteracy is not a glitch in the system. It is the system.

The Real Curriculum: What Financial Education Should Look Like

If we were to design a curriculum truly meant to equip young people with financial autonomy—not merely survival—we would begin not with budgeting apps or mock stock portfolios, but with a structural education in *power dynamics*. The curriculum would be built around five domains:

1. **Systems Fluency** – Understanding how economic systems are structured to distribute risk, reward, and responsibility. This includes taxation, debt issuance, banking regulations, and consumer protections (or the lack thereof).
2. **Contractual Literacy** – The ability to decode agreements, whether rental leases, employment contracts, subscription services, or terms and conditions. Most exploitation hides in clauses the average person is trained not to question.
3. **Psychological Defence** – Awareness of how shame, urgency, and manufactured desire are used to manipulate financial behaviour. This includes recognising behavioural nudges, algorithmic targeting, and the gamification of spending.
4. **Asset Fluency** – Knowing the difference between appreciating and depreciating assets, how inflation interacts with savings, and why wealth is built through ownership, not just income.
5. **Legal Awareness** – The basics of rights and remedies in financial disputes, including knowledge of small claims court, credit repair, legal aid, and consumer protection agencies.

A child armed with these tools is less likely to be seduced by payday loans, misled by flashy investments, or controlled by economic scarcity narratives. More importantly, they begin to see finance not as a personal failing or moral virtue—but as a language of systems that can be mastered, resisted, and reimagined.

What It Costs to Stay Ignorant

The absence of this education is not neutral. It creates intergenerational ripples of insecurity, fragility, and distrust. A teenager who enters adulthood without financial competence is:

More likely to accumulate predatory debt

Less likely to negotiate for fair pay

More vulnerable to financial abuse in personal relationships

Less prepared to identify scams, fraud, or exploitative services

More prone to rely on short-term consumption as a form of self-worth

And perhaps most insidiously, they are less likely to *trust themselves*—to believe they are capable of managing wealth, challenging authority, or designing lives outside the default settings of mainstream consumer capitalism.

When a society fails to teach financial literacy, it doesn't merely fail to educate. It actively *curates dependence.*

A Call to Educational Rebellion

We must not wait for state curricula to correct themselves. They will not. The incentive structures that suppress financial fluency are too deeply embedded. If change is to occur, it must be *parallel*, *grassroots*, and often *familial.*

Parents, mentors, and alternative educators must teach what schools refuse to: how to read the system, how to refuse predation, and how to design a life that is not captured by the mechanics of insecurity.

This is not just about money. It is about sovereignty.

Let us treat financial education not as a niche topic, but as a form of resistance, a civil right, and a cultural necessity. Because the question is no longer whether we can afford to teach our children differently—it's whether we can afford *not to.*

Raising Financial Rebels

Equipping the Next Generation to Question Defaults, Read Systems, and Build Autonomy

A child who never learns to ask *why* will grow into an adult who doesn't know how to say *no.* In a world engineered around compliance—economic, educational, social—the greatest act of parental care may not be protection, but preparation: the conscious raising of a child to question the systems they're born into.

It is tempting to teach children how to play the game—to budget wisely, save diligently, invest prudently. But financial fluency without systemic awareness is merely training for polite participation. It's giving a child tools, but not the ability to ask *who built the tool, who profits from its use, and whether there's another way to build entirely.*

To raise a financial rebel is not to raise a reckless rule-breaker. It is to raise someone equipped to *see rules for what they are*: designed structures, not universal truths. It is to raise someone who can decode manipulation, interrogate assumptions, and navigate finance not with fear or blind trust, but *with precision, autonomy, and clarity.* And in the long run, this form of financial parenting is not simply protective—it is revolutionary.

Why Conformity is Economically Dangerous

Let's be honest about what we're up against. The modern economy thrives not on informed, independent citizens, but on predictably indebted, consumption-driven workers. From the moment a child is old enough to use a screen, they are targeted by ads not designed to inform, but to instil habits: *Want more. Spend quickly. Never pause.*

If a child is taught only to budget their allowance and save for the future, but never taught how advertising exploits psychological triggers, how industries benefit from their confusion, or how debt can be disguised as opportunity, we haven't protected them—we've primed them for capture.

Conformity is the default setting of most financial education. It teaches behaviour, not critical thinking. It encourages good habits, but rarely questions the contexts in which those habits operate. By contrast, raising a financial rebel involves cultivating scepticism, not cynicism; agency, not anxiety.

The cost of raising obedient earners is generational dependence. The value of raising dissenters—grounded, informed dissenters—is legacy.

Cultivating System Awareness: The First Layer of Rebellion

Financial rebels don't just understand *how* money works; they understand *why* it works the way it does—and who benefits. Teaching children this level of awareness means exposing them, age-appropriately, to concepts adults often struggle to confront:

Why banks lend money they don't have

How inflation benefits borrowers but punishes savers

Why tax laws are written to reward capital, not labour

How corporations price identity, attention, and urgency

This isn't conspiracy—it's curriculum. Financial rebels are taught to *read the incentives behind the institutions*. This is not merely academic; it is *survival intelligence.*

Take the example of credit scores. Most adults can explain what raises or lowers one, but few understand that credit scoring is a proxy for trust within an extractive lending system. Why teach a child how to get a "good score" without teaching them to interrogate the system that makes this score so powerful in the first place?

When children learn that financial systems are human-made, profit-driven, and subject to change, they begin to *participate with intention*—not submission.

Language as Armour: Teaching Vocabulary That Decodes Power

Every system has its own language. Legalese. Contract terms. Financial acronyms. These are not merely technical—they are political. They form barriers to understanding, keeping outsiders from challenging insiders.

Financial rebels must be taught to wield language as defence. This includes:

Understanding what *interest-bearing*, *adjustable-rate*, or *secured debt* really means

Recognising phrases like *limited offer*, *subject to terms*, and *authorised access* as red flags, not details

Knowing how to parse contract clauses for hidden obligations or penalties

This isn't about becoming a lawyer. It's about ensuring your child can *read power when it presents itself in paper form.*

Just as we teach children not to sign things they don't understand, we must also teach them how understanding can be gained. Financial rebellion begins not with refusal, but with comprehension.

Role-Modelling Resistance: Parents as Financial Subversives

No child absorbs financial worldview from lectures alone. They inherit it from *observation.* If parents are afraid of money, deferential to financial institutions, or ashamed of their financial history, children absorb this posture long before they understand its logic.

Raising a financial rebel means modelling *healthy defiance.* It means showing a child what it looks like to:

Say no to offers that don't serve your values

Question prices, contracts, and "expert advice"

Design a career path outside traditional employment

Discuss wealth, debt, and scarcity without shame

This modelling cannot be performative. It must be lived. It is not about appearing financially savvy—it is about showing that *economic autonomy is a life stance, not just a set of tactics.*

And just as crucially, parents must be willing to share their financial mistakes. Rebels are not built through illusion. They are built through *honesty, repair, and transparency.* When a child sees a parent challenge a system—and survive it—they learn that risk is navigable, and that autonomy is possible even after failure.

Autonomy is Built Through Exposure, Not Shelter

One of the gravest errors in modern parenting is the conflation of protection with insulation. A child who never sees money discussed becomes an adult who treats it like taboo. A teenager who never handles real money—or its real-world consequences—is less prepared to make intelligent financial decisions than a peer who has experienced earning, spending, losing, and recalibrating.

We must treat economic exposure not as a threat to innocence, but as the *training ground of autonomy*. That includes:

Letting children manage a real (not pretend) budget, with real stakes

Inviting them into conversations about family financial decisions

Showing them how to research, compare, and challenge financial products

Encouraging them to build small, real income streams—not as hustles, but as labs for learning

If a child can run a lemonade stand, they can understand profit margins. If they can negotiate screen time, they can negotiate rates. *Financial intelligence is behavioural before it is technical.*

Teaching Against the Culture

Raising a financial rebel is often an act of cultural resistance. You will be teaching your child to decline what others embrace: limitless consumption, performative wealth, blind obedience to career ladders. This may isolate them at times. It may frustrate them. It will certainly make them harder to market to—and that is precisely the point.

The goal is not to raise contrarians. It is to raise *builders of parallel paradigms*: children who see alternatives, create structures, and shape their lives around *principles*, not programming.

To do that, you must name the programming. Speak openly about how advertising works. Point out when "education" is really indoctrination. Discuss how financial advice is often thinly veiled sales. Children are not too fragile to hear these things. They are too valuable *not* to.

The Tools That Matter Most

What do financial rebels actually need? Not perfection. Not a parental lecture series. Not early access to crypto. They need:

Language, to decode systems

Courage, to ask unpopular questions

Exposure, to real choices and consequences

Permission, to disagree with authority—even yours

And most of all, they need adults in their lives who will teach with clarity, lead by example, and *trust them to become smarter than we were allowed to be.*

Multigenerational Wealth Without Manipulation

How to Pass on Money and Meaning Without Creating Dependence, Guilt, or Dysfunction

The most delicate conversations in finance rarely concern numbers. They concern people. Inheritance. Expectations. Power. Regret. The myth of the wealthy yet broken family is not fiction—it's a cautionary tale repeated in the homes of the affluent and the aspirational alike. At the heart of these fractures lies not money itself, but *the way money is used to control, reward, withhold, or define the next generation.*

We are accustomed to thinking of legacy in material terms—property, portfolios, businesses, trusts. But the harder, more consequential inheritance is emotional and philosophical: what we teach (or fail to teach) our children about power, responsibility, value, identity, and freedom. Without intentional design, wealth transfer too easily becomes a proxy for control. Parents aim to protect but end up scripting. Children seek to honour but end up confined.

The question is not just how to pass on wealth—but how to pass it on without passing along manipulation.

This article aims to examine precisely that. It's not a financial planning guide. It's a rethinking of wealth as a multigenerational stewardship that must include dignity, autonomy, and transparency—not just net worth.

The Hidden Cost of "Security"

Every generation wants to provide more security than it received. But security, when interpreted narrowly, often leads to dependency. Over-involved financial guardianship can erode initiative, distort incentives, and replace confidence with compliance.

Children raised under constant monetary oversight often internalise one of two dangerous ideas: either that *money equals love*—and must be obeyed accordingly—or that *wealth is a burden*, one that requires sacrifice of self to preserve peace or approval.

Well-meaning provisions—trusts, allowances, safety nets—can become leashes if not paired with *respectful boundaries and philosophical clarity*. Ask a trust fund recipient how often financial support came with commentary about their career choices or life partner. Ask a successor in a family business how often succession planning came with identity erosion. The answers are sobering.

Security without sovereignty is a gilded cage. The goal must be *empowerment without enmeshment.*

The Emotional Infrastructure of Legacy

To pass on wealth without dysfunction, you must invest in more than accountants and estate plans. You must cultivate an *emotional infrastructure* that can support the weight of money.

That begins with explicit conversations—*early and often.* Not just about amounts or conditions, but about *intentions, values, and uncertainties.* What do you hope this money enables? What fears do you carry about its effects? What choices do you hope your children will make—and which are not yours to influence?

Many families avoid these discussions, telling themselves they're sparing their children worry. What they're often sparing is *their own discomfort.* The result is confusion, silence, and sometimes deep resentment.

Transparency doesn't mean full disclosure of every financial detail at every age. But it does mean progressively sharing *how decisions are made*, *what principles guide your wealth*, and *what you want to remain flexible in the face of changing futures.* It also means leaving room for children to *disagree with your priorities*—and still feel respected.

A 19-year-old might not yet understand your investment strategy. But they can understand your intention to ensure they're never trapped by debt or geography. A 27-year-old may not want to carry on the family business. But they can inherit the principle of building rather than extracting. *The transmission of wisdom must be adaptive, not doctrinal.*

Consent Over Control: Rethinking Inheritance Structures

Wealth transfers often default to mechanisms of control: conditional gifts, incentives for certain behaviours, punitive clauses for divergence from parental ideals. These structures may appear rational—designed to "protect" assets or "ensure" values—but they frequently backfire.

Control-based legacies breed secrecy, rebellion, and guilt. Autonomy-based legacies breed dialogue, agency, and trust.

One of the most radical concepts in multigenerational wealth planning is *intergenerational consent.* Instead of dictating terms from the grave or behind closed doors, it is possible—and powerful—to engage heirs in the design of their inheritance.

Ask questions like:

"What kind of support would feel empowering, not controlling?"

"What role would you want this money to play in your life?"

"Are there forms of help—emotional, relational, entrepreneurial—you value more than financial?"

By treating legacy as a living conversation, not a legal document, families shift from compliance to *collaboration.* And this shift can reduce the emotional residue that so often haunts "well-prepared" families who never actually discussed *how* or *why* wealth was being passed on.

Teaching Responsibility Without Transactional Love

Parents often struggle with how to instil responsibility. They fear entitlement, laziness, or wasted potential. But many end up teaching responsibility as a *test of worthiness* rather than a principle of stewardship.

Children shouldn't feel they have to "earn" love through their economic productivity. Nor should they fear that a career choice—artist, activist, primary caregiver—will forfeit their family's support.

True responsibility arises when children are given *freedom, context, and consequences*—not when they are bribed or punished into obedience.

Consider replacing conditional gifts with contextual ones:

"We're happy to support your further education. Here's the cap. Here's why we believe in this investment."

"We'll fund the down payment on a home—but we'll do the same for your siblings regardless of lifestyle or location."

"We've set aside capital if you want to start a business. There's no obligation, just a conversation about your plan."

These approaches affirm *agency*, while inviting accountability without judgement.

Wealth as Dialogue, Not Monologue

A multigenerational legacy is not a soliloquy. It's a dialogue—a series of interlocking narratives that must be updated as context evolves.

Grandparents may have built wealth through land ownership. Parents through education and globalisation. Children may see opportunity in decentralised systems, digital currencies, or lifestyle design. *Each generation will interpret risk, value, and work differently.* That's not dilution. That's *evolution.*

Families that remain cohesive over generations do not enforce uniformity. They encourage *reinterpretation of legacy in light of new realities.*

This requires humility. It requires recognising that the next generation may be smarter, braver, or more visionary than we were allowed to be. And it requires stepping back when we'd rather lean in—*not out of disengagement, but out of trust.*

Ending the Inheritance of Dysfunction

The most damaging inheritance is not bad money management—it's *unprocessed emotional baggage attached to money.* Guilt. Scarcity mindsets.

Status obsession. Identity collapse. Many family wounds are transmitted not through conflict, but through avoidance.

If you want to leave your children something truly valuable, leave them:

The *freedom to define success* for themselves

The *tools to repair relational strain*, not just financial strain

The *capacity to be generous without resentment* and independent without shame

This means doing your own work. It means addressing the parts of your financial story that remain unhealed. It means being honest about your mistakes without demanding moral repayment from your children for avoiding them.

And yes, it means giving up the fantasy of control—*because a legacy of freedom will always outlast a legacy of fear.*

Passing on wealth without manipulation is not an act of detachment. It is an act of deep respect: for your heirs' intellect, for their individuality, and for the world they will inherit—different from your own. This is not abdication. It is stewardship of a different kind: quiet, brave, and rare.

Creating Culture Shifts at Home

Redefining the Family's Role in Challenging Financial Norms and Seeding New Paradigms

The great unspoken curriculum in every household is culture. Long before a child opens a textbook or starts their first job, they absorb unspoken signals about money, worth, work, success, and security—often without anyone ever naming them aloud. Dinner table silences, emotional reactions to bills, celebrations of certain jobs over others, subtle dismissals of financial questions—all of it forms an internalised script. That script becomes the foundation of a worldview. And for most people, that worldview is inherited by default rather than design.

This chapter is about refusing that default.

Families are not passive transmitters of culture. They are *factories of norms*. They either perpetuate existing paradigms or challenge them. And the economic system we live in—predatory, extractive, consumption-driven—depends on families doing the former. It thrives on obedient workers, anxious consumers, and unexamined beliefs passed down like heirlooms. To disrupt this, we don't just need individual awakening. We need *cultural insubordination*, beginning at home.

The work of shifting economic consciousness doesn't start in boardrooms or political arenas. It starts in kitchens, living rooms, and bedrooms. It starts with what we celebrate, what we shame, what we fund, and what we forbid. And perhaps most critically, it starts with what we *question*—especially when our children begin to ask those same questions themselves.**Deprogramming Begins with Awareness**

You cannot change what you cannot see. The first step in challenging inherited economic norms is recognising the ones you've internalised. Most families operate under an invisible operating system that includes ideas such as:

Hard work is inherently virtuous—even when it's poorly paid, soul-crushing, or exploitative.

Saving is morally superior to spending—but only if you're saving for "respectable" goals.

Talking about money is gauche unless it's cloaked in performance—grades, promotions, degrees, mortgages.

Asking for more is dangerous—whether in salary negotiations, service interactions, or familial dynamics.

These aren't facts. They're scripts. And like most scripts, they were written to serve someone else's interests.

A family committed to cultural shift begins by *interrogating these assumptions aloud.* Why do we value university more than apprenticeships? Why do we describe someone as "doing well" simply because they bought a home? Why do we panic when a child chooses flexibility over stability, or creative expression over salary?

The point is not to arrive at a "correct" answer. The point is to *normalise economic thoughtfulness*, not economic obedience.

From Scarcity Scripts to Possibility Language

One of the most toxic hand-me-downs in family economic culture is the scarcity script—the idea that there is never enough, that life is a zero-sum game, and that financial safety requires relentless vigilance. Scarcity is not just a material state. It's a *psychological atmosphere*, and it seeps into everything: trust, joy, generosity, risk.

To shift this, families must actively practise what psychologists call *possibility language.* This does not mean vapid optimism. It means reframing decisions and conversations in terms of agency, opportunity, and design. For instance:

Instead of: "We can't afford that."
Say: *"That's not something we're prioritising right now—let's talk about why."*

Instead of: "Don't aim too high, you'll get disappointed."
Say: *"Let's break down what aiming high might actually involve—and what your alternatives are."*

Instead of: "You have to do X to be secure."
Say: *"Let's define what security actually means for you—and how flexible that definition might be."*

This reframing helps children develop a financial orientation rooted not in fear, but in *discernment.* It teaches them that life is a series of conscious trade-offs—not moral imperatives dictated by outdated norms.

Redesigning Incentives Without Replicating Capitalism

Too often, parents try to instil financial "responsibility" by mimicking the very system they hope to shield their children from. They offer performance-based rewards, chore payments, or punishments for "wasteful" spending. The implicit lesson? Money is moral. Earning is approval. Consumption is character.

Instead, a values-driven household decouples money from identity. It offers tools and consequences, not praise or punishment. It treats financial conversations as *experiments in design*, not evaluations of worth.

A child who receives an allowance, for example, can be invited into basic budgeting, saving, and investment conversations. Not to train them into mini-capitalists, but to give them fluency in the language of autonomy. A teenager making money from art or digital projects can be encouraged to understand taxes, contracts, or platform risk—not to "professionalise" them prematurely, but to *equip them with informed leverage.*

Economic skills are life skills. But unlike traditional schooling, they need to be taught in the context of *values, not just rules.*

The Family as Micro-Economy: Practising New Norms Inside the Home

Every household is a micro-economy. It has its own flows of capital, labour, rewards, and risks. It also has its own culture around those flows—who gets to make decisions, whose labour is recognised, how conflict is resolved, what failures are tolerated.

Families that wish to challenge financial norms must redesign their internal economies. This might include:

Democratising financial conversations: Age-appropriate transparency about household expenses, budgeting priorities, or major purchases.

Recognising invisible labour: Acknowledging caregiving, emotional support, and maintenance as *essential economic contributions*.

Modelling ethical trade-offs: Choosing to shop locally, refuse exploitative companies, or divest from harmful industries—and explaining those choices with clarity, not shame.

These shifts don't require perfection. They require *intention*. The goal is not to create a utopian household. The goal is to *practise resistance in real time*, where it matters most.

Building Intergenerational Fluency, Not Obedience

Too often, financial values are treated as one-directional: passed down from elders to youth. But in a post-industrial, rapidly digitising world, younger generations often have *superior insight into emerging paradigms*: decentralised tools, new markets, digital security, creator economies.

To ignore this is to rob the family of one of its greatest assets: *reciprocal learning*.

A culture-shifting household sees economic wisdom not as a monologue, but a conversation. It allows young people to challenge outdated strategies, test new ones, and offer feedback on family practices that may no longer serve their context.

This requires humility from parents and guardians. It also requires a willingness to be *disagreed with*—and to welcome that disagreement as evidence of critical thinking, not disloyalty.

The Endgame: Culture as the Ultimate Inheritance

The most durable inheritance is not a trust fund or a portfolio. It's *a worldview*. One that says:

You are not owned by your job, your income, or your assets.

Systems are designed—but also redesignable.

Wealth is not what you have, but what you can build, protect, and give without selling yourself in the process.

Families who seed this worldview may never be profiled in glossy magazines. Their homes may not look wealthy by traditional standards. But they will produce something rarer than success: *sovereign thinkers*. Children who are not seduced by status. Partners who don't mistake sacrifice for virtue. Elders who model evolution, not entitlement.

This is how culture changes. Quietly. Slowly. At the dinner table. In shared decision-making. In the stories we tell and the ones we refuse to pass on.

Shifting culture is not about breaking with tradition for its own sake. It's about refusing to pass along unexamined defaults that no longer serve the lives we want to live or the world we hope to leave behind. It's not a rejection of family—it's the deepest honouring of it: building a culture that liberates rather than binds.

Chapter 11
Radical Clarity – Designing Your Self-Defence System

Every system, especially those quietly faltering, survives best when you're lost in the weeds. Confusion is not a by-product—it's a feature. The less fluent you are in your own financial ecosystem—your real numbers, personal thresholds, unspoken values—the easier it becomes to steer you, softly and persistently, into dependency. Hustle culture thrives in that haze. So do legacy finance institutions and their shapeshifting cousins: the motivational speakers, the subscription-based experts, the algorithmic coaches who package overwhelm as opportunity. But here's the paradox: the antidote isn't more hustle. It isn't more knowledge, either. It's clarity. The sort of clarity that doesn't shout; it just works.

Not the superficial clarity of vision boards and bullet journals filled in on tired Sunday nights. Not the resolution-type clarity, which rarely survives its first encounter with fatigue. What we're talking about here is operational clarity—a scaffolding of decisions, routines, and boundaries that does the heavy lifting for you, even on the days when you can't. A system that guards your peace not through force, but by design.

This chapter is not an invitation to consume more information. Quite the opposite—it's an invitation to deprogram. To peel away the layers of performance and productivity you were told were essential. To unlearn the beliefs that have kept you grinding instead of growing. And to replace all that noise with structure—quiet, firm, functional structure. The kind that doesn't just support your financial life; it expresses it.

The first myth we'll dismantle is the one that undergirds nearly every burnout story: that survival, and then success, is a function of sheer effort. That waking at five, monetising your hobbies, and stacking revenue streams like poker chips is the path to safety. But what if it's not your ambition that's flawed? What if it's the scaffolding around it that's missing?

Discipline without infrastructure is exhaustion in disguise.

The difference between someone who treads water and someone who swims forward isn't always effort. It's leverage. The person with infrastructure—a reliable system of decisions, automation, and constraints—expends less energy to stay afloat. They're not stronger; they're smarter about friction. And they've stopped treating willpower as a permanent resource.

Operational clarity is built, not found. And it starts by rejecting the gospel of busyness as proof of worth. You are not behind because you're not doing enough. You're behind—if at all—because the system you're trapped in was never built for your liberation. The rules of the game reward motion, not meaning. Consumption, not clarity.

So this chapter asks you to pause. To interrogate the inputs. To examine which habits, metrics, and "best practices" were inherited rather than chosen. To step back from the dashboard and ask: *Whose definition of success am I optimising for?* And *what would change if I replaced hustle with design?*

Because financial peace—real peace, not the performative kind—is not born from heroic effort. It's born from alignment. When your routines reflect your values, when your thresholds are clearly marked, when your goals are not abstract but operationalised—then you stop reacting. You start responding.

And that's the goal: a system that responds on your behalf. A choreography, not a chaos. Where you are no longer fighting fires of your own making, but following a map you drew yourself—awake, informed, and unafraid.

Systems Over Hustles: The Fallacy of Effort as Strategy

Productivity culture has colonised the language of self-worth. Work ethic is now fetishised. Hustle is marketed as moral. And financial struggle is often framed as a lack of effort, not a symptom of a structurally rigged environment.

But hustle, in its raw form, is not a system. It is a *short-term compensation for systemic absence.* It works until your health fails. Until your attention fractures. Until your bandwidth collapses under the weight of too many spinning plates.

The self-defence mindset rejects this model. Instead of asking, "How can I work harder?" it asks: *"How can I remove decision fatigue, automate resilience, and reduce surface area for exploitation?"*

That might look like:

Automating savings and bill payments to eliminate emotional bandwidth drain.

Designing strict no-meeting blocks or client filters to enforce energetic boundaries.

Setting firm parameters around acceptable work, fees, and time investment—*then codifying them into policy.*

These are not hacks. They are *financial firewalls*—not built from complexity, but from consistency. The goal is to *own your time* as fiercely as you defend your money.

Designing for Resilience, Not Riches

One of the great bait-and-switches of capitalist psychology is that it subtly changes your target. You set out wanting enough to feel safe—but somewhere along the way, that morphs into chasing more to feel worthy. And because "more" has no ceiling, you remain perpetually insecure. Always just shy of peace.

This is not an accident. It is a feature of an economy that requires your discontent to function.

Radical clarity means refusing that premise entirely. It means defining *enough* on your own terms—and then *designing around it like a sovereign architect.* Not to excuse mediocrity. But to protect yourself from performative accumulation that leaves your nervous system shredded and your life hollow.

Designing for resilience means optimising for:

Margin, not maximalism

Optionality, not endless scale

Low-maintenance income, not volatile highs

It means understanding that stability is not the opposite of ambition. It is the *infrastructure that makes sustainable ambition possible.* True wealth is not what inflates your net worth on paper—it is what reduces your exposure to collapse.

The Financial Code of Honour: Your Operating System

Every sovereign system needs an internal constitution. Not just a budget. Not just goals. But a clear articulation of *what you stand for and what you will no longer allow.*

This chapter invites you to create a *Financial Code of Honour*—a short personal manifesto that governs your financial choices, behaviours, and boundaries. This is not an affirmation list. It is a precision tool. Its purpose is to:

Anchor you during times of decision paralysis

Filter out noise that does not serve your blueprint

Create *non-negotiables* that protect your time, energy, and integrity

For example:

"I do not work with clients who disrespect my boundaries—even if the fee is high."

"I invest only in businesses whose practices align with my values, regardless of returns."

"I will never again enter agreements I do not fully understand—no matter how urgent or tempting."

This code isn't a performance. It's a shield. *It removes the need for reactive decision-making because the hard decisions have already been made in advance.* That is clarity at its most radical.

The Shift from Emergency Response to Peaceful Precision

Most people manage money like emergency responders. They patch holes, chase income, scramble for deals, panic over invoices, and respond to crises. Their financial life is a perpetual fire drill. The nervous system never rests. Every new tax, fee, expense, or market tremor triggers a fresh cortisol spike.

What's missing is a philosophy of *preemptive design.* A system where decisions are made while calm, where risk is mitigated at the architecture level, and where your lifestyle *does not require you to be a superhero to function.*

The chapters that follow provide the tools for building such a system. You'll learn how to:

Identify fragility points in your current financial design

Shift from ad hoc decisions to rules-based living

Redefine your engagement with money not as a source of status, but as a tool of sovereignty

You'll also be invited to ask hard questions: Have you confused volatility with opportunity? Are you actually building freedom—or just debt-funded flexibility? Is your financial life an expression of your values—or a reflection of your fear?

These are not rhetorical questions. They are design questions. And the answers determine whether your system can protect you when the winds change.

A Culture of Overwhelm Requires You to Opt Out—Not Keep Up

One of the most subtle forms of oppression in modern life is informational overwhelm. You are constantly flooded with strategies, trends, and warnings. Everyone has a list. Everyone is screaming urgency. And beneath it all is a quiet implication: *If you don't keep up, you'll fall behind.*

But the person who is clear does not need to be fast. The person who is deliberate does not need to be loud. The person who designs with rigour does not need to "hustle harder"—because their system makes speed optional, not necessary.

Radical clarity is not a personality trait. It is a cultivated stance. It requires subtraction. Focus. Iteration. And, ultimately, the courage to build a financial life that *feels peaceful*, even if it looks unimpressive to the outside world.

This chapter will show you how.

The Financial Firewall – Designing a System That Says No for You

Exploitation rarely arrives as a brute-force attack. More often, it slips in through open ports: a poorly understood lease clause, a "limited-time" investment pitch, a subtle pressure to accept less than your worth. In a hyper-financialised world, economic extraction is ambient, decentralised, and disguised in the language of convenience, loyalty, or status. This is not paranoia—it's pattern recognition.

What protects you isn't just intelligence or effort. It's *architecture.* Specifically, *a personal financial firewall*—a curated system of values, filters, and pre-committed boundaries designed to block coercion before it even reaches your attention.

This chapter isn't about building walls. It's about building *filters*—selective permeability that lets in opportunity while keeping out opportunists. And it begins not with spreadsheets or apps, but with *a deep articulation of what you no longer permit.*

Exploitation Thrives on Ambiguity

If you're unclear on your rules, someone else will write them for you. This is the foundational vulnerability in most people's financial lives—not a lack of income, but a lack of thresholds. What kind of contracts will you sign? What kind of clients will you serve? What kinds of work will you never do, no matter the reward?

Without this clarity, every financial decision becomes a negotiation in real time. And that is exhausting. It's also dangerous—because when we're tired, rushed, or uncertain, we are most easily manipulated.

Predatory systems understand this. They depend on it. The fine print in a payday loan agreement isn't accidental; it's engineered confusion. The ever-shifting language in tech terms of service isn't the result of laziness; it's a feature designed to create legal ambiguity. *Your defence is not greater diligence—it is preemption.*

A well-built financial firewall ensures that *you don't need to analyse every detail in the heat of the moment—because your policy is already in place.*

What Is a Financial Firewall?

Unlike traditional financial advice, which focuses on maximising returns or minimising taxes, a financial firewall is about *minimising harm and reducing surface area for exploitation.* It is a living system composed of:

Filters: Predefined criteria that screen out misaligned opportunities

Rules: Codified behaviours and boundaries you do not violate, regardless of circumstance

Values: Deeply held principles that guide decision-making, especially under pressure

Together, these elements form a *behavioural perimeter*—a kind of decision architecture that protects not just your finances, but your *integrity, energy, and long-term peace.*

Consider the way major institutions operate. Investment firms have compliance checklists. Companies have risk frameworks. Militaries have rules of engagement. Why should your personal financial life be any less strategic?

The Filter Layer: Who and What Gets Access

The first layer of your firewall should deal with *inflow*—what gets through, and why.

This means developing *filters for offers, relationships, and transactions.* Examples might include:

Never accepting work without a written agreement

Rejecting any client who questions your pricing model

Declining partnership opportunities that involve vague upside and high urgency

This is not about rigidity for its own sake. It is about reducing decision fatigue and shielding your bandwidth. When every offer requires a bespoke moral calculus, you will eventually default to convenience over alignment.

Filters turn chaos into policy. They allow you to act with calm confidence instead of reactive confusion.

The Rule Layer: Non-Negotiables That Reduce Fragility

Rules are where your firewall gains its structural integrity. These are not vague intentions. They are *hardcoded defaults* that pre-decide what happens when reality tests you.

Consider these illustrative rules:

"I do not sign contracts with arbitration clauses that waive my legal rights."

"I always sleep on major financial decisions—no matter how urgent they appear."

"I never give more than 30% of my time to clients or employers who offer less than 70% alignment with my values."

Notice that these rules are not about how much money you want to earn or save. They are about *how you operate*, especially when others might pressure you to bend.

Rules are how you hold the line when the incentives to self-betray are high.

The Values Layer: What You're Actually Defending

At the core of every resilient financial system is a clearly articulated value set. Not in the abstract—but *in applied form.* Most people have generic values: integrity, freedom, fairness. But when money enters the picture, these often get overridden by fear or desire.

A strong firewall demands *operationalised values.* That means values that have been translated into specific behaviours and decisions.

For example:

If you value autonomy, your firewall might include refusing income sources that require 24/7 responsiveness.

If you value fairness, it might mean turning down contracts where power is unequally distributed, even if they're lucrative.

If you value truth, you may choose to forgo marketing tactics that exaggerate results or use psychological manipulation.

These are costly decisions in the short term. But *firewalls are not designed for short-term optimisation—they are built for long-term sovereignty.*

Why Most People Don't Have One

There's a reason few people operate with a defined financial firewall: the culture incentivises *compliance and complexity*, not clarity. Schools teach algebra before taxes. Employers offer perks instead of protections. And online financial advice focuses on strategy without ethics—"what to do with your money" rather than *what you're willing to trade for it.*

Moreover, the idea of personal financial policy is often reserved for the ultra-wealthy: trusts, attorneys, tax architects. The rest are encouraged to make it up as they go. But *you do not need wealth to have policy.* You need *boundaries, discernment, and language.*

The Cost of Not Having a Firewall

Without a financial firewall, you will absorb the costs of other people's urgency, sloppiness, and ambition. You'll waste hours renegotiating contracts that should have been clear. You'll lose peace of mind over offers that sounded good but weren't aligned. You'll find yourself entangled in work, relationships, or deals that cost you more than they reward you.

Over time, the cumulative erosion is massive.

It doesn't show up as a line item on your budget. But it does show up in your nervous system, your trust in people, and your relationship to money. When the world feels predatory, even abundance can start to feel like a liability.

How to Start Designing Yours

A financial firewall is not built overnight. Nor should it be. It is a process of iterative refinement.

1. **Audit Your Past Breaches**: Where have you felt used, unclear, or compromised in financial matters? What agreements did you wish you'd declined?
2. **Write Your Rules**: Choose 3–5 rules you will never violate, even under pressure. Be specific and practical.
3. **Define Your Filters**: List clear criteria that help you say no without guilt or delay.
4. **Anchor in Values**: Translate your top 2–3 personal values into *actionable decision heuristics*. Ask: What does this value look like under stress?

Then test them. Observe how your decisions change. Update as needed. *Your firewall is a living document—not a shrine.*

Final Reflection: This Is Not About Fear. It's About Alignment.

Some will argue that strong boundaries limit opportunity. That saying no too quickly could cost you growth. But this perspective assumes that *all growth is worth having*. It is not.

Growth without alignment leads to burnout. Wealth without boundaries leads to moral erosion. Influence without integrity becomes entrapment. The point of a financial firewall is *not to block life—it is to curate it.*

And once you experience what it feels like to make money, decisions, and moves that are fully aligned—you'll wonder why you ever accepted less.

This chapter is your toolkit to begin building that line of defence. Not just for your money—but for your *mind, time, dignity,* and long-term freedom.

Let's make the next "yes" cost someone more to earn—because the default is no, *unless it serves your system.*

Systems Over Hustles – Why Predictability, Not Pace, Builds Real Financial Defence

We live in an age that glorifies exhaustion. Entire subcultures romanticise the "hustle"—that endless sprint of monetising every hour, mastering ten income streams, sleeping four hours a night, and branding it all as ambition. But beneath the polished productivity porn lies a fragile architecture: burnout, inconsistency, and an illusion of control. What passes for progress is often just motion without direction.

Financial self-defence is not about sprinting. It's about designing repeatable systems—frameworks that quietly build resilience whether you're watching or not. And yet, because systems are unglamorous, they are undervalued. They don't perform well on social media. They don't spike dopamine. But *they work*. And they work when you're sick, distracted, burnt out, or simply living.

This chapter dismantles the cultural bias toward frenetic financial striving and replaces it with a more durable, intelligent standard: systematisation. Not in the abstract, Silicon Valley sense, but in the personal, strategic sense—*how you build routines that protect your time, automate your values, and make overwork obsolete.*

Hustle Culture: The Mirage of Mastery

To understand why systems matter, we must first examine why hustle seduces. Hustling promises autonomy. The language is intoxicating: be your own boss, grind till you shine, build your empire. But the reality often swaps one master for another. Instead of answering to a manager, you now answer to market volatility, algorithmic demand, or the treadmill of content, clients, and side gigs. Time is no longer structured by an employer—but neither is it protected by boundaries.

Psychologically, hustle works because it rewards effort visibility, not effectiveness. We conflate *busyness with productivity*. The brain likes the immediate feedback of a packed calendar, even if that calendar leads nowhere. In contrast, system-building demands delayed gratification: it is invisible, slow, and often unacknowledged until something goes wrong—and you remain standing.

Systems are what replace your energy with structure. Hustles are what deplete your energy in place of structure.

Defining a Financial System: The Anti-Hustle Toolkit

What is a system in this context? Not a rigid spreadsheet or a financial planner's checklist. It is a **repeatable method** that reduces decision fatigue, shields attention, and allocates resources without constant input. A system can be a rule, a routine, or a layered set of automations—but at its core, it must:

1. Reduce dependency on your day-to-day willpower
2. Work under stress, distraction, or personal change
3. Align with your values without requiring constant vigilance

For example:

A rule-based investing protocol: Automating contributions to a low-cost index fund on a fixed date, removing the need to "time" the market.

A psychological firewall: A pre-committed "no" to lifestyle upgrades until passive income exceeds expenses by 20%.

Time design: Blocking one day per week as *non-commercial*—no clients, no consumption, no monetisation allowed.

These are not tactical hacks. They are *architectural reinforcements*—structures that carry your principles forward even when you're tired, distracted, or tempted.

Why Systems Succeed Where Hustles Fail

Hustle culture depends on infinite personal energy. But energy is a depleting resource. Systems rely on *leverage*—on infrastructure doing the work once you've designed it well.

Consider two people with identical incomes. One manages it through continual vigilance—tracking expenses weekly, resisting impulse purchases, rebalancing portfolios manually, negotiating bills monthly. The other sets up a system: automated savings, expense caps, alerts for overages, rebalancing rules embedded in a once-a-year calendar review. In month one, both achieve similar results. In month twelve, the system wins. In year five, the difference is staggering.

Systems compound. Hustle exhausts.

This is not about laziness. It is about strategic laziness—allocating your finite energy toward high-leverage decisions *once*, so you don't have to make them weekly.

Complexity as a Form of Self-Sabotage

Many high performers confuse complexity with sophistication. They design systems so convoluted—multiple banks, obscure crypto wallets, layered spreadsheets, subscriptions to twelve productivity apps—that the system becomes another full-time job. This is not design. It is a disguised form of self-punishment.

True systemisation means *removing moving parts*. The goal is not elegant spreadsheets but *unbreakable simplicity*. Systems should reduce your mental load, not increase your sense of control. Because, as history has repeatedly shown—*systems that survive shocks are those that can be run under duress.*

During economic stress, pandemics, or personal upheaval, your system shouldn't ask you to optimise. It should simply hold.

Automate What You Can. Ritualise What You Must.

Automation is a powerful tool—but not everything can be outsourced to code or apps. Certain behaviours—like reflection, discernment, boundary-setting—require human input. These must be ritualised rather than automated. That is, they should *occur by design, not default.*

A monthly review of your finances—scheduled and protected—is a ritual.
Checking your net worth impulsively each week is a compulsion.

A Sunday check-in with your partner to align on spending values is a ritual.
Splitting every bill down to the penny over texts is a stress pattern.

Automation reduces friction. Rituals sustain meaning. The intelligent financial self-defence system blends both.

Designing Anti-Fragile Systems

The gold standard is not just a system that *survives* chaos—but one that *grows stronger because of it.* This is what Nassim Taleb calls "anti-fragile"—systems that adapt, evolve, and strengthen under volatility.

In practical terms, this could mean:

A spending cap that *lowers automatically* when your income drops, without you having to panic.

A rule that directs all unexpected income (bonuses, gifts, refunds) into "resilience reserves"—a separate fund that can be drawn only under strict conditions.

A "no-hustle clause" you sign with yourself: in economic downturns, you do not add new income streams—you instead review, optimise, or rest existing ones.

This is how systems become *intelligent agents of self-defence*—not rigid cages but evolving protocols.

Culture Will Not Reward You for This

A sobering truth: building systems will make you less legible to a culture that reads stress as significance. You will appear calmer. Quieter. Less interested in signalling your grind. Your financial moves may be invisible to peers who equate change with movement. And yet, this invisibility is power.

Noise signals effort. Silence often signals mastery.

The decision to systemise, to opt out of hustle theatre, is a philosophical one. It is a refusal to be defined by the pace of capitalism, and a move toward rhythm—your rhythm.

You may still work hard. You may still pursue goals. But your foundation will not be effort—it will be *design.*

Final Thought: Your System Is Your Signature

In the end, a financial system is a form of identity. It encodes your values, your boundaries, and your beliefs about what is worth preserving. It doesn't just manage your money. It *models your philosophy.*

Every filter you add, every rule you codify, every automation you install is a message to yourself: *this is how I protect my time, my peace, and my future from erosion.*

That's not optimisation. That's sovereignty.

Designing for Resilience, Not Riches – Realigning Financial Ambition Toward Peace and Permanence

If modern capitalism had a sacred text, it would read something like this: earn more, faster; acquire, scale, display. Financial success has been reduced to a game of accumulation, optimised for visibility and validated by metrics that have little to do with security—and even less with sanity. Wealth, once a means of freedom, is now a performance. We are no longer building lives. We are building audiences.

In this climate, financial goals are rarely examined for what they *mean*—only for how they *look*. A six-figure salary. A seven-figure portfolio. A beach house, a Rolex, a passive income funnel. These are not inherently wrong, but they are often *proxy goals*: borrowed desires serving someone else's script. Beneath the surface of aspiration lies a quieter truth that goes largely unspoken: *most people don't want to be rich. They want to feel safe.*

This chapter is a recalibration. It proposes a new standard of financial design—one built not for theatre, but for *resilience.* Not for speed, but for *durability.* Not for external approval, but for *internal coherence.* Wealth, in this frame, is not the pursuit of ever-larger numbers. It is the deliberate crafting of a life that bends under pressure without breaking.

The Hidden Cost of Chasing Riches

To understand the distinction between resilience and riches, we must begin by examining the false premises embedded in modern financial culture. We are taught, subtly and repeatedly, that the primary goal of work is to escape it. That the pinnacle of financial achievement is not contribution, but cessation: retire early, automate everything, buy your way out of effort. *But peace is not the same as escape—and autonomy is not a byproduct of income alone.*

The data tells its own story. Study after study shows that beyond a certain threshold—often cited around £60,000 to £80,000 in individual income—the emotional returns on extra money begin to diminish. What improves well-being is not merely more money, but more *control*: over your time, your decisions, your environment. That's what resilience actually offers.

Consider this: many of the wealthiest individuals in the world live in states of extraordinary fragility. Their lifestyles require armies of assistants, tax strategists, security systems, performance facades. Their privacy is compromised, their time spoken for, their every decision filtered through layers of risk management. They are not free. They are *leveraged.* And when markets crash or scandals erupt, their empires, often hollowed out by overextension, collapse fast.

Resilience, by contrast, is the architecture of *survivability.*

What Is Financial Resilience, Really?

Financial resilience is not simply about having an emergency fund. It is a layered, strategic posture that protects your autonomy, sustains your values, and adapts to volatility without demanding crisis-level reactivity. A resilient financial life doesn't just withstand shocks—it *absorbs and recovers from them with minimal drama.*

To build such a life, your systems must be designed with stress in mind:

Can your lifestyle survive a 30% drop in income without emotional freefall?

Are your obligations reversible, flexible, or fixed?

Do your goals still hold value if no one sees them?

These are not hypothetical questions. They are design principles. Resilience is less about "how much you have" and more about *how what you have behaves under pressure.*

From Extraction to Regeneration

The logic of "getting rich" in today's dominant narrative is extractive. It pulls energy from your body, attention from your family, creativity from your dreams—offering, in return, status badges you're too tired to enjoy. It's a game optimised for acceleration, not stability.

But resilience is regenerative. It recognises that the most vital financial decisions are rarely grandiose. They are cumulative, unsexy, and often invisible. Protecting your energy, honouring your values, and designing systems that grow stronger in chaos—*these are markers of sophistication, not passivity.*

Regenerative design starts with redefining success. Not as "more", but as "enough"—and then engineering your life around *what that enough requires in structural terms.* This is not minimalism for aesthetics. It's minimalism for sovereignty.

Goal Rewriting: From Vanity Metrics to Functional Metrics

Modern personal finance is rife with goals that read like marketing slogans: "£1M net worth," "Own five properties by 35," "Retire by 40." These targets may be relevant for some. But they are often *decorative*, disconnected from lived context. And when goals are designed without functional context, they become dangerous: they drive unnecessary risk, overexertion, and emotional dissonance.

The resilient alternative is to define goals as *functional thresholds*:

What level of income gives you full control of your calendar?

What amount of savings lets you walk away from a toxic client or job without fear?

What form of housing provides security without locking you into inflexible commitments?

By anchoring goals to *utility*, not optics, you reclaim the right to define success on your own terms—and escape the treadmill of ever-shifting benchmarks.

Trade Visibility for Optionality

One of the most radical aspects of resilience-focused design is its resistance to external validation. Resilient people often look *unremarkable* from the outside. Their cars are used, their wardrobes timeless, their portfolios boring. They are not building brand empires. They are building *buffer zones.*

In a world where financial worth is measured by how much you *show*, this quiet posture is a kind of cultural rebellion. But it buys something no amount of applause can replace: *optionality.* The freedom to say no. The power to walk away. The ability to pause, pivot, or disappear—without financial collapse.

Resilience makes you less dependent on the compliance of others. It is your firewall against exploitation.

Fragility by Design: How Most Financial Products Keep You Exposed

Much of the modern financial infrastructure is designed to exploit fragility. Adjustable-rate mortgages, buy-now-pay-later schemes, aspirational investing apps—they all presume a future where your income *always* rises and your energy *never* fails.

But real life is cyclical. Illness, caregiving, grief, burnout, layoffs—these are not edge cases. They are statistical certainties. Designing for resilience means *baking unpredictability into your plan.*

It also means being suspicious of products that require perfection to perform. Any investment, career plan, or tool that assumes linear growth is *a liability in disguise.*

The Peace Dividend

Ultimately, resilience is not an aesthetic preference. It is a form of peace. It lets you sleep without scanning for threats. It lets you make decisions from values, not fear. It lets you *age with agency*—free from the humiliation of forced dependence.

And that peace produces dividends. You show up differently in relationships. You parent with more patience. You contribute with more clarity. When your survival isn't constantly threatened by money anxiety, your bandwidth expands—for ethics, for vision, for depth.

That is the overlooked benefit of financial resilience: *it doesn't just preserve your capital. It preserves your character.*

Redefining the "Plan"

Designing for resilience also requires rethinking how we plan. Most financial plans are linear spreadsheets: forecast income, track expenses, save, retire. They assume stasis. But humans do not live in linear arcs—we live in *chapters.*

A resilient financial plan isn't a projection. It's a *navigation system.* It assumes fog, weather, detours. It is built around waypoints: stable anchors that allow you to shift course without capsizing. And its true metric of success is not net worth. It is *nervous system calmness during crisis.*

In this model, you are not trying to win the game. You are trying to *stay in it without losing yourself.*

Resilience is not anti-ambition. It is ambition with a memory.

It remembers that your future self will have different needs, energies, and truths than your current one. And it builds with that future in mind—not as a fantasy, but as a design constraint.

The Financial Code of Honour – How to Write Your Own Rules for Money and Refuse Exploitation Ever Again

At some point, many of us look at our bank accounts, our contracts, our calendars—and feel a quiet, bone-deep discomfort. Not just with how much we have or how hard we work, but *with what we've agreed to tolerate.* We sense we've been participating in a system that rewards obedience more than intelligence, passivity more than clarity. And somewhere along the way, money ceased to be a tool and became a test—of worth, of loyalty, of endurance.

This article offers a rupture point. A place to say: *enough.* Not in the way of financial surrender, but of personal clarity. The Financial Code of Honour is not a spreadsheet. It's not a vision board. It is a personal manifesto—a deliberate and explicit declaration of how you will *engage* with money from this point forward. What you will pursue.

What you will reject. What you will *never again trade for peace, health, or dignity.*

Every system we interact with—banks, employers, markets—has rules. Most are opaque, selectively enforced, and designed to benefit those who wrote them. But most people operate without rules of their own. And in the absence of personal policy, *you default to theirs.* You obey their defaults. You accept their framing. You perform their goals.

Writing your own code interrupts that cycle.

The Lie of Neutrality

In every financial interaction, there is an embedded power structure—explicit or implied. Some of it is legal, some of it cultural, some of it psychological. Your landlord can raise the rent with a typed notice. Your employer can freeze a promotion with a vague performance review. Your bank can reroute your funds, suspend access, or quietly charge you for their own inefficiency.

If you don't define your tolerances, someone else will define them *for* you. And it will be done in language that sanitises exploitation: "Just business." "Nothing personal." "It's company policy."

This is the myth of neutrality—that economic violence can be depersonalised. But the consequences are never neutral. The woman who accepts chronic underpayment "for experience" is not neutral. The family who loses a home over fine print is not neutral. These are not passive misfortunes. They are outcomes of systems designed for imbalance.

Your Financial Code of Honour is how you reclaim authorship. It's where you stop asking, "What can I get?" and start asking, "What will I never again give away?"

Codes Are Not Goals

It's important to distinguish your code from your ambitions. Financial goals are things you aim for: pay off debt, earn six figures, buy a home. They are outcomes. Your code is not about outcome. It is about *conduct.* It is a container of non-negotiables—behaviours you will no longer excuse, dynamics you will no longer tolerate, decisions you will no longer outsource.

This is not about purity. It's about alignment. You can choose to be strategic and still have boundaries. You can navigate capitalism *without becoming its servant.*

Examples of code statements might include:

"I will never again say yes to money that requires me to abandon my values."

"I refuse to monetise my identity for platforms I do not control."

"I will never confuse status with security."

"I will prioritise sovereignty over scale."

"I will not tolerate ambiguity in contracts or shame around asking questions."

Each one is a fulcrum of decision-making. When the next opportunity comes—job, investment, collaboration—you don't flail in indecision. You consult your code. Does this honour what I said I stand for?

If not, it's not for you. *No matter how shiny it looks.*

From Performance to Principle

In a financial system built on spectacle—Instagram wealth, startup hustle, scarcity marketing—self-worth is increasingly tethered to visibility. People are trained to chase not just income, but *optics*. To look busy. To appear high-status. To perform abundance even if it bankrupts them in private.

The Financial Code of Honour is your way out of that trap. It moves your compass from performance to *principle*. It asks not just "What's profitable?" but "What's *true* for me, even if no one applauds it?"

This principle-based approach doesn't mean you reject success or income. It means you stop *bending* for them. It means you value *peace over permission, privacy over performance, and clarity over complexity.*

A Code Is a Shield

At its best, a financial code is not just a guide. It is a *shield.* It protects you from bad contracts, exploitative clients, unpaid labour, and self-abandonment disguised as ambition. It guards your time from distraction and your energy from commodification.

It also gives language to what many of us have lacked: *an internal standard.* Too many people say "yes" by default—because they don't have a pre-written "no."

Your code becomes that pre-written no. It is a script of self-defence.

"I won't work for exposure."
"I won't take money from platforms that harvest user data without consent."
"I won't tolerate partners who demand urgency without respect."

When the moment of negotiation comes—when someone pushes, manipulates, pressures—you already have your line. It's not personal. It's policy.

Codes Create Calm

Another overlooked feature of the financial code: it simplifies your life. Much of financial stress comes from decision fatigue—endless debates over what to say yes to, how much to charge, when to walk away. A clear code removes that burden.

You no longer reinvent your ethics for every offer. You're not caught in loops of justification or apology. You operate from policy, not impulse.

This doesn't mean you stop thinking. It means you think *beforehand.* You design your responses in peacetime, so you don't panic in wartime.

Crafting Your Code: A Process of Distillation

Writing your code is not a branding exercise. It is not for display. It is a process of distillation—of identifying the moments in your financial life where you *betrayed yourself*, tolerated too much, or abandoned clarity.

Start by asking:

What financial decisions have I most regretted? What values did I violate in those moments?

Where have I felt disempowered in negotiation, payment, or work?

What behaviours have I tolerated in others that eroded my trust, energy, or time?

What compromises did I make that bought income but sold my integrity?

From these answers, you'll begin to see patterns. You'll find the phrases that matter. Keep them short. Keep them specific. Keep them *true even under pressure.*

Don't try to write a manifesto that pleases everyone. This isn't a press release. It's a *survival document.*

Money Without Memory

Too often, people engage with money as if each decision is isolated. But financial behaviour is cumulative. Every yes or no *builds your story.* And your story becomes your standard.

Without a code, people forget. They forget what they swore they'd never do again. They forget the pain of underpricing. They forget how long it took to recover from a toxic contract. And they repeat it—because *memory without a mechanism is just nostalgia.*

Your code is the mechanism.

It remembers for you. It speaks when you are tempted. It holds the line when your fear of scarcity whispers, "Just this once."

And in time, it becomes your posture. Not a document on your desktop, but a reflex in your bones.

To be financially sovereign is not just to have enough. It is to know what you will never again trade away in the pursuit of more.

That's what a Financial Code of Honour protects. Not your income. Your *alignment.*

And that alignment is what makes wealth *worth having at all.*

Conclusion
The Sovereign Mind

If you've made it this far, you're no longer a spectator in the financial machinery—you've crossed over into agency. That distinction matters. It's not just linguistic; it's structural. The vast majority will remain on the default track, quietly moving along a conveyor belt of predetermined economic choices—lulled by incentives they never selected, obedient to systems they never designed, vulnerable to risks they've barely been taught to name. To become sovereign in any real sense is to upend that trajectory. Not with superficial tweaks to spending or smarter budgeting apps, but by altering the scaffolding of your thinking.

This final chapter doesn't tie a neat bow around what's come before. Instead, it throws down a challenge: what would it mean to think—truly think—as someone who owns their decisions, defends their integrity, and cannot be quietly programmed?

At the heart of *The Sovereign Mind* is a deceptively blunt proposition: control does not begin with financial products or clever tools—it begins in thought. Not the aspirational kind. Not "vision board" clarity. But structural cognition. To live independently in a system designed for your dependence, you must interrogate the architecture of your beliefs. Where did they come from? Which serve you? Which are cages? And which must be dismantled entirely before you can begin to move freely?

This isn't motivational fluff. It's survival strategy. Because everything around you—banks, governments, tech platforms, advertising algorithms—has one objective: predictability. Your appetite for risk, your browser history, your emotional triggers, your digital purchases—all of it feeds into models designed to anticipate you. The easier you are to profile, the easier you are to manage. Sovereignty, then, is a practice of becoming illegible—an intentional disruption of your datafied self.

But let's get practical. What, precisely, does it take to live in this way?

Forget the gloss. Strip the term "sovereignty" of its modern gloss—no influencer rhetoric, no crypto maximalist cosplay, no soft-focus empowerment memes. Here, we define sovereignty as a mental operating system comprising three pillars: discernment, discipline, and design.

Discernment is the first filter. It's the art of recognising what you are tacitly consenting to—through silence, through habit, through unexamined participation. It's a skill honed in ambiguity. Modern systems do not speak plainly; they obscure. Financial products are layered with euphemism. Legal agreements are weaponised with complexity. Social norms are designed to hook your attention rather than earn your trust. To live with discernment is to see through the packaging. To pause and ask: who benefits if I proceed? What is being asked of me, and what am I being trained not to notice?

Take the rising popularity of "buy now, pay later" apps marketed to teenagers. It's not just clever branding—it's a curriculum in debt normalisation. Or subscription software that never ends—it's not progress, it's dependency rebranded. A sovereign mind reads the terms *and* the subtext.

Next comes **discipline**. Not the punishing, joyless brand touted by outdated finance gurus, but the quiet, sustained discipline of system-building. What routines have you constructed to guard your time, focus, and autonomy? What have you automated—strategically, not lazily—to conserve mental bandwidth? Who gets to access your energy? Your inbox? Your imagination?

Sovereignty in a distracted age requires strategic blindness. You must be willing to ignore even the interesting, the alluring, the promising—if it compromises the essential. Economic discipline is part of this. Real financial resilience isn't dramatic. It isn't a meme. It is unsexy, repetitive, and precise. It's about designing systems that work on your worst days, not your best. It's about recognising that freedom is not rulelessness. It's living by rules you authored, not rules you inherited.

Then there's **design**—where sovereignty becomes architectural. The sovereign mind doesn't just reflect. It builds. It constructs environments—financial, relational, digital—that are resistant to capture. What does your ecosystem look like when it's designed not merely to support your goals, but to safeguard your ethics?

Perhaps it means moving your income streams to decentralised platforms, where cancellation isn't one keystroke away. Maybe it's structuring contracts with exit options—clear, enforceable, not contingent on goodwill. Perhaps it means redesigning your children's education, not as rebellion but as protection. The goal is not to survive broken systems—it is to outgrow them, by creating alternatives that hold.

Importantly, this is not a manifesto for isolation. Sovereignty *sounds* like solitude, but that's a narrative sold by those who fear autonomous people banding together. The real threat to fragile institutions isn't the lone dissenter—it's communities of informed dissenters who can choose *when* and *whether* to engage.

And when sovereign individuals come together, what you get is not chaos but coordination. Voluntary. Transparent. Resilient. These are not cults or echo chambers. They're networks of mutual reinforcement. Places where tools are shared. Where contracts are non-extractive. Where blind spots are guarded, not exploited. The sovereign collective isn't utopian—it's antifragile. Not because it never breaks, but because it breaks cleanly and rebuilds faster.

So, what's asked of you here? This isn't a tidy conclusion. It's a provocation.

You're being asked to make explicit what has, until now, been implicit. What mindsets have taken root? Which can no longer coexist with who you're becoming? Which will need to be dismantled, no matter how comfortable, how familiar, or how deeply they've been reinforced by your past?

This is not a sentimental exercise. It's strategic. You're building a mental code—your own sovereign syntax. One that won't be legible to systems designed for predictability. One that will resist the pull to conform, comply, collapse.

Some relationships, routines, or beliefs may not survive that evolution. Let them go. That isn't failure. That's integrity.

And if you feel discomfort here—resistance, friction—lean into it. That's the edge of transformation. Sovereignty does not feel like applause. It feels like clarity—calm, steady, inconvenient clarity.

So, no summary. No wrap-up.

Only this: The capacity to think clearly. To choose without shame. To say "no" without explanation.

That is the sovereign mind. And it's yours now.

A Final Awakening

You were never meant to read this far.

Not because the material was too complex or the journey too long—but because the systems that shape our economic lives rely on one core assumption: that you won't ask too many questions. That you'll accept the defaults, reward the distractions, obey the incentives, and mistake comfort for safety. That you'll confuse financial literacy with obedience, confuse convenience with freedom, and confuse wealth with worth.

The fact that you're still here—still reading, still thinking—means something has already shifted.

This is not a book about money. It *began* with money because money is where the manipulation is most visible. It's where incentives codify power. It's the interface between your time, your autonomy, and your identity. But if you've paid attention, you've already realised that every chapter pointed beyond money. It pointed toward something more radical: *reclaiming authorship of your life in a system that profits from your submission.*

A final awakening begins with the recognition that engineered dependence is not a glitch in modern society—it is a feature. It is profitable to keep you financially anxious. It is efficient to keep you digitally distracted. It is politically expedient to keep you confused, fragmented, and reliant. And so, the real question becomes: how do you stay awake in a world that is constantly trying to *re-hypnotise* you?

Let's be clear: this isn't paranoia. It's pattern recognition. Consider the way financial education is omitted from public schooling—not due to lack of time, but because *disempowered citizens are easier to govern and market to.* Think about how your online behaviour is tracked, monetised, and used to shape your future options without your consent. Look at how banks, employers, governments, and platforms design choices for you—and then pretend they were yours.

Awakening is not an event. It's a discipline. One that must be practised daily, especially because the world will constantly give you good reasons to go back to sleep.

Sleep looks like the hustle that never ends because you confuse motion with meaning.
Sleep looks like the job you tolerate because the salary flatters your ego, even as it erodes your soul.
Sleep looks like letting your financial choices be dictated by social media, legacy culture, or outdated expectations.
Sleep looks like outsourcing your strategy, your ethics, and your future to people who profit when you don't think too hard.

To stay awake is to live in *active resistance* to that. But resistance alone is not enough. *You must build.* Sovereignty is not a posture of rebellion—it is a *design challenge*. You are now the architect. Not just of your budget or your retirement plan, but of your value system, your risk appetite, your economic alliances, your intellectual diet.

This means you no longer have the luxury of blaming the system without simultaneously building alternatives to it.

That is the ethical burden of awareness.

Yes, the financial system is rigged in favour of insiders. Yes, governments lie. Yes, the digital economy is mining your behaviour. Yes, wealth gaps are widening while narratives of meritocracy still circulate to pacify dissent. But *knowing that is not enough.* If all you do is become more cynical, then the system still wins. Your awareness becomes just another form of paralysis. *Awakening without action is just despair with a vocabulary.*

The challenge now is clarity, courage, and commitment.

Clarity—about your own values, your own limits, and your non-negotiables. What will you no longer tolerate? Not just in institutions, but in your habits? Your relationships? Your self-talk? Clarity isn't a mood. It's a set of enforced boundaries. It means deciding, *in advance*, what you will say no to—even when it's profitable, convenient, or socially sanctioned.

Courage—to live visibly in a way that contradicts economic norms. To question the default path, even when your peers applaud it. To move countries if the laws degrade. To walk away from deals that offend your ethics. To raise children who disrupt the system instead of conforming to it. Courage is not heroic. It's strategic. And often, it's quiet.

Commitment—not to a single tactic or tool, but to a lifelong practice of financial sovereignty. To continually assess whether your current systems serve your future self or merely preserve your past.

To build redundancy, decentralisation, and optionality into your life—not because you're fearful, but because you're *paying attention.*

Here's the uncomfortable truth: no one is coming to save you. There is no regulation, no app, no movement, no mentor who will permanently protect your autonomy. What you have now is *awareness*—and the obligation to use it.

You may lose friends.
You may alienate colleagues.
You may be called paranoid, difficult, or elitist.
But you will sleep peacefully. You will think clearly. And when systems fail, you will *not* be among the first to panic, because you did not build your life on their promises.

You built it on principles.

This, then, is your final task: write your own rules. Design your own contracts. Educate your children. Exit what offends your ethics. Align your earning with your values. Build backups. Guard your data. Reject hype. Say no, calmly and clearly, when everyone else is scrambling for permission.

This is not the end of a book. It is the beginning of an experiment: *what happens when someone builds a life that no longer requires permission to thrive?*

You've just spent an entire volume learning to see the mechanisms of control. Now comes the real work: living *as if* you believe what you've learned. Risking discomfort in service of dignity. Letting go of shortcuts in service of sovereignty.

No one can promise you safety. But if you stay awake, stay principled, and stay *designed*, you will have something far rarer: *agency.*

And once you've tasted that, you'll never go back to sleep.

About the Author

Darian Vos is a global thinker, financial deconstructor, and strategist who has spent the last two decades navigating and exposing the silent architecture of economic control. With roots in both Eastern and European traditions, Darian brings a uniquely cross-cultural lens to the psychology of money, systemic manipulation, and personal sovereignty. After years of consulting for private clients, whistleblowing against financial abuses, and studying behavioural economics and trauma-informed finance, he created a blueprint to help individuals defend their wealth, time, and autonomy. Darian's voice is sharp, compassionate, and unapologetically truthful—empowering readers not just to survive within broken systems, but to transcend them.

www.ingramcontent.com/pod-product-compliance
Lightning Source LLC
Chambersburg PA
CBHW031340230926
51848CB00002B/314